Turn the Guns Around

Mutinies, Soldier Revolts and Revolutions

By John Catalinotto

World View Forum

Turn the Guns Around
Mutinies, Soldier Revolts and Revolutions

John Catalinotto, first edition
Includes index and bibliography
ISBN-13: 978-0692813942
ISBN-10: 0692813942

Class struggle in the military
GI resistance to Vietnam War 1965-1975
Organizing the American Servicemen's Union
The Bond monthly GI newspaper
Franco-Prussian War – Paris Commune 1871
World War I – Russian Revolution 1917
Revolt of German North Sea Fleet 1918
Portuguese Carnation Revolution 1974
Leninist view of the state

Cover Design: Lallan Schoenstein

World View Forum
147 West 24th Street, 2nd Floor
New York, NY 10011

Books may be ordered through Amazon.com and other bookstores.

Book fonts: PT Sans; American Typewriter

This book is dedicated to the unknown soldier-resisters, who are the first to awaken to their own class interests and turn their weapons on the rulers who have sent them into vain battle.

Contents

Appendices

∞

Maps

Abbreviations: Ranks in the U.S. Armed Forces

Army	Army	Navy	Navy	AF	Air Force
PVT	Private	SR	Seaman Recruit	AMN	Airman
PV2	Private 2	SA	Seaman Apprentice	A1C	Airman 1 Class
PFC	Private 1 Class	PO3	Petty Officer 3 Class	SrA	Senior Airman
SP4	Specialist 4			SSgt	Staff Sergeant
CPL	Corporal				
SP5	Specialist 5				

Ranks order lowest to highest; Marine and Air Force ranks are similar to Army with slight differences. These abbreviations are used for U.S. enlisted troops and officers in this book.

SGT E6-E9 are lifer sergeants. Officers' abbreviations below.

	Army		Navy
2LT	Second Lieutenant	ENS	Ensign
1LT	First Lieutenant	LTJG	Lieutenant Jr Grade
CPT	Captain	1LT	Lieutenant
MAJ	Major	LCDR	Lieutenant Commander
LTC	Lieutenant Colonel	CDR	Commander
COL	Colonel	CPT	Captain
BG	Brigadier General	RDML	Rear Admiral (lwr half)
MG	Major General	RADM	Rear Admiral (upr half)
LTG	Lieutenant General	VADM	Vice Admiral
GEN	General	ADM	Admiral
GA	General of the Army	FADM	Fleet Admiral

Timeline of Vietnam War

1954 – French garrison at Dien Bien Phu surrenders to Viet Minh. Vietnam is split into North and South at Geneva conference.

1955 – South Vietnamese regime, supported by the U.S., refuses to participate in Vietnam-wide elections agreed to at Geneva.

1956 – U.S. "military advisers" arrive in South Vietnam.

1957 – Beginning of Communist insurgency in the South under the aegis of the National Liberation Front.

1960 – By the end of the year 900 U.S. troops in South Vietnam.

1961 – U.S. forces increase to 3,200.

1962 - Number of U.S. "military advisers" in South Vietnam rises to 12,000. Agent Orange, a deadly herbicide, is used to destroy crops and clear vegetation hiding guerilla forces. It also caused birth defects.

1963 – A U.S.-backed military coup overthrows and then kills South Vietnam President Diem. U.S. troops total 16,300 by end of the year. President John F. Kennedy assassinated In Dallas, Texas, Nov. 22. Lyndon Johnson becomes president.

1964 – August "Gulf of Tonkin incident": U.S. says North Vietnamese patrol boats fired on two U.S. Navy destroyers. (Later shown to be untrue.) U.S. Congress approves resolution authorizing military action in region. Troops increase to 23,300.

1965 – 200,000 American combat troops arrive in South Vietnam. Bombing of North Vietnam begins. **Between 1964 and 1973, the United States also dropped around 2.5 million tons of bombs on the neighboring country of Laos.**

1966 – U.S. troop numbers in Vietnam rise to 400,000.

April 12 – New York City, Youth Against War & Fascism demonstrates at Stock Exchange.

1967 – U.S. troops now 490,000. April 4: Dr. Martin Luther King, Jr. denounces war.

April 28 – Muhammad Ali refuses to be inducted into the U.S. Army.

August – Major rebellions in Black community in Newark, N.J. and Detroit, Michigan.

October 21 – 100,000 protesters in Washington, D.C. 30,000 march on Pentagon.

December 25 – Group of GIs announces formation of American Servicemen's Union.

1968 – January: Tet Offensive: a combined assault by National Liberation Front and North Vietnamese army on U.S. positions begins. U.S. troops strength grows to 540,000.

March 31 – President Johnson announces he will not seek another term. More than 500 civilians die in the U.S. massacre at My Lai. On April 4, Dr. Martin Luther King, Jr. assassinated in Memphis, Tenn. Rebellions break out in more than 100 cities.

August 23 – 160 Black GIs at Fort Hood, Texas, protest use in riot control in Chicago. Also major prison rebellions of GIs at Long Binh and Danang in Vietnam.

1969 – Troop level peaks at 543,000 in March. Starting in June, President Nixon begins to reduce U.S. ground troops in Vietnam, but begins secret bombing of Cambodia which continues for more than a year. Troops at 480,000 by end of year.

August-September, Sanctuary at Church of the Crossroads, Honolulu, Hawaii. Thirty-five GIs leave their units to protest war.

September 2 – North Vietnam's President Ho Chi Minh dies.

1970 – Nixon's national security advisor, Henry Kissinger, and Hanoi government representative Le Duc Tho start talks in Paris. U.S. troops drop to 280,000.

May 4 – National Guard kills four Kent State students at anti-war demonstrations protesting invasion of Cambodia. Cops kill two Jackson State students same week.

1971 – Publication of the first *Pentagon Papers*. 140,000 U.S. troops remain.

1972 – North Vietnam's Haiphong harbor mined in May.

1973 – Ceasefire agreement in Paris. U.S. ends conscription on January 27.

March, U.S. troop pullout completed. Of more than 3 million U.S. soldiers serving in the war, 58,000 died and 150,000 were seriously wounded.

1974 – President Nixon resigns following the Watergate scandal.

1975 – Vietnamese liberate Saigon. Remaining U.S. personnel flee on April 30.

Note to readers: Events noted in italics are discussed in this book in detail.

The Bond, **Sept. 22, 1969.** Photo: J. Catalinotto

Prologue 1 'As (U.S.) American as Apple Pie'

1846-48. 'Mexican War,' the U.S. government called it. The United States invaded and annexed the northern half of Mexico. This included all or parts of the present states of Arizona, California, Colorado, Nevada, New Mexico, Texas and Utah. Some of the U.S. Army units consisted of recent immigrants. U.S. officers were suspicious of them as new immigrants and Catholics and treated them badly. More than 200 troops deserted, mostly Irish and German Catholic immigrants, who switched sides and joined the Mexicans. Their unit was called the Saint Patrick's Battalion. Since the Mexicans had few cannons, the Saint Patrick's became the Mexicans' best artillery unit. Of the Saint Patrick's soldiers whom the U.S. Army captured at the end of the war, more than thirty were executed immediately after a kangaroo court-martial. The U.S. Army Brass reviled them as traitors. Mexico built statues to honor their courage.[1]

∞

1898-1901. Spanish-American War. The U.S. invaded and seized the Philippines, then a colony of Spain, and made war on the Filipino resistance to the U.S. occupation. U.S. troops killed hundreds of thousands of Filipinos — men, women and children — while trying to repress the resistance. Among the occupation troops were a few segregated units of Black soldiers, where Black troops fought under white commanders. These officers used the racist n-word to refer to Filipinos as well as to the African Americans. Some Black troops identified with the oppressed Filipinos because of this shared insult. The Philippine liberation movement recognized the segregated divisions and issued leaflets calling on the Black U.S. troops to desert and defect. At least a half dozen Black GIs fought alongside the Filipino resistance. One of the most famous was David Fagen, who became an officer among the Filipinos. U.S. officers put a price of $800 on Fagen's head. Some reports say he was executed as the war ended. Others say he pretended to be killed and escaped to live quietly on the islands.[2]

∞

1917-1919. World War I. Archangel. In 1917, some 13,000 U.S. troops landed in Archangel, Murmansk and Vladivostok, Russia with the pretext that this was needed to defeat Germany. It really was part of an allied attempt to aid the counterrevolutionary White Army against the Red Army of the workers' revolution that had swept into power in November 1917. The U.S. forces were underfed, poorly clothed for Russian winters and irate at the British commanders who were in charge of the allied intervention and who treated the U.S. troops with contempt. A movement demanding to come home arose among the 5,000 troops left in Archangel in 1919. A report in the February 18, 1919, *New York Times* gives a flavor of the events:

> Bolshevist propaganda, well written and printed in English, has been distributed mysteriously among the various allied units. Leaflets distributed in villages on the Onega front, where American forces are operating, call upon the American soldiers to organize soldiers' committees and demand of the officers that they be returned home, as the war with Germany is over and there is no reason for remaining in Russia.

Worried by the resistance the U.S. troops showed, the Woodrow Wilson administration ordered them home by May 1919.

1941-45. World War II. There were more than eight million troops in the U.S. military toward the end of 1945, after both Germany and Japan capitulated. Nearly all of them wanted to go home as soon as possible. Some military and government officials wanted to use the U.S. troops against the USSR in Europe and to stop the revolution in China. When repatriation was going too slowly for the troops, some 4,000 demonstrated in Manila on Christmas Day 1945. Then some 20,000 marched on army headquarters there on January 6, 1946. This is what World War II veteran F.O. Richardson wrote about these protests:

> Millions of GIs, sailors and Marines won their freedom from the military in 1945 and 1946 because of mass pressure.
>
> Thousands of GIs marched through the streets of European cities after the war had ended. The Brass still wanted to hold them. The GIs demanded they be shipped home.
>
> These organized demonstration also occurred in the Pacific area.
>
> The demands of the soldiers were supported by the mass sentiment at home.
>
> They were shipped home.[3]

The GIs' actions in the Philippines prevented the U.S. from sending troops in large numbers to fight on the side of the Kuomintang in China. This military resistance aided the victory of the Chinese Revolution of 1949.

∞

1962-75. Vietnam War. Probably the longest sustained resistance from rank-and-file troops of the U.S. Armed Forces to date.

∞

2016. Standing Rock. In a full-blown North Dakota blizzard, veterans of the U.S. wars on Iraq and Afghanistan and others, including many of Indigenous background, came in December to show solidarity with the Lakota, Dakota and Nakota Nations of Standing Rock. Monica Moorehead writes that for eight months members of the

> ... Standing Rock Sioux Nation have been in the forefront of uniting hundreds of other Indigenous Nations throughout the Americas to stop the [Dakota Access] Pipeline that threatens the desecration of ancestral lands, violates the 1851 and 1868 treaties signed between them and the U.S. government upholding the Sioux people's right to land sovereignty, and poses a real threat of poisoning the water supply for at least 17 million people.[4]

The veterans were ready to act as human shields. Police have used concussion grenades, teargas, water cannons against unarmed water protectors. A delegation of the veterans

> ... made a public apology on bended knee to Indigenous elders for U.S. genocidal crimes committed against Indigenous peoples, their land, their culture and resources.[5]

Fifty years after resistance began among U.S. troops in the conscript Vietnam-era military, a new kind of veteran is joining the people's struggle.

Prologue 2 'Big Firms Get Rich, GIs Die'

On April 12, 1966, fifteen young women and men slipped into the New York Stock Exchange. They didn't belong there. They had no money to invest in stocks, nor did they care if the market was down or up that day. They had another purpose.

They had informed a few reporters they planned something dramatic, asking the reporters to keep the action secret. The young people hoped to act before police or guards could stop them.

As they gathered in the lobby before going up to the observation area overlooking the floor of the exchange, Douglas Robinson of the *New York Times* signaled his presence by folding back his coat and exposing a red lining. He assumed red would be the right signal.

Although a war was on and both Vietnamese and U.S. troops were dying, the only weapons these youth carried were leaflets and banners. They were sending a message.

On the trading floor, hundreds of brokers were staring up at the Big Board that showed the up-to-date information on all the important stocks. It was a captive audience. The fifteen young people moved to the edge of the observation balcony overlooking the arena of frantic trading.

On a signal, some threw leaflets thirty feet down to the floor while three others unfurled a banner right across the Big Board. A sudden silence was followed by a collective howl from below as the brokers read "Stop the War in Vietnam" and, in bigger letters, "Big Firms Get Rich, GIs Die."* The banner was signed "Youth Against War & Fascism."

In 1966 some 200,000 of these GIs, mostly from the Army and Marines, were in Vietnam fighting a war against the Vietnamese people. Lyndon Baines Johnson was president of the United States. Following a supposed confrontation between North Vietnamese patrol boats and U.S. destroyers in the Gulf of Tonkin in August 1964, which was later exposed as faked by the Pentagon,[1] Johnson gained Congress's authority to escalate U.S. intervention in the war.

Despite some voices in the U.S. Congress who by early 1966 were critical of the president's war policy, Johnson planned to increase the number of U.S. troops there to 380,000 by year's end.

Toward the end of March 1966 there were peace marches of some thousands of people in Boston, New York, Philadelphia, Washington, Chicago and San Francisco. At the time, the majority of the U.S. population still supported the government and the war. The protests' dominant slogans were pacifist: "End the war," "Negotiate now."

The young people at the Stock Exchange had a clearer view of what the war against Vietnam was about. This view was shaped by the gut revulsion they felt when seeing photos of Vietnamese peasants burned to death by napalm bombs that Dow Chemical manufactured; it was honed by the knowledge that the Vietnamese were determined to fight until they won.

The YAWF members were also sympathetic to the rank-and-file U.S. troops who were drafted or induced to enlist and then sent to die so that the stockholders of companies like Dow Chemical would grow richer.

The slogan, "Big Firms Get Rich, GIs Die," reflected an ideology. The ideology condemned the U.S. war against Vietnam as a bosses' war. The Pentagon fought to maintain and increase the profits of the military-industrial complex and also the profits of all the bankers and super-rich who wanted to keep exploiting workers all over the world. The GIs were working-class youth used as cannon fodder; that is, they were sent to kill and die to expand the interests of the rich.

How YAWF delivered the slogan also expressed an attitude: In your face.†

Implicit in the slogan was an approach toward the GIs themselves. The young people active in Youth Against War & Fascism, of which I was one, considered the ordinary soldiers, sailors, Air Force and Coast Guard members, Marines, WACs and WAVEs to be their class brothers and sisters.

We were aware that many of the GIs had patriotic and anti-Communist beliefs. Everyone who grew up in the 1950s and early 1960s had these beliefs pounded into them. But we were confident we could explain the truth about what their real interests were, indeed, that they would learn that truth from their own experience in combat. They did learn, and more quickly than we imagined.‡

A Look Ahead

By 1968, it was obvious that the experience in Vietnam had turned many U.S. troops against the war. Upon their return to the U.S., these combat veterans came into contact with a massive and youthful anti-war movement and with the Black liberation struggle.

By 1970, whole units on active duty repeatedly refused to go on offensive missions in Vietnam. If pushed too hard by their officers, sometimes one or more of the troops would kill the officer. This practice gave birth to a new verb, "to frag," because often the elimination of the officer was carried out by rolling a fragmentation grenade into his tent. The officer or lifer sergeant was thereby "fragged." In 1970, exactly 109 fraggings occurred in Vietnam, according to Pentagon sources.[2]

Entire units began to refuse to go on combat missions. Meanwhile, the troops of Vietnam's National Liberation Front understood that by killing U.S. officers while letting ordinary GIs live or by showing solidarity with Black GIs, they could win both the battle and the hearts and minds of the U.S. troops.

In mid-1971, a provocative article entitled "The Collapse of the Armed Forces," by military historian Marine LCL Robert Debs Heinl, showed how much the GIs had broken with military indoctrination. Heinl wrote:

> By every conceivable indicator, our army that now remains in Vietnam is in a state approaching collapse, with individual units avoiding

or having refused combat, murdering their officers and noncommissioned officers, drug-ridden, and dispirited where not near mutinous."[3]

Within a year, many of the fifteen young people demonstrating inside the Stock Exchange had turned their ideology and attitude into concrete acts of solidarity with the lower ranks of the armed forces. They were protagonists in this history of the struggle by GIs and their supporters to resist the war.

∞

Note to the reader: Chapter Notes at the end of each chapter are for supplementary points that provide additional background for the narrative. They are marked by * † ‡ § symbols in the text. Superscript numbers are for endnotes, which mainly indicate sources.

Chapter Notes

* GI was the popular term for a lower ranking enlisted or conscripted person in the U.S. Armed Forces. Its use began in the 1930s, apparently from military jargon referring to all sorts of equipment: General Issue.

† The Stock Exchange traders picked up on this hostile attitude and, taking no chances, within days management had builders install a hard, transparent wall on the balcony to separate future visitors from the traders. The wall is still there.

‡ By 2015 researcher James Lewes finished compiling a list of all the anti-establishment publications that GIs produced during the Vietnam War period. Lewes told me in a December 6, 2016 email that they totaled about 1,150 newspapers, newsletters and mailings and 1,000 pamphlets/leaflets, petitions, posters and personal letters. About two-thirds were issued from within the U.S. Armed Forces; others included material from anti-war German and French troops. At least one copy of each of these is now available in digital form at the Wisconsin Historical Society GI Press Collection.

Introduction

This book's main goal is to reveal the relationship in a developed country between a rebellion inside the armed forces and a social revolution that changes which class rules society. Its central focus is how one small group of Marxists whose goal was socialist revolution tried to build a union of rank-and-file GIs during the U.S. war against Vietnam to break the chain of command.

At the time, we hoped a union of GIs would at least make the U.S. war against the Vietnamese people impossible. That all Vietnam would be independent was our hope and our dream. The broad movement of anti-war GIs, in which our organization played a role much bigger than our numbers and our resources might predict, did contribute to achieving that goal, as this book shows.

During the Vietnam War a tremendous mass movement developed among the drafted and enlisted U.S. troops in the Army, Navy, Air Force and Marines. This movement impeded Washington's use of massive numbers of troops to invade and occupy other countries.

Our part of this GI movement was to found and build the American Servicemen's Union (ASU). This book covers, step by step, how this process developed in the context of the tumultuous social movements of the late 1960s and early 1970s.

The ASU was made up of low-ranking GIs — no officers and no career noncommissioned officers. Like any union, it demanded higher wages and more benefits. But it also fought against illegal wars like the war against Vietnam, it fought racism, and it challenged the chain of command. Though the Pentagon refused to recognize the ASU, it felt the thorn in its side.

The ASU also fought the deployment of U.S. Army and National Guard troops against the civilian population of the United States, as they were used against African-American rebellions in the 1960s. Chapter 10 shows how the ASU helped Black troops resist such duty.

10

ASU organizers also agitated against using soldiers to break the two-week postal workers' strike of March 1970.[1]

The movement against the U.S. war in Vietnam was strong among all youth and influenced the troops. The Black Liberation Movement also had a tremendous impact, especially on African-American GIs. Chapter 8 shows how the ASU aided two Black Marines, who were persecuted for holding anti-war political discussions with their peers.

Most people today know little to nothing about how many young, low-ranking GIs opposed the war by the late 1960s. The ruling class's enormous anti-history machine has scrubbed out the political ferment from portrayals of that period. People may know of the Beatles, the Rolling Stones and the Woodstock concert of August 1969. Chapter 13 shows how, while Woodstock was unfolding, thirty-five GIs were taking refuge at a church in Honolulu, Hawai'i, the nerve center of the U.S. military machine in the Pacific, to resign from the war.

Chapters 18-20 show how even in stockades and brigs, GI resistance grew. And Chapters 27-28 show how the ASU also mobilized "retired" GIs to fight for veterans' benefits, protest the war and ultimately join the struggle for socialism. Young workers who the U.S. rulers had trained to fight and kill began using their courage and training to serve their brothers and sisters and fight the bosses.

While there were few women in the 1968-1974 Armed Forces, compared to today's military, Chapter 24 shows how the women's liberation movement had an important impact on the ASU and on the GI struggle.

∞

Left-wing political activists in the United States in the twenty-first century have quickly learned that whenever they are in motion, they become targets of a powerful state.

In 2011, heavily armed police swept those in Occupy Wall Street from a New York City square and from similar occupations all across the country. These youths were not only up against the 0.01% super-rich, but their hired enforcers.

Black Lives Matter organizers protest the guns of the police that are shooting down Black and Brown people without pretext or punishment. (See Appendix A) They too have run up against a powerful state that rarely fires cops who have gunned down an unarmed person, let alone puts them on trial.

Indigenous peoples and their allies, gathered in North Dakota to defend sovereign lands against the Dakota Access Pipeline, face attacks from State Police, National Guard and company mercenaries.

Is It Possible to Overcome State Power?

This book does not pretend to provide a blueprint for confronting that state. However, in it are descriptions of events during three wars that led to revolts in the armed forces, which were the first step in political or social revolutions.

Chapter 5 covers the Franco-Prussian War leading to the Paris Commune of 1871 — the first revolution led by the working class in a European power. Its lessons served as a template educating revolutionary organizations in how to smash the state.

Chapters 14-16 discuss World War I, which led to upheavals in Russia and Germany. These were the two Russian revolutions of 1917, the first deposing the Czar's empire and the second establishing a socialist republic that lasted seventy-two years; and the revolt of the German North Sea Fleet in November 1918 that ended the monarchy but stopped short of socialism.

Chapter 29 discusses how the army of the small European country of Portugal, worn down by liberation wars in its African colonies, revolted in 1974 and brought down a forty-eight-year-old fascist regime. This last revolt opened up a democratic space for eighteen important months and facilitated the liberation of Angola, Mozambique, and Guinea-Bissau and Cape Verde in Africa.

In all these events the armed forces start out as a weapon in the hands of the ruling class. Through the troops' contact with rebellious workers or their wartime experience, their political consciousness changes. Military discipline shatters and part of the armed forces joins the revolution, opening a struggle for state power.

An introduction should also outline the book's limitations. This book does not claim to discuss all paths to revolution, only those that fit the above pattern. For example, it omits the heroic revolt of enslaved Africans in Haiti that in 1804 expelled France and ended slavery there. This event had an enormous impact worldwide and on ending the institution of slavery in the U.S.[2]

The Communist-led revolutions in China, Korea, Cuba and Vietnam in the twentieth century were based on guerrilla fighters in the countryside, with most fighters coming from and supported by the peasantry. The guerrilla armies grew into people's armies that surrounded the urban centers.

These revolutionary armies combined a movement for national liberation with class struggle. They smashed the old landlord-capitalist-colonialist state by defeating its army in battle. Then they replaced that army with a people's army.

In the United States and most industrialized countries today, farmers are a small minority of the producers. Any movement that attempted to dismantle the repressive state apparatus in the United States, Europe, Japan, Canada or Australia would undoubtedly follow a different path than the guerrilla pattern, which depends on organizing peasants against landlords and people against colonial rule.

It would also be impossible to do justice to the epic struggle for the liberation of Vietnam in this volume. The Vietnamese have been far better placed to write that history, which one can find in the works of Ho Chi Minh and Vo Nguyen Giap, among others. Here it is discussed with respect to its impact on U.S. GIs.

∞

The specific effort to organize the American Servicemen's Union was one part of an enormous panorama of GI resistance. Much of

TURN THE GUNS AROUND

this movement was spontaneous, driven by war experiences and contact with the courageous Vietnamese, but it was also organized.

One sign of its organization were the hundreds of GI newspapers. The ASU newspaper, *The Bond*, was published approximately monthly from 1967 to 1974 and was read by tens of thousands of GIs. Its most popular section was the letters page. This book has six chapters reproducing enough of those letters to give readers access to a sample of the raw material of history.

A big part of the GI movement was anti-war "coffeehouses" that civilians set up near military bases to attract dissident GIs and give them a place to meet. Another was the live performances by anti-war actors like Jane Fonda, Donald Sutherland, Holly Near and Paul Mooney before massive crowds of GIs in towns near military bases in their Fxxx the Army tour.

Legal committees helped GIs fight courts-martial or apply for Conscientious Objector status. Ordinary people set up safe houses for GIs on the way to Canada or in London, Paris and Stockholm. The 1994 hit movie *Forrest Gump* gave the false impression that anti-war activists regularly spit on GIs. This was a conscious, contrived lie.[3] The anti-war movement was more likely to embrace the GI.

My children, then five and six years old, woke up through 1969 wondering what young man with a crew cut would be sleeping on the living room couch early on Saturday mornings and how much noise they could make before he woke up. On official leave or AWOL, the guys from Fort Dix, New Jersey were welcome.

No other country's military is as powerful today as the U.S. Armed Forces. The Pentagon is the self-appointed police power protecting the property and interests of those who own and exploit all over the world. It props up, defends and expands the property and privileges of a tiny part of humanity: those who own the banks, factories, power stations, mines, oil wells and technology. These few are the super-rich who own it all, including the land and seabed from which their workers extract resources.

The Pentagon played this same central role in the 1960s and 1970s, when the demonized enemy of global capitalists was communism. Even as today, the Pentagon was capable of enormous destruction. Few would have thought it was possible to stop the Pentagon by helping to change the consciousness of the human beings who hold the weapons.

∞

In part, this book is based on my personal experiences as a civilian organizer with the ASU between 1967 and 1970. I was the circulation manager for *The Bond* and corresponded with hundreds of GI organizers. I worked closely with the principal ASU organizers, who were active-duty GIs and recent veterans. Besides checking my facts with these participants, I also checked all chapters about the ASU narrative against documents from those times, mostly original sources like stories and letters in *The Bond* and in *Workers World* newspaper and, where possible, original documents by others, including U.S. government sources.

To write the descriptions of military revolts and revolutions in France, Russia, Germany and Portugal, I also used original sources and authoritative interpretations, translating them where necessary. Since I could not find the leaflet by African liberation leader Amílcar Cabral elsewhere in English, it is published in full in Appendix G-I.

Readers seeking more details about the early days of the American Servicemen's Union can find Andy Stapp's book, *Up Against the Brass*, published by Simon and Schuster in 1970.

Those interested in the overall GI movement can read *Left Face*, which my friend and forty-three-year collaborator Max Watts co-authored with SP4 David Cortright (ret.). Now a university professor, Cortright wrote another excellent and well-sourced book, *Soldiers in Revolt*. *Bloods*, by Wallace Terry, provides insight into the experience of African-American GIs. (See Bibliography). The article "Perceptions of Race and Class Among Chicano Vietnam Veterans," by Ybarra Lea, focuses on the experience of Chicanos.[4]

In 2005, a film director named David Zeiger, who was active in the coffeehouse movement, put together a fine film of GI resistance: *Sir! No Sir!* A DVD version with extra features includes an interview commentary by ASU organizers Terry Klug and Andy Stapp.

∞

For complete transparency, I should let readers know that since shortly after the October 1962 missile crisis I have been a member of Workers World Party and since 1982 I've been a managing editor of the newspaper, *Workers World* (see workers.org).

From 1962 on, I was appalled and horrified by the U.S. military intervention in Vietnam. Like my party, I took the side of the National Liberation Front and the North Vietnamese Army over the U.S. occupation army and the Saigon puppets. I also supported the rebellions in the Black communities, the Black Panther Party and the right of African Americans to armed self-defense and self-determination.

Many key ASU organizers in the national leadership shared similar positions. Not everyone in the GI movement or in the ASU aimed at turning the guns around, but all contributed to forcing the U.S. to leave Vietnam. Of course, it was the Vietnamese people who made far greater contributions and sacrifices for this victory.

In the spring of 1969 the Richard Nixon administration, aware of declining morale within the U.S. military, refused a request from GEN William Westmoreland to expand the U.S. occupation force in Vietnam from 540,000 to one million. Instead the U.S. Armed Forces, while continuing to bomb the people of Vietnam, Laos and Cambodia, slowly withdrew land forces. The Vietnamese revolutionaries liberated their country in April 1975.

Chapter 32 shows how from then until January 1991 Washington avoided placing ground troops in a war, a reluctance known as the "Vietnam Syndrome." This reluctance to put "boots on the ground" still haunts the U.S. rulers, who know that by demanding sacrifices from millions of soldiers they can awaken the entire working class to struggle.

∞

Any phenomenon deserves attention if it has caused so much disruption in the most powerful military force the world had known. Those who want to change society inevitably run up against this monster problem: How do you battle the repressive state apparatus?

This state has changed little since Marxists first described it in the nineteenth century: Police, courts, prisons and "armed bodies of men" (now including women), an entrenched government bureaucracy — and in the twenty-first century — enormous standing armies, navies and air forces for international policing and the big corporate media for mind control.

Powerful? Yes. Omnipotent? **Only if it's not challenged.**

Chapter 1   Send a Salami

Mathematics Exam 1. Problem 2. A U.S. helicopter hovers 400 feet above the ground in Vietnam and drops a napalm bomb directly on a small hut. At the same moment the bomb drops, a Vietnamese woman carrying her baby starts running away from the hut in a straight line at 7 feet per second. How far away from the hut are she and the baby when the bomb hits the ground and explodes?

Fall 1963. I included that problem on a test for an evening mathematics course I was teaching at the City College of New York. My students, many older than my twenty-three years, greeted it with nervous laughter. I don't know how it affected them afterward, but I had an infant daughter and the image I created kept haunting me. It still does. Four years later I found the most effective way to stop that bomb.

Youth Against War & Fascism, which held the April 1966 demonstration in the New York Stock Exchange, was allied with Workers World Party. In February 1967 I was hanging out on my lunch break in the Workers World Party office. The office was in a run-down wooden building, four stories high, wedged between larger brick buildings on a block in the now-gentrified Flatiron district, then filled with small factories. Another YAWF member, Mike, showed me a letter addressed to Workers World newspaper. It read:

> The January 6th edition of Workers World was of particular interest to us, since it gave the full text of President Ho Chi Minh's New Year's Eve address to the American people. We are with you in the fight for a communist America."[1]

What made this letter special was that those who signed it were three GIs stationed at Fort Sill, Oklahoma. "It must be a joke," I said.

Having grown up in the fiercely anti-Communist 1950s and early 1960s, I was surprised that anyone declared themselves to be pro-communist, let alone three soldiers. Mike was sharper. He said, "It's no joke, John. We can organize inside the U.S. Army."

These three GIs had no desire to die for Wall Street's big firms. On the contrary, they identified with Vietnam's liberation fighters. The letter offered an excellent opportunity to help end the war against the Vietnamese by reaching out to the U.S. troops themselves. These soldiers were young workers, extremely low-paid young workers with hazardous working conditions, long hours and brutal discipline.

The first signature, in big letters like John Hancock wrote on the U.S. Declaration of Independence, was from PFC Andy Stapp. Mike wrote a friendly answer, and to underline this sentiment, he included a gift: some cookies, a can with the words "Party Nuts" and a salami. The signs on Katz's Delicatessen on New York's Lower East Side must have inspired him: "Send a salami to your boy in the Army." This little gift was a good start.

Left, Andy Stapp. Photo: Family **Right, from a sign hanging in Katz's Delicatessen, New York City.** Photo: Ellen Catalinotto

Andy Stapp was special. A little over a year earlier, on October 16, 1965, Stapp had burned his draft card at a protest that was part of a student demonstration. He soon changed his mind regarding tactics in fighting against the war. Stapp decided he could resist the war more effectively inside the Army than on campus. That might not have been true for everyone. But in his case, he was so right. In December 1965 he showed up for his physical and entered the Army.

Stapp wasn't a great soldier. He was ambidextrous and was likely to turn left when ordered "Right face!" A competitive long-distance runner in his high school in suburban Philadelphia, he

TURN THE GUNS AROUND

managed to get through basic training. Still he had trouble carrying out the routine tasks that soldiers are ordered to do that require "normal" coordination.

He had one talent, however, that made him one of the most popular GIs in his barracks. He told great stories. Stapp was a humorous raconteur like radio storytellers Jean Shepherd and Garrison Keillor. This wonderful spinner of tales had a photographic memory, a deep knowledge of history from the Roman Empire to World War II, and a great imagination to spice up the narrative.

Specialists Fourth Class Richard Wheaton and Paul Gaedtke were two of the GIs Stapp first won over. They signed the letter to Workers World. Wheaton, who became one of the key leaders of the ASU in New York when he "retired" from active duty, wrote this about Stapp:

I first met Andy when he transferred to the 2nd Battalion, 2nd Artillery, Fort Sill, Oklahoma in the early autumn of 1966. The night before he arrived, we were warned by the First Sergeant that a troublemaker would be arriving the next day—a communist. We were told not to have anything to do with him, and were urged to freeze him out. Most of the guys just went back to whatever they were doing without giving it another thought. They had more important things to worry about: like, when would they draw orders for that meat-grinder known as Vietnam? Paul Gaedtke and I, on the other hand, were curious, and looked forward to meeting a fellow troublemaker.

The next evening there he was, stretched out on his bunk, head propped up on a pillow, his pencil moving down the page of a book, reading faster than we'd ever seen anyone read. As we approached, he let his book fall to his lap, removed his glasses, and gave us a cautious once-over.

Are you that Stapp guy?' we asked. He admitted he was. "They say you're a communist, is that true?" He admitted to that also. Paul and I sat down on the bunk opposite his and started asking some pretty pointed questions about his politics and his position on the war. He answered us directly and openly. We weren't prepared for such forthrightness, having been brainwashed to expect "commies" to be devious and deceitful. That night, we three went into town for beers and conversation, and became instant friends and, soon thereafter, comrades.

The conversations never ended, and eventually grew to include other members of the unit, won over by this charismatic and, oh yes, very funny guy.[2]

Stapp once said the Army made it easy for him to organize. "Most organizers have to keep chasing after the workers, trying to find them, get a few moments together to win them to the union. In the Army, I had access to the guys in my barracks 24/7."[3]

Stapp's stories targeted the chain of command, starting with President Lyndon Johnson and trickling down to the top generals and admirals at the Pentagon, the general running Fort Sill, the colonels and majors, all the way down to the company commander and various lieutenants and lifer sergeants who made life miserable for the troops. Listening, the GIs laughed with Stapp and got mad at Johnson — or at their sergeant. One by one, he convinced a half-dozen GIs not only to oppose the war against Vietnam, but to stand against the whole racist, imperialist system.

Sooner or later the officers were bound to confront Stapp. It finally happened. On May 13, 1967, his commanding officer, a Lieutenant Urquhart, ordered him to open his footlocker, which was filled with newspapers and magazines, some of them from various communist or anti-war organizations. Stapp refused.

Charged with refusing a direct order to open his locker, he was to be court-martialed in June. Stapp had his own civilian lawyer, supplied by the National Emergency Civil Liberties Committee. When the NECLC press release reached the Workers World office, we answered with more than a salami.

Youth Against War & Fascism organized a delegation to go to Stapp's court-martial to show solidarity in the courtroom and make sure the Fort Still Brass knew they were being watched. Among the ten or so people going were YAWF leaders Key Martin, Maryann Weissman and Sharon Eolis, who had all been at the Stock Exchange protest, and a young Black man from Brooklyn named Eddie Oquendo, a draft resister who later received a five-year sentence, of which he served twenty-six months.*

These young anti-war fighters drove from New York to Lawton, Oklahoma, the base town of Fort Sill. They set up operations at the Lawtonian Motel and met with seven soldiers, including Wheaton and Gaedtke, who had signed the letter. They were all low-ranking enlisted men, who were Stapp's closest allies and friends.

For the three nights before the court-martial, the YAWF delegation and the GIs planned their strategy. Armed with a portable mimeograph machine, they prepared press releases to attract the media to the base. The civilians would demonstrate when the decision came down.

When Stapp took the stand, he said:

> We GIs say this is not our war. It's Wall Street's war. I'll cite an example: Dow Chemical's stocks have soared as a result of the twenty-five million pounds of napalm it sells each month to the military forces in Vietnam. At the same time the death toll of American GIs has risen in proportion to profits and has now reached a new high last week alone of three hundred thirty-seven. Many men in the unit are opposed to the war and have literature in their lockers similar to what was in my foot locker. ... The ruling class needs robots in its Army, but we refuse to be unthinking cannon fodder.[4]

The YAWF civilians burst out in applause and five GIs who had defied their officers' warning to stay away from the trial joined them. When Stapp was found guilty, the YAWF delegation chanted, "The Brass is the tool of Wall Street's rule" and "End the war in Vietnam, bring the GIs home now." It was, to their knowledge, the first such protest at a military court-martial.

Stapp was found guilty at the court-martial and was sentenced to forty-five days unconfined hard labor, forfeiture of twenty days pay and reduction to the lowest possible rank, private. Stapp was proud to stay at that rank.

This was the first of two courts-martial that Stapp faced between June and August that cemented his relationship with Workers World Party and launched the American Servicemen's Union.

Up Against the Brass, Stapp's political memoir published in 1970, provides details of these events. Most important is that YAWF's solidarity built solid bonds between the civilian activists and the GIs.

Looking back on the events, Wheaton wrote:

> Even though the trial ended in a legal defeat, it was a win for us. Andy had garnered the sympathy of a large number of enlisted men in the battalion, and not just those who'd met him and talked to him. His bravery and refusal to be intimidated by the Brass had earned him their admiration; by attacking him, the Brass had handed us a huge victory and clarified the class lines within the military machine.[5]

At that first court-martial, some of the YAWF delegation, including Martin and Weissman, received restraining orders barring them from the base. The Army used the orders when the two tried to attend the second court-martial Stapp faced at the end of July.

During that summer, YAWF members in New York founded an organization called the Committee for GI Rights, whose first task was to defend Stapp and others in his group at Fort Sill who faced charges or simply harassment.

The objective lessons of the war aided Stapp's organizing. GIs were sent to serve a year in combat or for support work — logistics — in Vietnam. Since 200,000 were serving there in early 1966, that meant by early 1967 these troops, having experienced the war, were returning to bases in the U.S. for their last few months of service before exiting the military.

These combat veterans were angry, not with the Vietnamese "enemy," but with their officers and with the government that sent them to kill and die. Their own stories convinced the troops in training that they should stay far away from Vietnam.

During the early years of the war, the Army and Marine infantry had a disproportionately higher number of African Americans. Black troops, concentrated in the combat units, were taking more than their statistical share of the casualties in Vietnam from 1965-1969, although later this disproportion diminished.[6]

Many young white men who had the choice stayed as long as possible in college, hoping to postpone conscription or even to avoid the draft entirely. As the war went on, thousands left the United States for Canada, which offered asylum to draft resisters.

The college door was closed to most Black youth and only a few sought asylum in Canada, where there were no large Black neighborhoods. A growing number were looking to disappear from official records and some managed this by living "underground" with the tacit support of their communities.

That left a large number of Black, Puerto Rican and Chicano youths and working-class white youths still subject to conscription. In 1968 at the peak of the war, some 343,000 were drafted into the military and another 513,000 voluntarily enlisted,[7] many in the hope it would get them a post anywhere but Vietnam.

Both draftees and enlistees were often from union families and were almost always from the families that had household incomes under the median.[8] They were more likely to have a strong working-class consciousness than the better-off students who had first protested the war. To many of the troops facing assignment to Vietnam, Stapp's explanations of the war and capitalist society were more compelling than the lies of their sergeants and officers. He gave those of us already committed to stop the war a path to the troops. Now we had to reach out to thousands of rebellious GIs.

Chapter Notes

* Oquendo wrote, in 2014:

I did not want to fight in an unjust war. With the guidance of the late Gil Banks, a CORE Activist group called BAND [Blacks Against Negative Dying] was started. At the same time I became a member of YAWF, the only group I knew of that without reservation supported a group of Black nationalists opposed to the war. ...

I could not grasp the concept of antiwar GIs. However, YAWF sent a group to Fort Sill, Oklahoma, to meet and offer support to a group of soldiers and I just had to be a part of that.

Meeting Andy Stapp was almost surreal. We drove to Oklahoma through what seemed to me like a wasteland. Before we got some rest, we listened to Coltrane with a group of antiwar soldiers. Talking with Andy laid out part of my near future. Andy was totally anti-draft, impressing upon me that all I could get was five years and a $10,000 fine. Oh, sue me!

These courageous GIs faced much more dire consequences for their antiwar stance and activism. This was right in the face of the leadership of arguably the most powerful organization in the world, the US Army. Forgive me, but ¡que huevos!

Andy's opposition to the war was exceeded only by his deep aversion to racism, which he expressed in no uncertain terms. Our bond was natural, with mutual support for each other. Andy was a catalyst in my coming to the belief in class struggle.[9]

Chapter 2 **From Struggle to Structure**

July 1967. I was about to leave for work. The phone rang in our Brooklyn apartment. I picked it up and heard: "Don't go to work today. Fascists are outside the motel in Lawton. They're threatening to kill Key and Maryann. Get in to the HQ. We have to help."

I called my boss. "Hi, Steve (cough). John here. I feel lousy (cough). I think I'd better take a sick day." I ran through the building to the Eastern Parkway IRT stop across from the Brooklyn Museum. Soon I was at the Workers World office on Manhattan's West 21st Street, taking the creaky wooden stairs three at a time to the second floor. It was emergency mode.

After the first court-martial took place in June in Fort Sill, Oklahoma, Maryann Weissman and Key Martin set up operations in the Lawtonian Motel in Lawton, the base town. The local media's front-page articles warned of the "red" invasion of Oklahoma. Photos of Weissman showed her as a *femme fatale* out to lure GIs to their red doom. In his book, *Up Against the Brass*, Stapp showed the impact of that rabble-rousing:

> A radio announcer from a local station was standing in front of Maryann's window and saying, "A crowd is gathering here ..."
>
> No crowd had gathered until he had started to talk. ...
>
> Within fifteen minutes, more than three hundred people were pushing and elbowing for position. The crowd became ugly and the announcer left. Soon there was kicking and hammering at the door.
>
> "Get out of town, you Communist," someone yelled. ...
>
> "Do we kill her first? Or do we fuck her and then kill her?"[1]

Maryann and Key faced a lynch mob. Though we didn't trust the Oklahoma governor, our priority was saving the comrades' lives, so I called him with this message: "If anything happens to Key Martin and Maryann Weissman, we will hold the governor responsible." To my surprise, the governor's aide called back for details.

Meanwhile, Wheaton, Gaedtke and some of Stapp's other GI buddies didn't wait for the governor. They were bringing M-16 assault rifles to the motel to defend the YAWF organizers. In the end, the rightists backed off after police arrested Martin and Weissman.[2]

The Army Brass were used to winning courts-martial easily. The Judge Advocate General (JAG) prosecutors had prepared a sloppy case against Stapp that July 31. He had been charged, with no basis, with illegally leaving his barracks. The sergeant testifying at the trial had to admit that Stapp had not been ordered confined to barracks, but only to the base. The court-martial found Stapp not guilty.

Courts-martial are supposed to be open to the public. YAWF organized two carloads of supporters to drive from NYC to Lawton for the court-martial. But the military set up roadblocks at the entrances to the base to keep them from attending. When the cars stopped at the roadblock, Weissman and Martin were arrested. They were charged with violating the earlier bar order issued against them.

The solidarity trips cemented the relationship between the radicals and the GIs. SP4 Richard Wheaton described his own reaction:

> When Andy was under attack and we were casting about for civilian support, it was Workers World, and no one else, that stepped up to help us. No one else wanted to "mess with the military," but the party could see that that was just what we were itching to do, needed to do; it jumped at the opportunity and put its resources at our disposal to take the story of our struggle to the world, and the struggle itself to the belly of the beast.[3]

The other YAWF people were then taken to the JAG office and given bar orders against returning to the base. Martin and Weissman, tried in federal court on August 25 for violating the order to stay off Fort Sill, were handed maximum sentences of six months in federal prison. Even this apparent setback to organizing GIs had a positive side: It showed the GIs that the civilians in YAWF and WWP were willing to take risks and make sacrifices.

During the Oklahoma trips, I did support work in New York with Shirley Jolls, who co-wrote one of the pamphlets defending dissident Black Marines, and Fayette (Richie) Richardson,* a World War II paratrooper. Earlier, we had formed the Committee for GI Rights in New York. The committee published leaflets and pamphlets explaining the legal cases of the Fort Sill soldiers, demanding Constitutional rights for GIs and building support for dissident troops.

In September, Stapp visited New York. Workers World Party Chairperson Sam Marcy spent hours with him. Marcy raised the idea of organizing a union of rank-and-file soldiers. Stapp thought this was a great idea. It fit his experience.

A labor union represents the interests of the workers in a factory or store or school or hospital against the owners of those enterprises. Human labor adds value to the product. The union battles management over how much of that value is paid as wages and benefits; the owner takes the rest as profits. The ultimate weapon of the union is the strike — withholding labor.

About 30 percent of U.S. workers in the 1960s belonged to unions and considered them to be what they needed to fight for a better life.[4]

In the U.S. Armed Forces, military hierarchy mimics the structure of capitalist society. The low-ranking GIs are like workers. The sergeants in the professional army, also known as "lifers," are like lower level supervisors, who receive higher pay and perks and tell workers what to do. The lieutenants, captains and majors are similar to mid-level management, with the colonels and generals playing the role of top management.

Because military decisions concern the life and death of the soldiers, its top management depends on a rigid chain of command to function. Top officers order lower officers, who order sergeants, who order soldiers: The military depends on obedience.

Marcy and Stapp agreed that GI organizers could present the ASU as the most logical class organization of rank-and-file GIs. At the same time, the ASU would raise demands that rank-and-file GIs elect their officers, and that would legitimize a GI's right to refuse illegal orders, like orders to fight against Vietnam. The ASU would fight not only for higher pay and better food, but against racism, to prevent any use of troops against strikes, protests and rebellions. The ASU would break the chain of command.

∞

Looking back nearly fifty years, I see we must have had enormous audacity to think that with such a tiny number of people we could take on the U.S. Armed Forces. Yet what we Marxists call "the objective conditions" were moving in our favor.

Civil Rights leader the Rev. Dr. Martin Luther King Jr. made his famous anti-war speech in early April 1967.

Three weeks later, heavyweight boxing champion Muhammad Ali refused to be drafted. This cost him his title for three years and got him a five-year jail sentence that was later reversed. His action reflected growing anti-war sentiment among the African-American population and magnified it.†

In the summer of 1967 there were major rebellions in the Black neighborhoods of Detroit and Newark. In the fall of 1967 the overall mood in the country opposing the war continued to grow, although a poll would show anti-war forces were still a minority.

When the Brass broke up the groups around Stapp at Fort Sill in late 1967 by sending the individual GIs, one by one, to other bases, this did more to spread the struggle than disperse it. One of the GIs, an 18-year-old private from Vermont named Dick Perrin, soon deserted and wound up in a group of GIs in Paris that became another pole of resistance. Meanwhile, casualty rates of GIs increased in the Central Highlands of Vietnam, and more and more GIs turned against the war, at a faster rate and with more vehemence than in the civilian population.

After his court-martial in July, Stapp met Workers World member Deirdre Griswold, a young political leader who had been working with the Bertrand Russell War Crimes Tribunal‡ in Europe earlier in the year. She was one of the group that had driven from New York hoping to attend Stapp's court-martial. The attraction was mutual and immediate, and the two got married that fall in Oklahoma.

Stapp wrote in *Up Against the Brass*, "Asked by the *Daily Oklahoman* to comment on our marriage, the head of Military Intelligence said, 'Like a Rockefeller marrying a duPont, it's a political merger.'"[5] For Deirdre and Andy's marriage, no property was involved.

In December 1967, I organized a series of meetings in the Philadelphia area featuring Stapp and Eddie Oquendo, the young Black draft resister who had bonded with the GIs when he was at the court-martial in June. The two argued that both forms of resistance, draft refusal and organizing within the military, could contribute to ending the war. They convinced me.

Eddie Oquendo, draft resister. Photo: Workers World

On the morning of December 25 in New York, Stapp called together a small group of GIs on Christmas leave, who approved the eight demands (later expanded to twelve) that Stapp and another of the Fort Sill group, PFC Dick Ilg, had drafted. That group founded the American Servicemen's Union with Stapp unanimously elected chairperson.

Stapp's in-your-face attitude and his ability to interact with even a hostile media were beginning to attract more support. This turned out to be important in helping the ASU grow.

In early 1967 in Berkeley, California, a civilian named Bill Callison began publishing a monthly four-page newspaper that would reach out to GIs. Callison called this paper *The Bond*, referring to the bond he wanted to establish between the civilian anti-war movement and the GIs. He published it from June to December, when, feeling he was at a personal breaking point, he bequeathed the newspaper to the ASU. Stapp and SP4 Richard Wheaton had already been contributing articles to *The Bond*.

Over the summer, as part of his work with the Committee for GI Rights, Richie Richardson wrote a pamphlet, *GI Rights and Military Injustice*. Richie, a schoolteacher, was also an experienced writer and editor.

A Workers World Party member, Richie was a veteran combat paratrooper. In 1967, pro-war superpatriots would label anti-war people "cowards." Richie easily shut them up. At 44, he still fit into his old paratrooper's uniform, which he wore for public speaking. Starting in January 1968, Richie was editing *The Bond*.

The ASU needed someone to take care of *The Bond*'s circulation, keep the small office at 156 Fifth Avenue running and answer the mail. Most of the active union GIs were still on military bases. Martin and Weissman were in prison. Marcy asked me to take it on.

I leaped at the task. For the next thirty-three months, I did only what work was needed to stay on the payroll at my day job, which was a ten-minute walk from the ASU office. I could do this until the summer of 1970, when I was nearly fired and faced hard choices. As an ASU volunteer, my thirty hours a week grew until this project was absorbing all my waking hours and informing my dreams.

In the spring of 1966 at the Stock Exchange, all we young radicals in YAWF had was ideology and attitude. By New Year's Day 1968 we had a newspaper, a national office and a core of GI leaders committed to building a union that could jam up the gears of the Pentagon's terrible war machine.

Chapter Notes

* Richardson parachuted into Normandy, France, with the 82nd Airborne Pathfinders the night before D-Day, June 6, 1944, when the U.S. and British troops invaded as part of the drive against the German occupation of France. Richardson also fought in the Battle of the Bulge, which was the name given to the German army's last World War II offensive in France.

† Muhammad Ali: "Why should they ask me to put on a uniform and go 10,000 miles from home and drop bombs and bullets on Brown people in Vietnam while so-called Negro people in Louisville are treated like dogs and denied simple human rights? No I'm not going 10,000 miles from home to help murder and burn another poor nation simply to continue the domination of white slave masters of the darker people the world over. This is the day when such evils must come to an end. I have been warned that to take such a stand would cost me millions of dollars. But I have said it once and I will say it again. The real enemy of my people is here. I will not disgrace my religion, my people or myself by becoming a tool to enslave those who are fighting for their own justice, freedom and equality. If I thought the war was going to bring freedom and equality to 22 million of my people they wouldn't have to draft me, I'd join tomorrow. I have nothing to lose by standing up for my beliefs. So I'll go to jail, so what? We've been in jail for 400 years."[6]

‡ Philosopher and mathematician Bertrand Russell, Jean-Paul Sartre and other European intellectuals set up a people's war crimes tribunal in 1966 and 1967 to put the U.S. leaders on trial for crimes in Vietnam. Deirdre Griswold worked as an administrative assistant for the tribunal in London and Stockholm after the French government refused to permit the tribunal to take place in Paris. Maryann Weissman also worked for the tribunal.

**Left, Andy Stapp, Maryann Weissman, Key Martin.
Circa 1969.** Photo: ASU collection

F.O. Richardson, 1945.
Photo: ASU collection

Chapter 3 Dear Andy — Letters to *The Bond*
The Soldiers Set the Rules

"Dear Andy." That's how many of the hundreds of letters we received each month began. As chairperson of the American Servicemen's Union, Andy was the face of military resistance for what would become tens of thousands of rebellious GIs.

Every month we published the newspaper of the ASU, *The Bond*. Of the four pages, a full page in small type was a selection of these letters. *The Bond*'s content was great. But for many of the GIs reading it, their favorite section was the letters page. In 2016, when even email is considered old media, and most messages are sent in 140-character sound bites, it's hard to remember that even snail mail can build tension and excitement. But it did. It's easy to see why.

More than punishment, what held the anti-war GIs back from expressing themselves was the feeling of isolation. All it took was reading a full tabloid page of letters in small type from people who shared their thoughts and reactions for them to conclude: "I am not alone." And for those who subscribed and read *The Bond*'s letter page each month, this conclusion would grow to: "We're everywhere!"

For us in the ASU office, the letters opened a window to the consciousness of the GIs. In the beginning, most expressed individual needs, from anger at bad treatment to a wish to escape the horrors of a posting to Vietnam. Month by month more of the letters showed a desire for organization and solidarity. They also showed us what we needed to do. For example, it was a letter, included below, that led to our issuing union cards.

Here is a small sample of the letters we received between January and April 1968 (the dates refer to publication of *The Bond*):

January 28, 1968 - CONSCIENTIOUS OBJECTOR

I am a Conscientious Objector. I am very much interested in your program.

I am wondering what my rights are as an Army private concerning C.O.'s. Would you please send any literature available to me on the rights of C.O.'s. I have not as yet declared my status on paper to the Army.

Right now I'm trying to get a medical discharge.

Fort Sam Houston, Texas

∞

January 28, 1968 - WANTS INFORMATION ON ASU

Gentlemen:

We have been advised that you can supply us with information concerning the GI union. We are privates in the Army, inducted and against the war. After induction we enlisted because we were to be sent to an infantry unit. While at Fort Sill we learned that the information we are requesting could be obtained from you. Any information would be appreciated. Thank you.

Fort Sill, Oklahoma

∞

January 28, 1968 - FORT BENNING SOLDIERS SUPPORT UNION

Dear Andy,

As fellow soldiers, some veterans of Vietnam, the rest waiting to go, we are in fullest solidarity with your fight for GI rights. We stand in opposition [to] the Army's attempts to silence you, first by harassment and outright coercion, and then failing there, by trying to throw you out of the service via an "undesirable discharge." We must stick together!

Your example has inspired us, likewise, to openly declare ourselves against the war of aggression in Vietnam and to support the National Liberation Front as representing the hopes and aspirations of the Vietnamese people. We have seen too many of our buddies die just so Big Business can continue making the fast buck. We pledge ourselves to organize in the Resistance against this filthy war and the System which spawned it.

Free speech for GIs!

Bring our Buddies Home, Now!

Alive!

A Soldiers' Union, Now!

Yours in the struggle,

PFC Maury Knutson, PFC Thomas Wake, PFC Andrew Holloway

January 28, 1968 - THINGS MOVING RAPIDLY

Dear Friends,

Things are moving quite rapidly here. Our movement for GI rights received quite a lift as our threat of outside legal help removed the threat of a bust against Al, the veteran of both Vietnam and Newark. The Black GIs are moving to the forefront in organizing efforts. The company officers and the First Sergeant are all quite upset. "Top" counseled (name*) and (name*) [*name* means name deleted*] not to associate with me, as it meant "bad trouble," and to hand over literature. Both refused. They are also taking Article 31 on security aspects on DD 398 which is the start of a national agency check being initiated against them. The harassment against me is terrific though not unbearable.

An important new member of our group is (name*). He's a black GI from Birmingham, Alabama and served with the infantry in Vietnam. He has freely told of atrocities he saw while over there. He has been quite impressed with the handling of Al's case. (Name*) previously had beaten the hell out of the joker in the company who is a Klan member. While I debated him in front of white guys, (name*) eliminated him as a physical threat. This was important, as they, the Ku-Klux boys, were my only real "rivals." An important part of my work has been fighting racism. Under the slogans, "Racism is for losers" and "Why cut your own throat" we've had some good solid success.

Georgia

∞

February 1968 - U.S. AGGRESSION 'CRIMINAL'

Gentlemen:

I was inducted into the Army in August 1967 as a 1-A-O. Through lectures and "Battle Glory" films they think they can remold my beliefs into theirs.

It will never work.

The American aggression against North Vietnam is criminal; they can't tell me otherwise.

In January [1968], I MAY get orders to go to Vietnam. I will refuse them.

Fort Sam Houston, Texas

February 18, 1968 - UNION COULD GIVE SUPPORT TO GIs WHO REFUSE VIET DUTY

I am a soldier at Fort Campbell who is interested in the GI union which Andy Stapp represents. I am still in basic training but I applied for a 1-A-O classification so I haven't been taking any combat training and will probably be here for some time while my application is processed. I have introduced the union to other trainees and have found a lot of potential support for it here. I don't have anything concrete to give them though, but hope that maybe you can help me. Should I send in names? Do you have membership cards?

As I see it, in addition to gaining better working conditions this union could provide a hard core of support for those refusing to be shipped to Vietnam. This should tend to strengthen and intensify the impact of these refusals — now the refusals are only on a personal level and don't have much effect if they aren't widely publicized.

I'd appreciate any leaflets, etc., you could spare.

Fort Campbell, Kentucky

∞

February 18, 1968 - PLAN A GIs' BASE PAPER

I got hold of my first copy of The Bond on a little trip to Houston; I do not want it to be my last copy. My friends and I have made duplicates of your subscription form and we are making them available to anyone here who wants them. Do you mind if articles from The Bond are reprinted in another paper?

My friends and I really appreciate your newspaper. Please keep up the good work.

Perrin AFB, Texas

P.S.: We are planning a paper here.

∞

February 18, 1968 - SO I CANCELLED MY 'BOND'

Last week my company commander obtained a previous issue of The Bond. He discouraged GIs from reading the newspaper and has agreed to hold a discussion concerning the facts and opinions presented in your tabloid.

Since the CO discouraged men in his unit from receiving The Bond, I have decided to discontinue mine — I have cancelled my U.S. SAVINGS BOND.

Ft. Carson, Colorado

February 18, 1968 - UP THE MEKONG RIVER

I have read your newspaper and truly believe that it is what servicemen need, and have needed for a long time. Everybody in the service gets shit on and are finally getting tired of it. Through the Bond you can see and hear only a few of the many faults and fuckups that one lives with when living under a dictatorship.

Right now we are up one of the rivers in the Mekong Delta. Life aboard this ship is miserable to say the least. We get liberty every three months supposedly. However, it has gone as high as seven months straight without any of the normal releases from tension and frustration.

Since we are stationed in Vietnam, we qualify for the three-day in-country R&R period every three months, and five-day out-of-country R&R every six months. However, the captain says he doesn't feel that we deserve it.

I think people like this should be suppressed and kept from decisions and responsibilities concerning the welfare and recreation of an entire ship and crew.

Snoopy, FPO, San Francisco

∞

February 18, 1968 - PLATOON 'DETERIORATES'

I've been passing out Bonds an issue at a time. They were well received. The Drill Sergeant knew about it but didn't know who. He let it ride until lately when it became apparent that our platoon was deteriorating badly. We now have five men AWOL and men have been splitting from night training for the barracks. Men from our platoon have received about 10 article 15s (mocked up kind, because they are not allowed to give trainees article 15s).

Finally one man in our platoon stood up in a class and let everyone know what he thought of the Army. He was later questioned — asked if he knew who was passing out anti-war literature. He said he didn't know.

I'm out of Bonds. I don't know whether the Bonds are responsible for the platoon's behavior, but the Drill Sergeant is beginning to think so; I'll take his word for it.

California

March 18, 1968 - WILL GO TO JAIL BEFORE VIET

I just started reading the Bond. I received it from a friend of mine, and for once I've found someone who believes as I do about the war in Vietnam. Yes, I too believe that it is a senseless war and it is nothing put plain Bull. I'm determined that I would rather go to jail before I'd go there — that god-forsaken place called Vietnam.

∞

March 18, 1968 - CONSIDERS WHAT HE SHOULD DO

I, along with countless fellow GIs, realize that we were wrong in more or less meekly submitting to the draft. In retrospect I feel that morally I should have either submitted to jail for refusing to take the oath or taken up residence in Canada.

Fort Gordon, Georgia

∞

March 18, 1968 - MANY ABOARD AGREE

I was unable to get the coupon for subscribing to your newsletter because there were too many people who wanted to read it. There are many of us aboard my ship who strongly agree with your editorial policy and we are sadly lacking in material which will tell us the truth...so any back issues or leaflets you could send us would certainly be put to good use.

FPO, San Francisco

∞

April 14, 1968 - BRASS HIT ONE, FAILED TO STOP MOVEMENT

We support your opposition to the war, the inhuman actions of this established course that is leading many to destruction and obliteration.

My friend wrote you a letter approximately a week ago with a list of subscribers to *The Bond*. He was arrested by the military police, investigated by Military Intelligence, and gave a sworn statement to give his unequivocal support to the Army. And his copy of "Military Injustice" was also confiscated. He didn't receive his issue of the last Bond, which leads us to wonder about the mail service at Bragg.

This doesn't stop our movement for a free America. And, gentlemen, there is a movement for peace here. Its members are doubling every day. Future plans include such things as an underground free press and a love-in in North Carolina. And eventually an end to all this blind slaughtering of mankind.

We together will have a free America.

Fort Bragg, North Carolina

TURN THE GUNS AROUND

Chapter 4   **From Fingers to a Fist**

At the end of December 1967, after that first important meeting when GIs founded the American Servicemen's Union, Stapp suddenly got violently ill on leave. We worried for his life. As he was visiting his parents in Merion, Pennsylvania, his appendix burst. He had an emergency appendectomy and was suffering from peritonitis.

The Army Brass had a Field Board Hearing waiting for him at Fort Sill, Oklahoma. Such a hearing can make an administrative decision, such as discharging a soldier. A court-martial is needed if he is charged with a crime punishable by confinement. The Brass wanted to show Stapp was a subversive and to get rid of him early with an Undesirable Discharge, which would deprive him of all GI benefits and stop him from organizing the union while on active duty.

Politically, Stapp was ready to fight the Army in Oklahoma, but physically, he was flat on his back in a Philadelphia hospital. He was still being fed intravenously just days before the scheduled hearing. Riding roughshod over the recommendations of Stapp's civilian doctor, the Army grabbed him out of his hospital bed and transported him to the Wilson Army Hospital at Fort Dix, New Jersey.

Once Deirdre Griswold learned what had happened, she borrowed a car and we drove to the hospital, ninety minutes from New York, on that icy winter night. The nurses tried to keep her out of his room. Deirdre rarely shouts. She just said, "I'm sitting in here until you let me in." After a half hour, they gave in. Stapp appeared to be in no immediate danger and we left after the visit.

Two days later, however, the Army put him on a Medivac plane back to Fort Sill. The propeller-driven cargo plane made fifteen stops letting sick passengers on and off and took fifty-six hours getting to Fort Sill, with the temperature in the plane dropping way below freezing every time the door opened. Stapp wrote:

The only food I had been allowed at the hospital was tea and soup, but the nurse on the plane offered me a ham sandwich. ... In my semi delirium I imagined the Brass were trying to kill me, but the saner part of my mind said that after all this is the Army, they always do things this way.[1]

For the rest of his life Stapp hated to fly.

He landed in Fort Sill in time for the January 4 hearing, but even the Army doctors knew he wasn't fit for it; he was moved to a bed in the base hospital and the hearing was postponed until January 30. It lasted three days. Deirdre Griswold Stapp and other civilian supporters were there in the courtroom, ready to applaud for him.

The command let every GI at Fort Sill know that a GI was going on trial as a subversive because he wanted to form a union. The officers instructed all to stay away from the hearing.

That pissed them off. The most defiant GIs showed up. One was SP5 Bob Lemay, who had spent a year in Vietnam. He was not in combat, but even in support functions he had learned enough to hate the war and to ignore officers' instructions.

Since the Army was trying to prove that Stapp was a subversive who could harm the military, they called a half-dozen GIs who had worked with him to testify against him. Instead of speaking out against Stapp, they spoke out against the Army and the war. The Army had one declared a hostile witness and sent another back to the stockade.

SP4 Richard Wheaton,* for example, told the board he was a Marxist and that he became one "since I came into the Army and as a result of the war in Vietnam."[2]

SP4 Mel Hoit told the board "[Stapp] is concerned with soldiers' rights and enforcing the Constitution within the Army."[3]

Stapp's attorney, Michael Kennedy from the National Emergency Civil Liberties Committee, set up a series of questions that Andy could use against the Army. Stapp turned the Field Board Hearing into a launching pad for the union, answering:

"[GIs] want to be able to sit on boards of courts-martial. They want an end to racism in the barracks. They want a federal minimum wage. They want a right to disobey an illegal order. They want a right to elect their officers."[4]

∞

The hearing coincided with bigger events beyond the Army's control. On January 29, the National Liberation Front of South Vietnam — what U.S. media called the Vietcong — opened a widespread surprise attack in all major cities during the country's Lunar New Year, or Tet. It lasted for three weeks. The liberation fighters even briefly seized the U.S. Embassy in Saigon, the southern capital.

While the Tet Offensive fell short of ending the war and driving out the U.S. occupiers, it destroyed confidence within U.S. ruling circles that the Pentagon would win this war and that the people in the U.S. would continue to support the effort. It boosted the anti-war movement's confidence in our success. And it convinced many GIs that for the U.S., the war against Vietnam was unwinnable. So why fight? The casualty figures, with 543 GIs killed and 2,547 wounded the week of February 11-17, smacked everyone in the head.

Meanwhile, on January 28, the ASU team in New York, with contributions from GIs at Fort Sill, produced its first copy of *The Bond*, proudly identified as Volume 2, Number 1.

∞

The field board delayed its decision for two months, then finally found against Stapp and discharged him from the Army as undesirable, with loss of all rank and benefits. PVT Andy Stapp (ret.) held the lowest rank possible, but he was the ASU's chairperson. He would build the core of the union in New York and spread the idea around the world.

The hearing convinced Lemay to join the ASU. Six months later he and his wife, Sherry Lemay, moved to New York and Bob took possession of the ASU office. He was the most consistent staffer, opening the ASU office daily at 9:30 a.m. and sorting through the mail. I can still picture Bob sitting at his desk with a pipe in his mouth, his hands on his typewriter and his lunch sitting in a brown bag at the side, probably along with a can of beer.

Lemay and Wheaton were the mainstays of the ASU office the first couple of years, and they also wrote for the newspaper. A Vietnam veteran Bill Smith, an excellent journalist, started working with Richie as Vietnam editor of *The Bond*. Wheaton once wrote about Smith:

> When Bill writes: 'We don't want to be shit upon any more and possibly killed in a war we know is unjust or sent back into a community that may very likely be attacked by National Guardsmen or green troops who never knew what it was like to be in 'Nam and kill blindly at some pig's whim. We're tired and pissed off and we're fighting back.' It comes from the gut with understanding and force.[5]

Some of the young people active in Youth Against War & Fascism also helped on ASU work around the office, getting *The Bond* ready for the printer or on newspaper mailings. Some of the civilians doing background work at the ASU office — Shirley Jolls, Laurie Fierstein, Sue Davis — would also organize and lead demonstrations with YAWF.

Mailing copies of *The Bond* to GIs was a complicated task. We made them appear to be personal letters from friend or family, never using a printed label or a return address with the union office. All envelopes were addressed by hand. The newspapers were then folded, stuffed and sent by first class mail. We needed a full crew of anti-war volunteers as the mailing list got longer.

The ASU office was a short walk from my job. My lunch breaks kept growing longer as I couldn't tear myself away from the letters that kept coming in larger numbers from the bases and APOs around the world.

∞

At the end of March a little extra money in the union budget allowed me to fly to a Students for a Democratic Society conference at the University of Kentucky in Lexington.†

At the conference, I tried to build support for the ASU among the radical students and meet any GIs who attended. I met Dave Ort from Fort Campbell, who was carrying the ASU membership card his letter had inspired. I imagined thousands of GIs like Dave joining the ASU simply because being a union member was part of their life.

Then I met John Lewis, a tall, working-class, anti-war youth who was on a razor's edge. He was trying to decide whether to resist the draft and how. We talked about the ASU and its potential.

At the time we were not urging youth facing the draft to enter the military.‡ I told him, however, "If you go into the Army and try to organize GIs, the ASU will give you full support. We don't want you to go to Vietnam. But if any soldiers wind up there and then decide they want to resist the military, we will back them."

Following our meeting, John Lewis chose to accept the draft. From the South, Lewis was polite and soft-spoken to his peers — as long as they weren't racists. Over the next two years he would stand up against any racist and every officer and sergeant who tried to hound GIs into submission from Honolulu, Hawai'i to the Fort Dix Stockade in New Jersey.

I missed the last flight home from Lexington and on Sunday, March 31, 1968, I spent the night in Louisville watching TV as President Lyndon Johnson announced that he would not run for re-election and that he was suspending bombing raids against North Vietnam. Those days, young demonstrators confronted Johnson all over, shouting, "LBJ, LBJ, how many kids did you kill today?"[6] The president had become a liability for the war effort.

Meanwhile, by the late summer of 1968 thousands of GIs were reading *The Bond* every month. We had a solid editorial and office staff. In Chapter 1, I wrote that Andy Stapp was special. The other ASU organizers may have seemed like "ordinary" guys. Now they were all special. We had become a fist. It was time to take on some bigger struggles.

Chapter Notes

* Wheaton exited the Army in September 1968 and immediately jumped into the middle of a struggle supporting Black soldiers at Fort Hood, Texas (see Chapter 10). He then started working with the ASU in New York, spending the first month at our apartment in Brooklyn until he found an apartment of his own.

† This was a few months before SDS became really radical. That happened after the assassination of Civil Rights leader Rev. Dr. Martin Luther King Jr. in Memphis in April 1968 and the sit-in at Columbia College in New York in early May. The Columbia occupation ended when the New York Police Department attacked a large group of students and bloodied their heads.

‡ The ASU had two reasons: One was that we knew that once the military had their hands on you, the officers had many ways of punishing rebellious soldiers. They could cut orders to send you to Vietnam. They could perpetually assign you the hardest and most unpleasant tasks, like cleaning latrines. It was a future of tremendous harassment and real threats. (Later the organizing climate improved because so many other GIs would be on your side.) The other reason was that we wanted to avoid putting people in a position where they might have to kill Vietnamese liberation fighters in order to survive.

Chapter 5 The Paris Commune

When I was 17 years old, I was surprised to find that my Sicilian-born grandfather was all excited about a new book he had just obtained. It was a recent translation to Italian of a journal relating events during the Paris Commune of 1871, which was ten years before he was born. Though I was oblivious to its importance, for my *nonno*, a retired cigar-maker, textile worker and communist, the Commune was worth a lifetime of study.

The Commune was the first historical experience of how it would be possible for the working class to change society and replace the oppressive capitalist class that exploited it. The workers needed to control not only the productive forces but the state − a state that had been the key organ that kept them oppressed. The experience of the Paris Commune showed how this could be done.

This uprising of Parisian workers was the essential prologue to the European revolutions of the twentieth century. This uprising was different from the peasant revolts in Persia in the Middle Ages or in Germany in the seventeenth century and different from the glorious revolution in Haiti against slavery that expelled French colonialism in 1804.

The Commune was the first revolution in a European capitalist society where the workers − those who lived by selling their labor power, the modern proletariat − succeeded in setting up their own government and their own state.[1] And the Paris Commune burst into existence through a soldiers' mutiny in the army of the French Empire.

The Franco-Prussian War, 1870-1871

On July 19, 1870, after four years of growing tension between the two major continental capitalist powers that were contending for domination of Europe, France declared war on Prussia.*

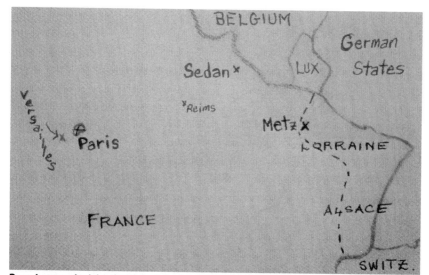

Prussia won decisive battles at Sedan and Metz (175 miles from Paris) by fall 1870. The French ruling class later ceded Alsace and Lorraine to Prussia. Map: J. Catalinotto

To Louis-Napoleon's chagrin, in the beginning of September 1870, the Prussian army took the city of Sedan, in northeast France near the French-Belgian border. The Prussians routed the French forces, which surrendered *en masse*. The Prussian army captured some 83,000 French troops, among them Emperor Louis-Napoleon III himself.[2] His empire fell and Parisian deputies established a republic, called the Government of National Defense, which had some republican forces and some who still supported the monarchy. This government was supposed to continue trying to protect France from an invading Prussian army intent on seizing French territory and imposing war reparations. On October 27, another massive section of the French army surrendered to the Prussians. These 143,000 troops had been under siege in the town of Metz, the capital of Lorraine.[3]

As the Prussian soldiers neared Paris, the French army moved three hundred of its heavy cannons out of their grasp, placing them on the hills within the city. Some 171 cannons sat on the high ground of Montmartre near the mostly working-class and poorer districts. This action set the stage for the coming social revolution, which was to combine an acute class struggle with the defense of national sovereignty.

The Prussian army marched into Paris in an attempt to force the French government to capitulate. When the government hesitated to surrender, the Prussians set up a siege outside the city, blocking all shipments, including food. In January 1871 the Prussian army fired thousands of shells at Paris.

The only serious defenders of the city against the Prussian invasion were the troops of the National Guard, which had been formed to protect Paris from the foreign invasion by the Prussian troops surrounding the French capital. This was an army of volunteers, especially strong in districts with the poorest workers, many of them unemployed, and impoverished shopkeepers. It was half militia, half political organization, with strong participation of the parties and groups that had been suppressed by Louis-Napoleon's Empire.

Throughout the fall of 1870 and the winter of 1871 the siege of Paris and the ensuing collapse of the French economy had driven the already poor population to near starvation. Many joined the National Guard out of patriotic sentiments; the Guards' work was now concentrated on protecting their own homes and neighborhoods. Many who joined the Guard had been unemployed, so the Guard's pay of thirty cents a day, though a pittance, was better than nothing. National Guard committees and subcommittees became the structure for political committees that represented the local population.

On January 28 the French national government capitulated to the Prussians, but the National Guard still defended Paris. On February 1, 1871, new national elections, dominated by areas outside Paris, put a majority of representatives who supported the monarchy into the French National Parliament. That political body sat in the town of Versailles, about ten miles west-southwest of Paris' center.

The new pro-monarchist government then provoked the working people by ending a moratorium on rents in Paris. With ruling-class arrogance, the monarchists and capitalists actually demanded that the already destitute tenants and small shopkeepers pay up all they owed in back rents. This new pro-monarchy Parliament feared the National Guard and the Parisian workers more than it did the Prussian army. They had a reason. Though the Prussian army might seize

French territory, it defended the property of landlords and capitalists in Germany, and would do the same in France.[4]

August Thiers headed the 1870-71 governments that replaced the Empire. Thiers had been prime minister of France twenty-two years earlier, when he ordered the army to crush the June 1848 workers' uprising in Paris that had terrified the French capitalists. The ruling class and its representative, Thiers, had their priority: Disarm the National Guard and leave the workers' organizations at the mercy of the Prussians.[5]

The National Guard, in turn, passed out an appeal to the national army troops, asking them to "unite with us to save the republic."[6]

March 18, 1871

This set the stage for the first day of the Commune. On March 18, 1871, Thiers sent the national army into the neighborhoods of Paris controlled by the National Guard. Their official orders were to take the big guns then under the control of the workers and urban poor and round up and arrest individual leaders of revolutionary workers' organizations. Specifically, the army was commanded to go into the high ground of Montmartre and collect the cannons under the peoples' control.

Before dawn, the government sent forty thousand troops to collect the three hundred cannons in Paris. These troops neglected, however, to bring along the horses that would be needed to move the cannons. Many analysts speculate that the whole operation was aimed at provoking a battle with the workers that would lead to the mass arrest of their leaders. Troops were reluctant to fire on people they viewed as their own compatriots.

The central committee of the National Guard ordered barricades set up to defend the cannons. More important than the barricades, however, was the action of the local population, especially of the women in Montmartre and in the nearby Eleventh District neighborhood with its many poor and working-class inhabitants.

Louise Michel

Historical records place one of the most famous of the women Commune leaders, Louise Michel, on the hill or Butte of Montmartre that morning. One can imagine the gray-haired Michel, a fifty-year-old schoolteacher who became the outspoken leader of the Women's Union for the Defense of Paris and Aid to the Wounded — *l'Union des Femmes* — hurrying from block to block, from hovel to hovel, mobilizing her forces. According to most descriptions, she was giving medical care to a wounded sentry as the confrontation was taking place.[7]

At 8 a.m., the people, especially the women, began to speak with and appeal to the national army troops sent by the Thiers government. At first there was mutual fear. Then recognition. Soon there would be solidarity.

Writing about that day, Michel was modest about her own role:

> The soldiers of the reactionaries captured our artillery by surprise, but they were unable to haul them away as they had intended, because they had neglected to bring horses with them.

> Learning that the Versailles soldiers were trying to seize the cannon, men and women of Montmartre swarmed up the Butte in a surprise maneuver. Those people who were climbing believed they would die, but they were prepared to pay the price.

> The Butte of Montmartre was bathed in the first light of day, through which things were glimpsed as if they were hidden behind a thin veil of water. Gradually the crowd increased. The other districts of Paris, hearing of the events taking place on the Butte of Montmartre, came to our assistance.

> The women of Paris covered the cannon with their bodies. When their officers ordered the soldiers to fire, the men refused."[8]

The troops of the 88th Regiment were under the command of General Claude Lecomte. His operation was threatened by the obviously friendly interaction between the revolutionary people and his army. Wanting to break up the contact, he ordered his troops to fire on the people. But they were no longer **his** troops. The general repeated his order. The troops again refused and the crowd moved closer, so the troops could not obey the order to use their bayonets. Thomas March wrote of it:

> The women at once cried out, 'Would you fire upon us and our children?' The soldiers hesitated; one of their officers, revolver in hand, threatened them; he was surrounded by the women, several of his men broke away from their ranks and openly deserted, while the others reversed their guns and lifted the butt ends into the air in token of sympathy with the people.[9]

The general, now shaking with anger tinged with fear, gave his order a third time. Again the troops refused. And in another giant step, they pointed their weapons at the general, taking him prisoner and marching him to a local dance hall, the Chateau Rouge, while the eighty gendarmes who surrounded him were brought to the City Hall of the Eighteenth Arrondissement.

Soon another prisoner joined General Lecomte, General Jacques-Léon Clement-Thomas. The people had a special reason for hating Clement-Thomas. He was one of the officers who had commanded the troops that buried the workers' uprising of June 1848 in blood. Though he was wearing civilian clothing, the people recognized this notorious figure.[10]

Around 10 a.m., the Thiers government learned that the troops under General Faron had also fraternized with the people and had abandoned their weapons and transport to them. The regime and General d'Aurelle de Paladines, the regular army commander in chief of the National Guard, then attempted to organize an offensive against the popular movement, with the support of National Guard troops from a wealthy neighborhood in the center and west of Paris. Of 18,000 troops Thiers was counting on, barely 600 answered the call to arms.

The rich Parisians knew whose side they were on, but they had no taste for the front line. These 600, when they saw how few they numbered, decided it was wiser to go home. The governor of Paris, General Joseph Vinoy, decided at this point to retreat with his troops to the Military School.[11]

At about 3 p.m., the government reconvened to discuss what to do: Leave Paris to return later in strength, or stay in the ministries at the Paris City Hall and organize their resistance to the uprising in the western part of the city. Meanwhile, the revolutionary National Guard was marching *en masse* past the ministry where the heads of the government were meeting. Frightened by the power of the armed masses, Thiers decided to withdraw the government completely to nearby Versailles. He ordered all the troops to retreat from Paris and all the government officials to leave as well.

As is often the case on the day of a revolutionary outbreak, the masses refused to be held back, even by their new leaders. Although the Montmartre vigilance committee tried to moderate the action of the angry masses, the crowd, furious over Lecomte and Clement-Thomas, stormed the Chateau Rouge where they were being held and executed the hated generals. Most of the bullets later found in their bodies came from the regular army's weapons.

Before midnight, the uprising seized the headquarters of the National Guard, the central police headquarters and Paris City Hall. The forces of revolution held most of the city.

At dawn on March 18, 1871, before all this happened, the central committee of the National Guard had no plan to seize power. They merely set out to defend themselves from a military coup by the Thiers government. Despite the absence of intent, what happened on March 18 became Day One of the seventy-two days of the uprising that grew into the Paris Commune.

By the end of that day most of the 50,000 rank-and-file troops of France's regular army who had been in Paris had either changed their allegiance to the National Guard, deserted, or been withdrawn from the city. Half of Napoleon III's army — the more than 200,000 troops captured at Sedan and Metz — were being held as prisoners of war by the Prussian forces at that time.

This meant that within Paris, the National Guard **constituted the new state.** The National Guard was both the political body directing the new state and the armed force keeping order in Paris. The National Guard defended the unemployed, the workers and the small producers and shopkeepers who saw the new state as **their** government.

In the short time of its existence, the Commune was able to introduce social and economic measures that inspired workers around the world. These included replacing the standing army with the armed people, separating church and state, ending state support of religious bodies and pay for priests, making education secular, forbidding night work in bakeries, and supporting the takeover of abandoned factories by their workers. The Commune also declared that officials' salaries could not exceed those for skilled workers.[12]

The revolution was only strong enough to establish the rule of the Commune within the city of Paris, the capital of France, its largest city and the largest working-class concentration in this centralized capitalist state. Commune rule arose in some of the other major cities, like Lyon and Marseille, but could not be sustained in these provincial cities. Without support from the provinces, the Commune was unable to control the destiny of all of France from Paris alone. Nevertheless, the historical lessons from this first workers' revolution allowed later revolutionary leaders to prepare the ground for successful insurrections in the future.

Marx Showed How Commune Smashed Capitalist State

For the theoretical leader of the International Workers Organization, Karl Marx, who with Friedrich Engels wrote *The Communist Manifesto* in 1847, the Paris Commune provided the first historical experience of how the working class could overthrow the capitalist ruling class and begin to run society in its own interest and in the interest of all the oppressed classes. Until the historical experience presented by the Paris Commune, there had been no living example allowing early Marxist leaders and theoreticians to outline how state power could be transferred from the capitalist rulers to the working class.

The experience of the Commune showed that it is impossible for the working class and oppressed sectors of the population to simply win over parliament and start building a new social system. The old government, bureaucracy and armed forces were tied by innumerable strings to the old ruling capitalist class, and only by destroying this old state and building a new one, bound to the working class, could society be changed, which is exactly what the revolutionary events of March 18 accomplished, at least within Paris.

Marx wrote of all this in his pamphlet, *The Civil War in France*, published in 1871. Marx's pamphlet and the history of the Commune also became the basis for key chapters of the pamphlet *State and Revolution*, which Russian revolutionary and communist leader Vladimir Ulyanov, known as Lenin, wrote in the summer of 1917 while waiting in hiding outside St. Petersburg on the eve of the revolution that was to shape the twentieth century. He was writing in the midst of a revolutionary crisis and — allowing for references to people or events that are certainly obscure one hundred years later — his pamphlet provides as clear as possible an explanation of why a revolution is needed to overturn capitalist rule.

Lenin showed it was necessary to smash the old state, which enforced capitalist rule, and replace it with a new state based on the rule of the working class. Only then could one change society.

Anyone seriously interested in a revolution that frees the downtrodden and oppressed should read these works by Marx and Lenin in full. For the convenience of readers, I reproduce in Appendix B some important excerpts from Chapter 3 of Lenin's pamphlet, in which Lenin quotes from Marx. These excerpts focus on how the Paris Commune showed what Marxists mean by "the state" and how it is necessary to smash this state and erect a new workers' state to put the working class in charge of society.

The Commune lasted seventy-two days. The French ruling class and its government in Versailles made what must be considered — from the point of view of any French patriot then or now or anyone aspiring to overturn capitalism — a "treasonous" deal with the Prussian generals. In return for the use of the French prisoners of war to repress the Commune, they ceded the province of Alsace-Lorraine to Prussia.

The *Journal of the Paris Commune* of May 22, 1871, reproduced the leaflet we publish here.

Soldiers of the army of Versailles,

We are fathers of families.

We fight to prevent our children from being, one day, as you are, under the yoke of military despotism.

One day you too will be parents.

If you fire on the people today, your children will despise you, as we despise the soldiers who tore apart the bellies of the people in June 1848 and December 1851.

Two months ago, on March 18, your brothers in the army of Paris, the wounded heart confronting the cowards who sold out France, fraternized with the people: Follow their example.

Soldiers, our children and our brothers, listen to this carefully, and let your conscience decide:

When the orders are an abominable crime, disobedience is a duty.

May 22, 1871

The Central Committee[13]

Though this leaflet and others like it were heartfelt appeals to the French regular soldiers, the call was, unlike on March 18, ineffective. Why? At least in part because the mostly peasant troops, who had been held as prisoners far from Paris, had had no contact with the Parisian workers. They remained brainwashed by the lies of the rulers in Versailles. This time the troops failed to rebel. They obeyed their officers and slaughtered the Communards who dared to defend Paris, including many of the women fighters of *L'Union des Femmes*. Some 30,000 Communards were massacred and 43,000 more imprisoned or exiled to New Caledonia, a French-held territory in the South Pacific called Kanaky by the Indigenous people.†

Despite its defeat, the lessons of the Paris Commune remained alive and valuable for Lenin in 1917 and my grandfather in 1957; they remain valuable for revolutionaries today.

Chapter Notes

* **Emperor Louis-Napoleon Bonaparte**, nephew of Napoleon I, was the dictator who ruled France since 1852. In 1870 he was threatened by uprisings of peasants and urban poor at home. He had also been humiliated by the Mexican revolt that threw out French rule in 1867. This French emperor hoped that defeating the Prussians would restore his prestige and unify the country behind his conquest of territory up to the Rhine River. **Otto von Bismarck** was the general and political leader who was minister-president of Prussia, the most powerful of the German-speaking states whose territory included parts of what in 2016 is Poland and even a small area of Russia. Other regions not yet united with Prussia in 1870 included Bavaria, Baden and Saxony. Bismarck lured Napoleon III into declaring war on Germany and then pulled the other German states into a defensive alliance that would then seize the Connecticut-sized French area called Alsace-Lorraine, a majority of whose population was German-speaking, and complete the unification of Germany. (continued next page)

† **Louise Michel**, a leader of *l'Union des Femmes*, fought alongside the working people defending the Commune and then escaped. She turned herself in only after finding out the authorities were holding her elderly mother hostage. In court, Michel refused to submit to the reactionaries or promise to hold her tongue in the future, demanding instead that they shoot her. They didn't. Michel was among those sent to New Caledonia.[14]

In subsequent years there was an uprising on the island of the Kanak Indigenous people. Unfortunately, French imperialism was able to use many of the imprisoned Communards to fight against the Native uprising. Not Louise Michel, however. She distinguished herself as a revolutionary leader by standing in solidarity with the Indigenous uprising against French rule. Here is an excerpt from Michel's writing on the Kanak revolt of 1878:

> The Kanaks were seeking the same liberty we had sought in the Commune. Let me say only that my red scarf, the red scarf of the Commune that I had hidden from every search, was divided in two pieces one night. Two Kanaks, before going to join the insurgents against the whites, had come to say goodbye to me. They slipped into the ocean. The sea was bad, and they may never have arrived across the bay, or perhaps they were killed in the fighting. I never saw either of them again, and I don't know which of the two deaths took them, but they were brave with the bravery that black and white both have. ...
>
> The Kanak Insurrection of 1878 failed. The strength and longing of human hearts was shown once again, but the whites shot down the rebels as we were mowed down in front of Bastion 37 and on the plains of Satory. When they sent [Kanak leader] Atai's head to Paris, I wondered who the real headhunters were.[15]

There is a large square in Paris named after Louise Michel; this revolutionary anarchist certainly earned the honor.

Chapter 6 The Tet Offensive of 1968

This is a transcript of Andy Stapp's last public talk, given at a meeting organized by Workers World Party in January 2013. It serves as an excellent overview of the history of the American Servicemen's Union.

The Tet Offensive was a countrywide uprising by the National Liberation Front's guerrilla forces throughout South Vietnam that began on January 29, 1968, the first day of the Asian New Year, called Tet. While this offensive did not lead to an immediate military defeat of the U.S. occupation force and the South Vietnamese puppet army, it completely changed the political atmosphere regarding the war. This eventually led the U.S. to sign an agreement in 1973 to pull out U.S. troops, leading to the Vietnamese liberation of the South in 1975.

Stapp's talk was preceded by a slide show with scenes from the anti-war movement in the United States inside and outside the Armed Forces, to which he refers.

The last picture in the slide show of the resistance to the U.S. war against Vietnam reminded me of that notorious case of the two GIs who defected to the National Liberation Front. They were the bane of the Pentagon, which had orders out to kill them on sight. They were one Black and one white GI, united in their solidarity with the NLF, and of course the Pentagon code-named them "salt and pepper."

I was amazed as I realized this is the 45th anniversary of the Tet Offensive. It seems to me that it happened yesterday. Of course these days I can't always remember what did happen yesterday.

It made me realize how long the U.S. war on Vietnam was. I was in the ninth grade at school when the first U.S. soldier was killed in Vietnam — his name was Captain York — that's a really useless piece of information. I see some of you remember his name. I was thirty-one years old when the last two Marines died. Then liberation forces took over Saigon — now Ho Chi Minh City — in the spring of 1975.

I'm not going to try to analyze the events of that period. Maybe more I'll paint a picture of what things looked like to me and to others as those events unfolded.

On the first day after the Tet uprising began, I was brought before a military tribunal and charged under the Espionage Act of 1918 specifically with causing disobedience, disloyalty and refusal to duty among members of the Armed Forces. I tell you it was one of the happiest days of my life, made even happier by the screaming headlines in all the local newspapers about the Tet Offensive.

You heard the list of all the places captured — the U.S. Embassy, for one. The attack on the U.S. Embassy was led by the ambassador's Vietnamese chauffeur.

As you know, the U.S. Army was and is a violent, anti-democratic organization, with a wide gap between a group of upper-class officers and back then a very suppressed class of enlisted troops. During the Vietnam War it was packed with draftees furious that they were being asked to fight and die for something they did not believe in. The American Servicemen's Union was founded to harness this anger and unleash it.

Now, to Tet. Specifically I want to mention a guy named Bob Chenoweth. He was an ASU organizer in Hue, Vietnam, when the National Liberation Front overran the city — their city — in January 1968. He was an Armed Forces radio guy in the northern part of South Vietnam — sort of a "Good Morning Vietnam" kind of DJ.

As the National Liberation Front got closer and closer it was "Good night, Irene," and they were all sitting around in the basement waiting to be captured. He had a Vietnamese girlfriend and I remember him telling us she was sitting across from him, and he said: "Sun Oh, I saw you yesterday and you were pacing from the front of the station to the wall and from the wall to the wall. You were counting how many steps it was, weren't you — you were doing that so you could tell the Vietcong how far they had to go to get to the bunker."

She answered him: "You know, Bob, you are a really nice guy ... but this is **my** country." She was right, he said. He had to agree with her. He ended up spending five years in captivity as a prisoner of war.

By the time of the Tet Offensive the soldiers and sailors and Marines had begun to hate their own officers more than the so-called enemy. Repression in the military was very harsh. One of our organizers, Mitch Smith, got six months in prison for not saluting an officer, and that was kind of typical.

Two Black Marines, Harvey and Daniels — who you also saw in the slide show — just for saying the war was racist, they were convicted under the Espionage Act too. I remember reading the trial transcript and the presiding judge said, "Well, you know what I believe is 'right or wrong my country,' I don't know about this free-speech stuff."

Ken Stolte and Dan Amick got four years in prison just for handing out union leaflets at Fort Ord, California.

It's actually kind of shocking to look back and recall how radicalized the GIs had become in those days. Looking back I can hardly believe it myself. I'll give an example. Deirdre [Griswold] had given me a ring to wear that was made out of aluminum from the first U.S. airplane shot down over Vietnam by the Vietnamese. She had gotten it in Prague, Czechoslovakia, where she had met with the Vietnamese. It had the date, 1964, engraved in the aluminum.

So that was my ring — and I'm a soldier in the Army.

They have reveille in the morning in the Army. You get up very early. I reach out and I notice that I don't have the ring on. I said, "Where's my ring?"

A soldier answered, "What happened?"

I said, "I lost my ring."

So there's these forty guys there, saying, "Stapp lost his ring, you know, the one made from the first airplane shot down in Vietnam." And the forty guys are all crawling around the ground trying to find my ring. That seemed kind of normal, but looking back on it, it was pretty radical.

The barracks would be blasting Phil Och's anti-war songs day and night with these demoralized sergeants going around shaking their heads.

As the population at home turned against the war, the soldiers joined in and became even more militant — and the soldiers were armed. There was a whole military base with forty thousand GIs confined to barracks.

Can you imagine it, on payday no less? The Brass confined forty thousand GIs to barracks because they were afraid the GIs would rebel in support of an anti-war GI who was to be court-martialed that day. Me. And they had fire hoses at the ready and machine guns on rooftops.

Now the ASU's anti-war and anti-racist message was spread by *The Bond*, which we saw in the slide show. Mike Gill, who I'm glad to see is here, worked in the Post Office in the Army and used to make sure it got around, also in Vietnam.

In *The Bond* you could clip out forms and send in your membership dues and we used to get them sometimes from a year-old paper because *The Bond* would be passed around from hand to hand and last a long time. Union chapters popped up at more than a hundred bases in the U.S. and abroad, in Korea, Japan, the Philippines, Thailand, Okinawa, Guam, of course Germany, and even Iceland and Spain, and of course in Vietnam.

By 1971 the U.S. war effort was beginning to show signs of collapsing. I remember the thing as early as August 1969 in Hawai'i — it seemed to be just hours from chaos there — sailors sabotaged ships, GIs printed and reprinted anti-war propaganda and attended anti-war rallies in uniform, they rebelled in stockades and brigs, rioted against deployment, held sit-down strikes, refused orders to go on combat patrols, deserted by the tens of thousands.

One battalion of eight hundred paratroopers in Pleiku held a meeting and voted out their commanding colonel — you know, of course, that you normally don't vote on anything in the Army — but the Army removed him right away because the command feared the consequences of not doing it.

Then the troops took the final, inevitable step, which was killing their officers. At first it was a couple, and then a few dozen, and then hundreds. One of those charged with killing his officers was Billy Dean Smith, an African-American union member whom we defended. He personally set some kind of record by working his way up and wiping out a good portion of his chain of command.

Billy Dean Smith had an encore performance in Cuba where Fidel Castro presented him with one of those old 1959 Marine Corps caps that were worn by guerrillas fighting the dictator Fulgencio Batista in the Sierra Maestra mountains.

I remember being in the ASU office one day when a former Army lieutenant came in. We didn't like officers much. Remember John Kerry? He was an anti-war officer but always putting a wet blanket on the struggle. Don't confuse him with Bob Kerry, who was an out-and-out war criminal who became president of the New School. Anyway, we were sort of in a mood of "Okay, boy, you can talk to us if that's what you want."

He surprised us all by saying, "I want to thank you."

"So what do you want to thank us for?" we asked.

"Well, when I was deployed in Vietnam I got this platoon and two guys came up to me on the first day and they said, 'Lieutenant, we're representatives of the American Servicemen's Union and we want to talk to you. We want you to understand that the Vietcong are very dangerous, but when you leave them alone they don't bother you. So this is what we do: If we go out on patrol and the command tells us that the Vietcong are ten clicks [kilometers] to the right, then we go ten clicks to the left. Do you understand, Lieutenant? If we do it that way then everything is nice.'

"I thought about it and it made sense to me, so I come to thank you because almost my entire platoon got back alive."

Some final observations: The Black and Latino soldiers were always at the forefront of this struggle. And although women were only 2 percent of the military back then, they played a key role as well. Susan Schnall was actually an officer, but that was because she was a nurse and a nurse was automatically an officer's rank. So Lieutenant Susan Schnall flew a small airplane over the Presidio base in San Francisco and dropped thousands of anti-war leaflets on it.

And then there were women organizing from the outside. In the slide show there was the picture of the demonstration at Fort Dix in New Jersey, seven thousand people, led by women and the majority women, to support anti-war soldiers. John Lewis and Terry Klug, who are here tonight, were among those soldiers.

Some of the people at Terry's trial did get some time in Leavenworth — not all were acquitted. It's correct that Terry had been in Leavenworth, and was acquitted because no one would testify against him.

There were also women in the ASU leadership or who contributed to its development like Joyce Chediac, Laurie Fierstein, Shirley Jolls and Maryann Weissman. Socialists and Marxists and Communists have been at the front of every progressive movement, in unions, the Civil Rights Movement, the Lesbian-Gay-Bi-Trans movement and all movements for equality, and that was true of the ASU, too.

Chapter 7 **Dear Andy**

Marines, Navy, Air Force

January 21, 1969 — 'BRASS DON'T SCARE THIS SAILOR'

I've had it, man — the Navy really sucks. Enclosed is a few bucks to help put a stop to the crap these Brass-Brained Bastards shove at us "citizens" in this "free and democratic" country. It's got to stop — NOW!

Sorry I couldn't send you much. I got busted recently — a summary court-martial for "willfully refusing" to stamp return addresses on a stack of envelopes. A WAVE officer wrote me up. Another WAVE officer presided over the summary. They were friends. That's what is known as "military justice." Anyway, I was found guilty, busted to E-2 and fined $75.60. Wow!

The Lifers here told me to keep my mouth shut and look like I was a dumb seaman. Typical lifer advice. They know the WAVE had it in for me; but no matter, their philosophy is to stay straight for 20 or 30 years so they can get that security that comes in the mail once a month. They trade their souls for this phony security. And I believe they would even kill you if so ordered — for God and Country.

My Fascist-talking CO, a LT Lamey, told me to my face that he would like to "get a piece of my ass" and that the Marines would take care of me in the brig — since that was the direction I was headed because of my "attitude" toward military service.

You can print my name if you like because the Brass just don't scare me.

Yours for a GI Union, Roger Priest

The Pentagon (War Building), Office of Navy Inform. (Ministry of Truth)

∞

January 21, 1969 — CAMP LEJEUNE BRIG

I am a prisoner in the Camp Lejeune Brig. I heard of you through (name deleted) who is now in a cell-block cell for instigating a riot last Monday night. I thought it was about time we rebelled against the Brass. Here at Lejeune we are treated like animals: stuffed in cells made to hold 15 and there are 30 or 40 in them; made to go out in cold weather in light weather jackets. The other night we were hosed down and everyone's clothing and beds were soaking wet. Then we were made to go out and work in the cold the very next morning. The reason I wrote is I think you and Servicemen's Union can do something about the way the prisoners here at Lejeune are being treated.

Prisoner, Camp Lejeune

January 21, 1969 — IN THE TREASURE ISLAND BRIG

I turned myself in here at Treasure Island on Dec. 20, and have been fasting ever since.

The brig here is pretty hard to take while you're fasting. It's pretty hard to take anyway. I could fill a book on what happened there the three days I was in. I'm in the restricted barracks now, and a bunch of us are getting together a letter of complaint to the Secretary of the Navy on the atrocities we witnessed and were victims of in the brig.

By the way, could you please send me four or five copies of the latest Bond? I'm sure most of the guys here could dig it. They're all really interested when I rap about the Union.

Treasure Island, California

∞

March 17, 1969 — 'A DAMNED GOOD FIRE FIGHT'

During this (fire) fight my platoon was reduced by one-half, my best friend was shot twice in the leg and died almost six hours later from loss of blood, another close friend had his brains splattered in the back of his helmet and still another (who, incidentally, had less than 20 days to do in the crotch and was married less than a year) died a slow death with several rounds in his stomach. Not to mention the wounded.

My CO's statement: "That was a damned good fire fight."

What else can I say? Phew!

Tom, USMC (regretfully), Vietnam

∞

April 15, 1969 — MARINES BEGIN CAMPAIGN FOR NEW 'MILITARY ID'

Around here we are going to start wearing some sort of identification (such as wristbands, rings or ringlets, etc.) to be able to identify one another immediately. We feel that with just such a seemingly small and imperceptible device we may be able to increase our enrollment and easily recognize one another, even though we may never have met.

Marine, Quantico, Virginia.

July 22, 1969 — HE'S DOWN THERE WITH THE MEN NOW

I wrote and told you that I was transferred from my job as Captain's Writer when my political affiliations became known — and cause for ridiculous panic — to my "superiors," notably the Commanding Officer of this vessel. Without a security clearance (sic) I am only reliable enough to work in the Engineering Dept. office, a position which effectively uses my talents as a yeoman, but which denies my participating in all the higher decision-making areas, where my knowledge of the real issues and answers might be put to use against the administration (a predictable military condition of acute paranoia). The job is a good one — down with the men who run the ship, who repair it and keep it going; the working men who are receptive to the promise of the ideals of the ASU.

USS F.D. Roosevelt, FPO N.Y.

∞

October 20, 1969 — FORRESTAL SAILORS HAIL DIX DEMONSTRATION

We wish to express our sincere appreciation to all the members and friends of the American Servicemen's Union who helped to make our brief visit to New York a pleasurable and extremely worthwhile one.

The Oct. 12 Fort Dix Demonstration was, of course, the high point of our visit. We are happy to have had the opportunity to legally express our deep disaffection with the military's blatant disregard for human and constitutional rights, and Washington's continued involvement — against the will of the American people and the people of the world — in its immoral and illegal war of aggression in Vietnam. We congratulate you, our sister organizations, and the thousands of individually concerned citizens who helped make the Fort Dix Demonstration a success.

In closing, we wish to affirm our right, as well as our responsibility, as moral human beings, as American citizens and as members of the American Servicemen's Union, to come to the forefront of support not only for our fellow GIs, but for oppressed peoples everywhere. To stand up against tyranny anywhere but in the forefront is, of course, to stand not at all, but is merely to submit, to validate and to perpetuate the injustices of the oppressor.

Yours for Peace,

Albert M. Rita, William H. Yeadon — USS Forrestal

NAVY ORGANIZER SHAKES UP THE "COMMAND"

I'm really digging the Union thing down here in Florida. The command here is really shaken up — I dig that too. They have been trying to give me a bad discharge, trying to bust me for drugs, "un- American activities" etc. They see the harm I'm causing the "Navy's image" here, and they really want me out. They couldn't give me a bad discharge, so now they re giving me an honorable — that's nice. Our move ment is alive and fighting here in the Jacksonville area. New members are received each day. It will take many months however to suppress the lifers here, but through continuous perseverance it will be done.

U.S. Naval Station Mayport, Florida

∞

December 16, 1969 — AIRMEN 'ROCK STEADY' DURING INTERROGATION

On Moratorium Day [October 15, 1969] ten of us from the unit and approximately 40-50 GIs from other units on base walked the streets of Shreveport, La., passing out literature of an anti-war nature. Fine. No hassle from cops or anyone. Then on Friday (Oct. 17), I was called into OSI headquarters to answer some questions. Naturally, I didn't tell them shit. So they took my fingerprints and "mug shot" and sent me on my way. They called all of us in over the next few days and we stood rock steady — no answers to any questions. The lifer bastards had no case whatsoever because they had no information.

Airman, Barksdale AFB, Louisiana

∞

December 16, 1969 — SEAMEN DEFY NOSEY PIG

The XO found a copy of The BOND in a package of "subversive material" sent to one of my friends. (We're still wondering how he happened to see it in there.) He said that if "this shit" gets around, my friend would be hung. It WILL get around.

Seaman Apprentice, FPO NY

Chapter 8 Black Marines Against the Brass

William Harvey, left, and George Daniels. Photo: ASU collection

Portions of a letter from George Daniels to a friend in his hometown.

AN APPEAL FROM THE BRIG:

Note that the last time we dealt with these beasts, we asked that I be released. This time we demand.

This may sound radical to you but what was done to us was radical. Two men sentenced to 6 and 10 years for dissenting against the war? The reason is because we are Black, intelligent, and refuse to be pushed. Nxxxers just ain't supposed to act like that!

While I was brainwashed into believing that the cause for going overseas was a just cause, I did show that I would put on a uniform and fight if necessary to protect people like you. Now that we are hip to what's really happening, it's the people's turn to protect me. Only they don't have to pick up rifles, just pens. Hang petitions in the Candy Store, Herman's, the Center, and every other place you can think of because now it's your turn.

Beginning in 1967, opposition to the war in Vietnam surged throughout the U.S. military. Soldiers, mostly from working-class families, stood up to fight against the war. After the rebellions in the inner cities from Harlem to Watts, from Newark, New Jersey, to Detroit, and after the inspiration from sports stars like Muhammad Ali and the rapid expansion of the Black Panther Party, a revolutionary spirit spread to Black GIs. This was true even in the Marines, considered an elite fighting force where obedience was brutally enforced.

This revolutionary sentiment manifested itself in the summer of 1967 at the Marine base in Camp Pendleton, California, when two Black Marines, PFC George Daniels and Lance CPL William Harvey, in discussions with other Black Marines, according to the charges leveled against them, advised them "to refuse to serve in Vietnam."

In December 1967 Harvey and Daniels, deprived of civilian counsel and with the Marine Corps succeeding in keeping the trial out of the corporate media, faced a general court-martial. They were tried separately and in secret. Their courts-martial boards were comprised completely of officers: one colonel, two lieutenant colonels, two majors, four captains, three first lieutenants, one lieutenant commander and one warrant officer. No surprise: Daniels received a six-year sentence and Harvey a ten-year sentence. They had served nearly a year of this sentence in the Portsmouth Naval Prison in New Hampshire when the American Servicemen's Union became aware of the case.

The ASU immediately decided to do whatever was possible to help them. We lined up the best civilian legal representation. The ASU used *The Bond* and reached out to other media to gain the widest publicity about the case, which was an obvious violation of the two Marines' constitutional rights of speech and assembly. "Free Harvey and Daniels" became a slogan on placards in many anti-war demonstrations in the streets of U.S. cities in 1968 and 1969.

Without the organizing of the ASU and the legal support, Harvey and Daniels might have stayed in prison for years. The following pamphlet was written after they were released from prison but before they left the Marines.

Kangaroo Court-Martial (excerpts)

Two Black Marines Who Got Six and Ten Years for Opposing the Vietnam War

Andrew Stapp: What do you feel that the attitude of the Black servicemen is toward the Vietnam War?

William Harvey: I feel that the Black man's attitude is that the war is one of genocide toward the colored people of the earth in general, in that the military can kill two birds with one stone. There is a little bit of the fear element inside the Black servicemen's makeup but it is slowly and surely disappearing.

George Daniels: I find that many Blacks seem to feel that the war in Vietnam is just another attempt to spread the racism that exists in this country. By their going over to Vietnam, they also view it as a fratricidal attempt.

Blacks view all people other than whites as their brothers. Because everywhere you look in this world where people of color are being oppressed, it is being done by the white man. And by seeing this, Blacks, in many cases rather than accept the white person as an individual, they'll judge them all beforehand and say such words as honky-devils and a reversal of the names they've pinned on us. Also, in more cases, we find this to be true in the names they've pinned on the Vietcong, the "gxxks," "chxnks," "wetbacks," "nxxgers," "kxkes," and things like that.

But the Black man's attitude has changed. Upon the advent of such songs as SAY IT LOUD, I'M BLACK AND I'M PROUD, Blacks who might have once straightened their hair, or been ashamed of their large noses or thick lips, are finally realizing that this is what they are and why they should be proud of it.

Black Rebellions in the Army

Andrew Stapp: What are the reasons for rebellions of the Black servicemen stationed in Hawai'i, Vietnam and North Carolina that have broken out in the last couple of weeks?

William Harvey: It is because the basic concept of the Afro-American's manhood is being challenged and he's stepping forward to take up the challenge. Upon going to Vietnam, the fear of what will happen to you if you don't go is what really makes you go over there.

George Daniels: As Harvey said, the attitude has changed. The riots of the Black servicemen that have been taking place are nothing but sheer manifestations of the frustrations that have been in them for months and months, if not years. And at long last, they're saying that they no longer accept this. They won't accept it as it is, and they must act accordingly. So they're in rebellion. They've tried to do things, I think peacefully, but in many cases violence is necessary.

Everything this country has, she achieved through violence. Back in the 1776s around here, when Britain had imposed an embargo act on this country she didn't just get around a coffee table and talk it over. They picked up arms.

Conditions in Military Prisons

Andrew Stapp: What were conditions like at Portsmouth Naval Prison?

William Harvey: Well, to start with the attitude of the guards. Over in Vietnam they love you and want to fight by you because they know that you can save their life. But once you put on a gray prison uniform and they're still wearing brown or green, you then become the dog and they are the master.

In Portsmouth it is psychological slavery. They try to beat a man down into the dust so bad to make him go along with the establishment, knowing that when he gets back on the streets then he won't take up arms against them. This can be seen in the work details they give and the attitudes shown by parole boards.

These boards ask you what you'll be doing when you get outside. Do you plan on joining any anti-government movements? They also like to ask Blacks, are you a Muslim, do you hate white people, would you kill them if you got out on the street? Of course, how can you answer something like this before a board? If you're truthful, you have to say what you feel.

Officers and the Days of Yes-Sirring

Andrew Stapp: You mentioned officers as being worse than the guards. Would you elaborate on this?

William Harvey: Yes, I would say so because even during inspections the officers would step before your cell and expect you to snap to attention like some kind of robot.

George Daniels: This is definitely true. The officers, they really have everything going. Their clubs are better, their quarters are better. During my last two months at Portsmouth, I was assigned extra hard duty because of the various marches you've had for us outside the prison. The job of typist was taken away from me. The officers said, well, since you're a political prisoner and you're causing so much trouble here you can't have a job of this nature. So I had to go up and make up their beds and things like that.

Andrew Stapp: How many Black officers did you see in the Marine Corps?

George Daniels: During my time in the Marine Corps, which is three years, I've seen approximately two Black officers. And at the Naval Disciplinary Institution there was only one.

Andrew Stapp: How many Black prisoners are there at Portsmouth?

George Daniels: Out of a total of 1,200 prisoners, about 400 are Black. Most of them are there for going UA [Unauthorized Absence], some for going to Vietnam and realizing what they were involved in and rioting.

The Results of Support

Andrew Stapp: There was a lot of agitation done around your case by the American Servicemen's Union. What effect do you think it had?

William Harvey: I believe that the military thought that this case wouldn't receive any publicity at all. That's why they tried us in secret. After all, who wants to hear about two Black Marines thrown into jail for speaking against the white establishment? The publicity definitely got us out earlier. If there wasn't any, I wouldn't be here giving this interview now.

George Daniels: I'm inclined to agree with Harvey. The publicity played a major role in dramatizing our plight and showing people just what takes place in the land of the free and the home of the brave.

Kangaroo Court-Martial

Andrew Stapp: Would you describe your "subversion" trials?

William Harvey: Mine was more or less funny, because the law officer would ask my lawyer: Do you have the arguments that you would like to raise at this time? My lawyer did have some pretty good ones. But they were being thrown out the window so quick both of our heads were swimming. The lawyers of the prosecution would scare the people sitting on the stand testifying against us so bad that they actually didn't know what they were saying. My lawyer would object, but the law officer would always overrule in order not to have it put in the record book on what is going down.

One of the reasons why I think I got six years and Daniels got ten was because of two of the fellows testifying against me didn't really want to do it, and when they got up there and found out what they actually were doing, they told the law officer, "If I had known this, I never would have come in here."

The law officer said, "Get this man out of court." And the other ones were just confused. All around, they should never have been there, and the law officer said, "Discount his testimony, too."

George Daniels: In my case, I think the law officer played a very major part. In one case a witness was called in and he gave his testimony that concerned how he felt about communism and how it stands up to the so-called capitalism or democracy we have here.

He said that he just couldn't believe that Blacks were deprived as they really are. He rapped about his driving through ghettoes and slum areas and not really feeling that this was as bad as the newspapers and Black people play it up to be.

And with this attitude in court, I guess it must have disseminated somehow among the jury. They must have also felt the same way. Because it's difficult for any white person to appraise a Black man's life when he's never been Black for one day.

White Juries, White GM, White DuPonts

Andrew Stapp: Did you have an all-white jury?

George Daniels: Yes, I did have an all-white jury. When testimonies were being made for me, most of the people on the jury were either writing things on paper or sharpening pencils or breaking things. They weren't paying attention. But when the prosecution brought its witnesses on, they were all looking at him keenly with their ears open. Really, as if to say, "This is true here, we'll really get this guy this time."

As my charge sheet has stated before, I was then overgeneralizing on many things. I felt the problem in America was then a racial war, per se, and nothing else. But now I view it as the few rich people exploiting large numbers of poor people.

The poor are inducted into the Armed Forces and used as cannon fodder; the rich people really gain from it. And whereas I once thought my enemies were all whites, I see now that it is the people on the Board of Directors of General Motors, DuPont, people who are getting their pockets lined with all this bloody money. I think that when the people realize this, that the people on top are purposely making poor whites fight poor Blacks, only then will we be able to solve the problems that exist in this country.

Andrew Stapp: Do you see a connection between the fight of the Black colony at home and the fight of the oppressed people around the world against U.S. imperialism?

William Harvey: Yes, there is a direct connection. If the Puerto Ricans, the Mexicans and the Blacks in the United States actually did what they are supposed to be doing in relation to the world revolution, less Vietnamese would be dying and less Africans would be dying down in Rhodesia.

George Daniels: As many people are realizing now, especially Blacks, as long as there are slaves in Africa, their own so-called liberty that they think they might possess here is in jeopardy. So Africa, Asia and Latin America and all other places, what happens there affects us and vice versa.

Chapter 9 Second Front

In Paris we anti-war GIs were getting radicalized quickly. Then came the explosive May-June events of 1968. This was an uprising of students and workers, with massive demonstrations every day, and workers in the CGT [General Confederation of Labor] asking their party [Communist Party of France (PCF)] and union to arm them. We would make Molotov cocktails* in our small room and then would be walking loaded down with them to Boul' Mich, to various corners on the Left Bank. I was all excited being part of a revolution there. If we had been captured by police while carrying the Molotov cocktails we'd have been expelled, but we were caught up in the struggle and so we ignored the dangers. – Terry Klug.[1]

After Fort Sill, Oklahoma, a second focus for GI organizing opened up in Europe, especially in Paris, France. There, a special group of more than a half-dozen GIs who had taken leave from the U.S. military rather than accept orders to go to Vietnam had gathered together toward the Fall of 1967 and the beginning of 1968. They coalesced into an informal organization.

Like some of the GIs who had worked with Stapp at Fort Sill, Dick Perrin was reassigned to another base in an attempt to keep all the American Servicemen's Union guys separated from each other. In the early fall of 1967 Perrin was sent to Germany, where he was working as a mechanic near the border between the Federal Republic of Germany and what was then the German Democratic Republic.

Perrin quickly got fed up with his experience in the Army, especially the gross racism he saw against Black GIs and the evidence that officers were watching him closely. To escape that situation, Perrin headed for Paris, hitching a ride with a sergeant for an auto trip from Heidelberg into France, complete with a car crash. He was happy to arrive alive and well in the French capital and out of the military. And happier still to find a network of support there.[2]

Along with Perrin, Terry Klug was another GI in the group. Klug was later to become one of the key anti-war leaders of the American Servicemen's Union.

Klug had enlisted in the Army in September 1966. If Hollywood had made a film about the ASU, the young Harrison Ford, with an Indiana Jones attitude, could have played Klug. As an enlistee, Klug had signed up for a three-year stint. Recruiters told him that by enlisting he could pick where he would be stationed, which was not Vietnam. Klug wasn't the first young man to believe the lies of military recruiters.

Because his father worked abroad in Europe and Central America, Klug had grown up living outside the United States. In a 2007 interview, Klug said:

> I thought I'd make out fine in Europe. The recruiters make it all sound reasonable. Of course, after basic training they have these rosters reading off where people are going. It says 'Posted' and you look for your name.
>
> Some were sent to Brussels, Belgium, where NATO headquarters is. Many went to Germany. I got sent to Fort Bragg, North Carolina, in early 1967, as a typist in a Military Intelligence unit. I found out the whole unit was going to Vietnam.
>
> Luckily, I found it out a couple months in advance of the actual deployment. This gave me a lot of time to think over what to do.
>
> I talked to the commanding officer and told him I couldn't go to Korea or Vietnam, but I'd be happy to go to Germany or Italy. He said he'd look into it. A week later he said he tried but was told there would be no exceptions.
>
> They gave us leave one month before we had to go to Vietnam. I went to my grandmother's house, since I knew my parents would not back me up on this. Grandma gave me $2,000, which got me from Indiana to JFK Airport and back to Rome where I had gone to high school and where I still had friends.
>
> This was in the summer of 1967. It was a one-way ticket. I loved being in Rome, but I also started reading that France had withdrawn from NATO, that people who left the military went to Sweden and France and these countries wouldn't send you back.

I hitchhiked to Paris and connected with someone at the Shakespeare & Company bookstore. They put me in touch with someone named Max, who was supposed to help me find places to stay and jobs. There were others there and we formed a loose group of young deserters. We called ourselves Resistance Inside the Army or RITA. I shared an apartment with Dick Perrin, which was formerly a maid's quarters in a posh building.[3]

We in the ASU office got to know Klug's friend "Max" for his work in Paris and in West Germany, over the course of the next few years. Max Watts was the *nom de guerre* of Tomi Schwaetzer, born in Austria in 1928, who grew up in the United States but left again at the time of the U.S. war against Korea.

Max was one of the more colorful characters in the revolutionary movement at that time in Paris. He operated independently of the traditional political parties, who were skeptical of the U.S. GIs.†

Max had a talent for staging revolutionary theater. His first bold media move in 1967 took advantage of a visit of one of the leaders of the Student Nonviolent Coordinating Committee (SNCC) who was in Paris. In 1967, before he chose the name Kwame Turé,‡ Stokely Carmichael had already gotten media attention as head of SNCC. He and H. Rap Brown (aka Jamil Abdullah Al-Amin) got credit for popularizing the slogan, "Black Power."[4]

Kwame Turé was politically astute all his life, and in Paris in 1967 he saw the potential of a movement of resistance inside the U.S. military, even if at that time all the GI deserters in Paris happened to be white youth. Thus he joined the press conference that Max Watts staged.

Watts hid the GIs behind curtains made of sheets while the SNCC leader was outside on camera. It was even more dramatic when PVT Perrin then emerged to give interviews to the media, whose coverage put RITA on the map.

From the point of view of its impact on GI resisters, Paris in 1968 was perfect. Not only did the Tet Offensive confirm massive opposition in Vietnam to the disastrous U.S. war, but in France there was a developing working-class struggle that in the spring of 1968 would shake the foundations of power.

The RITA group in Paris jumped right into the student and workers' strike during that spring. A mass student rebellion took to the streets. The spirit of struggle spilled over into the working class and sparked a general strike of ten million workers. Many RITA deserters participated in the street fighting in Paris alongside the revolutionary students and workers. This showed the GIs the potential of the class struggle. This is how Klug described the events:

> We were all eating at the Sorbonne, at the cafeteria, though the school was closed. Farmers and workers would bring in the food and donate it to those who were going out on the street. For most of the two months there was this great feeling of solidarity and that we could accomplish anything.

> Then the leadership of the movement pulled back from a confrontation with the French state. There was a referendum that Charles de Gaulle won. Then there was a letdown among the young people, including us, when this movement faded.

> During that time, I had been reading about what was happening back in the States, getting the ASU newspaper, *The Bond*, and I made a decision I would come back. I joined the ASU sometime in August of 1968. By then we wanted to do a lot more than just reform the service. By the fall of 1968 I knew we had to go back. I thought I would be more effective in the resistance back in the States — even if it meant risking jail.

> Perrin and I had someone go back to the U.S. Embassy to make initial contacts. We thought we could negotiate our safe return. I wasn't feeling good that day and passed out in the office. Dick came back and said they offered no deal.

> I decided to come back anyway. I thought if I turned myself in and returned to the U.S., I would go through a trial and maybe get a year in prison. I wanted out of the Army. I felt much more at home in the radical movement than I ever did in the Army.[5]

Back in New York, throughout 1968 the ASU office stayed in regular contact with the RITA activists, mainly in letters between Max and me.§ We sent them one hundred copies of *The Bond* each month to distribute.

TURN THE GUNS AROUND

In mid-January 1969, I got an urgent call at my job from Max. His call created some drama at my office, which was unused to dramatic calls from Paris. Max was in form: "Cat, Terry is on a plane heading for JFK Airport. Get the ASU people there to meet him."

I called Andy Stapp and relayed the message. He, Richard Wheaton and some others got out to JFK in time to greet Klug carrying signs reading, "Welcome home, Terry."

Klug had hoped he would be able to enter the U.S. and meet his new friends, along with some old ones, maybe get high, get lucky, and then turn himself in later. But when he arrived at JFK that January 18, 1969, the border agent looked at him, looked at a photo and said: "Are you Terry Klug?"

His luck had run out. Klug was quickly identified, arrested and brought directly to Fort Dix, New Jersey, a major basic training base.

That January the Fort Dix stockade was housing more than one war resister and plenty of young GIs in trouble with the Army. Unlike Klug, however, they had missed the experience of street fighting in Paris in May-June 1968.

One of the GIs Klug met on his first day in the stockade was PVT John Lewis, who introduced himself as an ASU organizer. "Damn," thought Klug to himself, "we're everywhere."[6]

Meanwhile, Perrin decided to go to Canada rather than putting himself once more in the hands of the military. He wound up staying and building a life there, as did many others who were unable to return to the United States before they received amnesty in 1977.

Klug was facing a court-martial on two counts of desertion, starting from his absence on April 20, 1967. One count was for "intent to remain away permanently" and one for "intent to shirk important duty." The latter referred to the orders for his Military Intelligence unit to go to Vietnam. These charges could each get Klug a sentence of five years in federal prison in Leavenworth, Kansas.

The ASU arranged for civilian defense counselors Jerry Moscowitz and Roland Watts of the Workers Defense League for Klug.

WDL lawyers represented many ASU GIs. The three-day trial for desertion ended with a conviction on April 22, 1969.

PVT Bill Smith (ret.) wrote this in *The Bond* about the trial:

> Terry Klug was sentenced to three years' hard labor, dishonorable discharge and forfeiture of all pay and allowances. He was taken from the courtroom by armed guards. But the Brass couldn't stop Terry from giving a clenched-fist salute — evidence of his personal strength and symbolic of the ASU's determination to win.[7]

In a letter, Klug wrote this about the sentencing:

> Especially when they were going through the preparations for sentencing me, was I scared. When they read off those three years I swear I could feel the pressure of the blood rushing from my head and I nearly fainted. But even though I was afraid, there was something else I felt that was much more overwhelming than fear — pride! As I stood there facing the enemy during the moment they sentenced me, I knew that that was the proudest moment of my life, and the tears that shone in my eyes for that one brief moment were tears of victory and pride! I wanted to shout at them and scream, "We're going to win, baby!" just so they'd know where they were at.[8]

This was no false bravado. Organizing went on within the Fort Dix stockade in the months following the sentencing. Before Klug was transferred to Leavenworth, he played a key role in a stockade uprising. The revolt was one of the heroic moments of struggle in the attempt to organize a union in the military and resist the war against Vietnam.

Reading Klug's words you can see that not only for Black GIs — as Harvey and Daniels showed — but for anti-war, class-conscious white GIs, the "enemy" was not the Vietnamese guerrillas or North Vietnamese Army. The GIs' enemies were the officers and noncommissioned officers who ordered the U.S. enlisted soldiers, sailors, airmen and Marines into battle.

After the political climate changed for the worse in France, Max and others working with him were forced to leave the country in early 1972. They set up a RITA center near Heidelberg, Germany, in the vicinity of some of the many U.S. bases in that country where

220,000 GIs were stationed. We continued to send even more copies of *The Bond* to RITA in Germany, where the ASU and resistance in general grew on all the bases. (See Chapter 30)

Chapter Notes

* Molotov cocktails were glass bottles filled with gasoline or other flammable substances, usually stopped up by a wick of some textile material, like a torn T-shirt. One could set the wick aflame and hurl it against a building or automobile, at which time it would burst into flames. It was named after Soviet Foreign Minister Vyacheslav Molotov. During World War II, sometimes anti-Nazi partisan forces used Molotov coctails when they were unable to get their hands on a more effective weapon like a bazooka.

† Unable to win official approval from the French Communist Party for the RITA group, Max did find aid from some of the most famous French leftists. Jean-Paul Sartre loaned the group a mailing address and provided other support. It was also at Paris RITA events where the actor Jane Fonda first became acquainted with GI resistance. She went on to entertain tens of thousands of troops with anti-war spectacles on bases all over the world.

‡ He took that name in honor of the first African postcolonial presidents, Kwame Nkrumah of Ghana and Sekou Touré of Guinea. H. Rap Brown now prefers to be called Jamil Abdullah Al-Amin; he is a political prisoner in Georgia.

§ Since international phone calls were expensive, this meant air-mail correspondence between Max and the ASU. Copies of these letters still exist at the International Institute of Social History in Amsterdam, where Max's extensive files on RITA are archived.

The Bond, May 20, 1969. Photo at bottom shows Terry Klug (left) and Andy Stapp.
Photo: J. Catalinotto

Chapter 10 Black Liberation at Fort Hood

A nger radiated through the barracks when orders reached the Black troops of the 1st Armored Division that they would be sent to Chicago on riot-control duty.

GIs spread a message throughout Fort Hood, Texas, on Aug. 23, 1968: They would meet on the grassy area at the main intersection of the fort to start an all-night discussion. More than one hundred GIs showed up to plan what to do. It was more than a rap session. It was a protest. To the generals and colonels whose orders must be obeyed, it was mutiny.

Some of the GIs had won medals for bravery. Some had been wounded. After a year of heavy combat in Vietnam, the fed-up Black troops were outraged at being ordered to occupy African-American neighborhoods in Chicago.

At the end of August, Chicago was the venue for the 1968 Democratic National Convention. Rebellious youth were coming by the thousands to protest the Vietnam War.* "Boss" Mayor Richard Daley wanted federal troops on hand to shoot down Black people should the anti-war protest spill over into the Black community.

What these soldiers believed – and it was true – was that the government feared a Black uprising and planned to use the U.S. Army to fire on their sisters and brothers.

Much had happened building up to this moment. Up to about 1966, African Americans had made up 20 percent of the killed and wounded in Vietnam, although they were only about 12 percent of the U.S. population.[1] They were still a high proportion of the rank-and-file combat troops in 1968.

The 1st Armored Division had been in Vietnam; many troops returning from the traumatic experience of combat were stationed at Fort Hood, Texas. Those not reenlisting in the Army were awaiting discharge orders, anxious to get back to civilian life. They were questioning their role in Vietnam.

84

On April 4, 1968, just a year after Dr. King had spoken out against the U.S. war in Vietnam, a racist sniper assassinated him in Memphis, Tennessee. Because of FBI head J. Edgar Hoover's open hostility to Dr. King, many people suspected the FBI was involved in the assassination.[2]

In response to losing their popular leader, who was committed to nonviolence, Black people erupted nationally in righteous revolt in a hundred cities. Along with local police, 22,000 federal troops and 34,000 National Guard were deployed throughout the country, most heavily in Chicago, Washington and Baltimore.†

Some 5,000 GIs from Fort Hood, Texas, many of them Black, were sent to Chicago. The Fort Hood troops received instructions from powerful Democratic Mayor Daley, relayed through the officers, "to shoot to kill any arsonist and to shoot to maim or cripple anyone looting."[3]

These orders were hard to swallow. When they got back to Fort Hood, many of the Black GIs vowed never to accept such a mission again.

Fast forward to August, as the Black GIs met to discuss resisting orders, the commanding officer of the 1st Armored Division, MG John Boles, tried to talk the men back to their barracks. That failed.

The Provost Marshal, who commands the Military Police, LTC Edwin Kulo, came out among the troops several times between 3 a.m. and 6 a.m. and "instructed" them, "Go back to your barracks. It's for your own good."

The Black GIs stayed strong: No commands from an officer would change their decision to refuse to kill their people. Hours passed. Orders went to the military police: "Arrest them at dawn."

At 6 a.m., two MP companies arrested forty-three soldiers and took them to the post stockade and then to the stockade annex. When the troops refused orders to enter the prison, MPs attacked and beat them, injuring some, reopening the stitches on the kidney of one GI wounded in Vietnam.

TURN THE GUNS AROUND

When the dust cleared, forty-three Black GIs were to be court-martialed. Thirty-one faced special courts-martial, with a maximum sentence of six months in prison. The other twelve faced general courts-martial and could be sentenced to years in prison. The officers considered six of the twelve "ringleaders." They faced years.

They were to be tried by officers under the command of the ranking officers of the division. In the normal operations of the Army, if the generals want convictions, they get them. In this case, however, the defendants had support.

How the ASU Got Involved

Andy Stapp and I were in the union office on Saturday morning, August 24, doing paperwork and discussing whether to go to the anti-war protest at the DNC. Buses and cars were leaving New York that day for Chicago.

The phone rang. Stapp picked it up. After a few seconds, he signaled for me to get on the extension. A SP5 from Fort Hood was on the line, saying, "The MPs arrested a bunch of Black GIs this morning. The guys were meeting all night. They didn't like being sent to Chicago."

It took only a look between us to decide this was our priority. I got more details while Stapp called the National Emergency Civil Liberties Committee (NECLC) — the organization of progressive attorneys who had helped Stapp during his Field Board Hearing. They told Stapp to get the names of the arrested GIs.

Getting that phone call was the kind of lucky break in organizing that comes from hard work, in this case, Stapp's skillful work with the media. The GI, who lived on the base, called us because he had just seen an article in the August 1968 *Esquire* magazine based on an interview with Stapp, and he "knew right away I had to join this union." His Black MP friend had already agreed to give the names of those arrested to the GI's spouse, who would call them in to us.

Whether or not the forty-three GIs had joined the union, their action made them eligible for support. The ASU considered all orders to fire on the Black population illegal. We would defend the Black soldiers. Organizing legal and popular support for these GIs could spark mass resistance inside the Army.

GIs facing courts-martial must be represented by an officer in the Judge Advocate General's office. But GIs also have the legal right to a civilian lawyer, an important asset. The ASU's experience was that most GIs didn't know how to get a lawyer or couldn't afford one. That meant the first thing the ASU had to do was find a civilian lawyer who would work on behalf of the GIs.‡ The ASU also needed to talk with the soldiers and find out how they wanted their story told. Then we could write about it in *The Bond*.

By the end of the weekend we had lined up civilian attorneys for the GIs and were sending an ASU delegation to Fort Hood to interview the arrested soldiers.

The National Emergency Civil Liberties Committee had top-notch anti-war lawyers like Michael Kennedy, who had advised Stapp at his hearing.§ Through the ASU's new contact at Fort Hood, we were able to give Kennedy the names of all forty-three GIs arrested, including the six who were considered the ringleaders.

Visiting Fort Hood

Stapp and I prepared to meet the leaders at Fort Hood, equipped with a letter from the NECLC that introduced us as Kennedy's legal assistants. I arranged to take a few days off my day job and joined Stapp on a flight to Dallas. With some borrowed IDs, we were able to fly half price as "students" on standby on the red-eye flight.

Dallas was a center of right-wing reaction we were aware of, particularly since President John Kennedy had been assassinated there in 1963. Stapp and I joked in the plane about how many years we might have to spend in a Texas jail.

We stopped laughing when, at Love Airport, we saw a giant statue of a Texas Ranger, his six-shooter on his hip.** The sign on the ranger's pedestal read: "One riot, one ranger."

We looked at each other and both said at once, "Get me outaheeere." But we swallowed our fear and scampered up a ramp to an old propeller-driven DC3 to fly the 125 miles to the Fort Hood/Killeen airport. The plane scared Stapp more than the ranger.

Killeen presented the depressing aspect of the typical base town — bars, pawnshops and little else, or at least little else with display windows. Added to this was the odor of rotting dead locusts, which the wind had blown into piles in every corner and curb. To connect with some friendly people before leaping into the abyss, we made a stop at the Oleo Strut, the anti-war GI coffeehouse in Killeen. Now at least somebody in the area knew that we existed.

Since we had no car, we walked to the 250-square-mile base. More than 40,000 soldiers and officers from the 1st and 2nd Armored Divisions were stationed there. We set out to meet with the six GIs facing a general court-martial and the longest prison terms.

Here is how Stapp described the meeting:

At the Judge Advocate General's office I handed Kennedy's letter to a Captain Henig. He must have thought I was a lawyer because he didn't even question my request to see the prisoners. He told Cat and me that the Black GIs had been temporarily released and were under barracks arrest because 'There isn't enough room in the stockade.' He added, however, that a group was due for release and he expected to fill the vacancies immediately.

We thanked Henig and headed for the barracks. ... We talked with a number of the Black GIs in the barracks and they said they were glad we had come. Among them was Alvin Henry, who had earned the Silver Star for 'risking his life to carry a wounded sergeant to a medical evacuation helicopter'; Walter Waites, who had served eighteen months in Vietnam even though he had lost a brother there; and Bob Rucker, who had received a Leadership Plaque, an Army Commendation and a Bronze Star.

Andy Stapp outside the Judge Advocate General's office at Fort Hood, Texas, September 1968. Photo: John Catalinotto

Cat and I told them about Michael Kennedy and the NECLC and how well they had handled GI cases before. Even though a few of the Black GIs were union members, they were at first hesitant to trust us. Bitter experience had taught them to question the motives of white men. But in the end they accepted our help. ...

Bob Rucker had had only three more weeks to serve in the Army when he had risked a five-year prison sentence to participate in the Fort Hood demonstrations. He could have stayed in his bunk that night and not one of his friends would have blamed him. It was no wonder they respected him. Yet this winner of the Bronze Star would be accused of cowardice at his court-martial because he had refused to go to Chicago.[4]

We learned that one of the six GIs, Ernest Frederick, was being held in the stockade. While we were waiting to see him, a lifer SGT E-8 at the stockade apparently recognized Stapp's name. As the minutes went by, we realized that something besides the locusts was rotten in Texas. Called in by Provost Marshall Gericke who had replaced LTC Kulo, we announced that we had to leave.

"Not so fast," COL Gericke said as we walked out the door. He and some MPs chased us, shouting, "Stop, Stapp!" They caught up and handed Stapp an order barring him from Fort Hood. This meant

TURN THE GUNS AROUND

that if he stepped on the base again he would be arrested and face six months in federal prison, as Key Martin and Maryann Weissman had a year earlier at Fort Sill when they tried to attend Stapp's trial. The Brass had no bar order for me.

The Army was subject to federal laws and sometimes obeyed them, at least when there was media attention. Off base, we knew the local sheriff set the rules. Or changed them however he wanted.

I rewrote my notes of the discussions with the five GIs into a coherent report while we waited at the stockade. The Black GIs were aware of their potential role in Chicago. They knew what National Guard and Army troops had done in Detroit, Newark and Baltimore. They wanted nothing to do with shooting people they considered their sisters and brothers.

As soon as we were chased off the base, I addressed an envelope and mailed the report to New York. If the sheriff picked us up, we at least would have gotten the story out. But there was no more drama that day.

∞

Over the next two days, we tried to build support with local sympathizers from Austin and in Killeen, where we met a local attorney whose daughter volunteered at the Oleo Strut. Two other recent veterans arrived. They had finished their service and were ASU organizers. Bill Smith flew from New York. Richard Wheaton came straight from Fort Sill. With an ASU team in place and more help on the way, I flew home to my day job.

Within a few days, the local cops acted much as we had anticipated. They arrested Stapp, Smith and Wheaton and charged them with "vagrancy." The judge, in collusion with the sheriff, found them guilty.

Wheaton asked the judge, "How can we be vagrants? I have $600." The judge answered, "You're guilty and are fined $600."[5]

With the collusion of the local police, the Army tried to keep the ASU from building connections with the Black GIs — and with any white GIs who might support them. The arrests and the bar order were obstacles to organizing, but they couldn't stop it completely.

The Bond broke the story that built support for the Fort Hood 43 to GIs all over the world. Word spread of the brave resisters to the growing anti-war movement all over the United States. And the legal work went on. The next step was to send support to the trial of the six GIs, which took place in late October.

The Trial of the Six 'Ringleaders'

The officers running Fort Hood knew they had a problem with the forty-three Black GIs they'd arrested: Letting everyone go might encourage disobedience. But a hard crackdown could also spark revolt, as it did in the Presidio case later that year.

For the Fort Hood 43, the military court allowed the defense to use a legal technicality to get many of the troops off without serving time; others got sentences ranging from three to eleven months.

Since Stapp couldn't appear on Fort Hood without facing arrest, the ASU asked my spouse, Ellen Catalinotto, a writer, and me to attend the trial. Some Workers World Party comrades, who also had young children, cared for our four- and five-year-olds. *The Bond's* Vietnam editor, Bill Smith, joined us.

From October 22-25 we three attended the court-martial of the troops Andy and I visited in August. To avoid the Killeen sheriff, our ASU delegation stayed at the on-base home of the GI and his spouse who had called in the names to the ASU. This hospitality indicated broad support for the Black soldiers, including support from some white troops.

From left, PFC Ernest Bess, attorney Michael Kennedy, PFC Guy Smith, SP4 Albert Henry, PVT Ernest Frederick, SGT Robert Rucker, and SP4 Tollie Royal. October 1968 at Fort Hood, Texas. Photo: Ellen Catalinotto

Ellen Catalinotto wrote at the time:

[In statements to the courtroom,] PFC Guy Smith ... told the court, "I demonstrated against Army policy here and in Vietnam. ... There is racism and prejudice here. GEN Boles said he would do something about it, but nothing has been done. ... There are clubs in Killeen where Black GIs can't go. ... The Black man has been held back because of his color. Your convictions add to the injustice." ...

The court-martial of six Black GIs who demonstrated along with 100 others against racism and riot control duty ended here tonight after four days. Two men were acquitted, two got sentences of three months hard labor and the others received bad conduct discharges. The sentences, considerably less than the maximum, were an indication of the Army's fear that harsher punishment might backfire and lead to open rebellion. ...

Morale was high as the men left the courtroom, shaking hands and gathering around the jeep that was to take Henry to the stockade. The relatively lenient sentences were a victory — not of justice, but of the strength and determination of the Black soldiers not to be used against their brothers.[6] [See Appendix C for more of article.]

BLACK LIBERATION

To the extent we could in the shadow of the courtroom, Kennedy, the six GIs, Ellen and I celebrated the successful outcome. Even the GIs who had to spend a few months in the stockade said they felt they won. Kennedy used the excuse that they had not heard the direct orders. The Black GIs still spoke out against the racism they had experienced in the Army.

The next morning, Ellen and I went to the Killeen airport and hopped on a six-seat plane to fly to Dallas and then back to New York and our children. Smith made his way back a few days later.

Through successful organization of the legal work — carried out by the NECLC attorneys — the ASU was able to establish its reputation of defending GIs who were willing to take actions that the military might decide were mutinous. In 1968 the most likely manifestation of this rebellious attitude on a mass scale was among the Black GIs, who suffered the legacy of centuries of slavery and discrimination and who often identified with rebellions in the inner cities or saw themselves as potential Black Panthers.

The meeting that the Black GIs held in August 1968 at Fort Hood raised the possibility of a mass refusal to follow orders, in this instance to occupy Chicago's Black community. Such an action would weaken the Army's role even if it couldn't prevent the occupation.

The ASU empowered its members to disobey the officers and noncommissioned officers who ordered them to repress the people. The ASU not only endorsed the rebellion of the Black troops. To further shatter ties to the chain of command, the ASU convinced others, including white GIs, to act in solidarity with Black resistance.

The lesson for the Pentagon was that the conscripted Army, especially one politicized by an unpopular war, might be unreliable if used against rebellions in African-American communities in the United States.

The lesson for revolutionaries was that they could weaken the imperialist state's main repressive organ: the U.S. Armed Forces.

Chapter Notes

* Some of the spokespeople for this demonstration called themselves "Yippies," a word they coined to combine the countercultural "hippies" with political protest. The media gave them lots of publicity. The convention had attracted protest from a radical sector of the civilian anti-war movement. Thousands of mainly young people camping out at a park in downtown Chicago protested the war and the Democratic Party Convention, which was to nominate the pro-war Hubert Humphrey over the supposedly anti-war Eugene McCarthy. Daley's brutal police force attacked the protesters mercilessly.

The cops, with backing from the National Guard, had enough heft and fire power to repress the anti-war demonstrators without the Army. The troops' real job was to stand by — in case the Black community in Chicago joined the protest of the mostly white anti-war movement. Thus the troops' potential role was to shoot down people in the African-American community, should there be a rebellion in August similar to the one in April following Dr. King's murder.

The leaders of this demonstration were later put on trial and became known first as the Chicago 8 and later as the Chicago 7 when Black Panther leader Bobby Seale's case was separated from that of the others.

On August 25, with additional troops from Fort Sill, Oklahoma, and Fort Carson, Colorado, a total of 5,000 U.S. Army soldiers were sent north and quartered at Glenview Naval Air Station and the Great Lakes Naval Training Center, both near Chicago. There was no Black rebellion, so they were not used during Convention Week.

† To go back a little further, federal and local governments were using federal and National Guard troops in 1967 and 1968 to fire on African Americans who were rebelling in the Black communities across the country. Opposition to the war in Vietnam by the most prestigious leader of the Civil Rights Movement, the Rev. Dr. Martin Luther King Jr., helped mass anti-war sentiment grow. And there was draft resistance by the famous and beloved heavyweight boxing champion, Muhammad Ali, after he joined the Nation of Islam. For the troops at Fort Hood, there was also the grind of having spent a year of combat in Vietnam. These factors influenced the soldiers and Marines, especially the African Americans.

To repress a massive rebellion in Detroit in July 1967, Michigan Governor George Romney — father of 2012 Republican presidential candidate Mitt Romney — had ordered up the Michigan National Guard. These troops fired 155,000 rounds at the population, killing most of the forty-three people who died during the struggle.[7] President Lyndon Johnson deployed the 101st Airborne. The National Guard and the U.S. Army together had 17,000 troops in Detroit. That same month in Newark, N.J., the National Guard entered the city and was responsible for most of the twenty-six deaths.

‡ A special court-martial can set a maximum sentence of twelve months. The more serious general court-martial can decree much higher sentences. The legal JAG officer tends to identify with fellow officers and is subject to pressure from his superior officers. That's true even in the unlikely event the GI on trial has an honest or a sympathetic JAG attorney.

§ Michael Kennedy, who handled Andy Stapp's Field Board Hearing, was a top lawyer for political cases during the 1960s and 1970s, like the Chicago 8. He later represented Black Panther leader Huey Newton as well as members of the American Indian Movement who were involved in the epic 1973 struggle at Wounded Knee in South Dakota.

** The origins of the Texas Rangers were closely connected to the 1829 Texas "uprising" against Mexico that was aimed at preserving slavery in Texas and at beating down Mexicans and Native peoples.

Chapter 11 A Day in the Life of a GI Union

Adapted from an unsigned article in Workers World, *April 3, 1969.*

At 9:30 a.m., Bob Lemay, a Vietnam veteran, opens up Room 633 at 156 Fifth Avenue, the first national office of the American Servicemen's Union. There is a pile of mail on the floor, letters from GIs. Six letters contain subs to *The Bond*, the union's newspaper. Four enroll new union members. They're from Okinawa, Vietnam and bases all over the states. Bob starts to sort out the mail and do some of the routine office work — making up new union cards, entering subs and any money receipts.

The office is small, jammed with letter files and supplies of all sorts, but surprisingly well organized. A couple of large bulletin boards add color: an officer's broken swagger stick is taped up on one, a memento of a press conference where Mark Rudd, one of the Columbia College SDS leaders, a future Weatherman, told how he would help organize soldiers in the Army if drafted; cartoons sent by GIs; a copy of ASU chairperson Andy Stapp's undesirable discharge; a poster on Vietnam; a letter from the head of the Navy, Admiral Thomas Moorer, refusing a request that the ASU be admitted to the investigation of the Pueblo incident as an interested party. The Pueblo was a U.S. spy ship captured by North Korea.

At 10:30 a.m., the phone rings. It's an AWOL GI in Detroit looking for help. Bob will call him back with the numbers of people to contact. Bob tries to keep going on the office work, but the interruptions are more frequent now.

At 11:00 a.m., a GI from Fort Dix who just got out of the stockade comes in. He spends about half an hour talking about what's happening with the guys on the inside.

At noon the second delivery of mail arrives, more of the same.

At 1:00 p.m., Andy Stapp and John Cat come in from work. They get the latest news from Bob, look over some of the letters and discuss what has to be done in the afternoon.

At 1:30 p.m., the husband of a WAAC calls from San Antonio. His wife has been in a severe state of depression but can't get admitted to Fort Sam Houston Army Hospital. Our union medic had referred him to the ASU.

At 2:00 p.m., the third mail delivery comes in with a batch of letters from Vietnam.

At 2:30 p.m., a union sailor calls from Virginia. His ship is due to sail to Guantánamo base on Monday. Some of the sailors working in the boiler room are talking about going "over the hill" (going absent without official leave) because they feel the ship is unsafe. Andy advises them to contact an ex-sailor in the area. This veteran can help them get out leaflets opposing the sailing of the ship, demanding that necessary repairs be made. He suggests that the leaflet compare the Navy officers' attitude toward the sailors' safety with the Brass's attitude toward GIs in Vietnam.

At 3:00 p.m., the buddy of a fellow refusing induction drops in for a stack of *Bonds*. He is going to distribute them at the induction center. Almost at the same time, the mother, sister and brother of a Puerto Rican GI arrive. He is thinking of refusing to go to Vietnam. Bill Smith, Vietnam editor of *The Bond*, talks to them about how the union can help. Meanwhile Bob is calling back to the GI in Detroit with numbers for attorneys.

∞

After the Puerto Rican family leaves, Bob gives Smith the Vietnam mail. Richard Wheaton, another GI who joined the ASU while stationed at Fort Sill, comes in after work, checks out all the letters to see what he can use on the next letter page of *The Bond*. Lemay is just leaving when Richie Richardson, managing editor, steps in and he discusses assignments for the coming issue, then picks up some copy already written by Bill Smith.

TURN THE GUNS AROUND

From left, SP4 Richard Wheaton (ret.) and Jackie Dornbos, SP5 Bob Lemay (ret.).
Photos: American Servicemen's Union

Andy Stapp calls from the National Emergency Civil Liberties Committee, where he is checking out steps they are taking to file writs of habeas corpus on behalf of Izaac Barr, a Black GI forced to board a plane to Vietnam against his will. The NECLC is demanding his return.

At 5:30 p.m., everybody squeezes into the office for a while, and it's pandemonium. But soon, the "day shift" has left, and Wheaton and Cat settle down to answering letters. Andy has gone to an SDS meeting on a demonstration for May Day. One of the demonstration's demands will be the release of GI political prisoners.

At 10:30 p.m., the last shift goes home. It's been a busy day — but no busier than tomorrow will be.

Chapter 12 **Dear Andy**
Letters from Vietnam I

June 11, 1968 — ROCKET ATTACKS IN VIETNAM

I guess you've read about the renewed attacks in Saigon lately. Well, every time Saigon gets it so do we. Time and other news media have played down this latest series, but things were pretty bad for about 10 days there. In fact we had Tet-like casualty lists. Several guys from our company were hit, one fatally. Everyone has skinned knees, like little kids, only in our case they come from diving in ditches rather than falling off bicycles or out of trees.

Rocket and mortar attacks are the most panic-inspiring events I've ever experienced. We mostly get the rockets, which are about 6 inches in diameter and somewhere around 6 feet long. If they're coming in close, you first hear a loud sound like that of a welding torch held close to the ear. Then before you can really react there is a loud "Wham!" which shakes the ground and throws out jagged bits of shrapnel.

The sound of the rocket exploding is not what you'd expect; instead of a "bang" it's more of a "wham" as I just mentioned, rather like the crack of a giant whip. The bad part of the attack is after the first rocket hits, for the first one shakes you up and gets the adrenalin pumping through you. You hit the ground and then wait, listening for the next ones, which follow in a few seconds. And as you hear them roaring in you wonder if they'll pass over or not. They're so loud that you're sure they're right on you but they're hundreds of feet away if you're lucky.

All this is nothing compared to what the guys in the field catch so I should consider myself lucky and I do. I've been reading about Columbia [University, where cops beat students, May 1968], etc. Unrest and dissatisfaction are the watchwords of the day it seems. There may be more action in the streets than even over here. It seems that's the case in France. Keep me posted.

PFC, Vietnam

October 16, 1968 — THE BOND SPREADS AROUND AT DANANG

I'll stand behind you 100 percent for the cause of the union. I agree with all the demands stated and also feel like you, we need to organize in order to get fair deals from the Brass.

The first 30 copies you sent me for distribution are going good. We've been putting them out to guys in our squadrons and from there they just spread around. You can hear different guys talking about The BOND in chow or on the bus and everyone in our ranks seems to agree (except the usual suck-ass types and potential lifers).

I can't enclose a dollar in M.P.C. because I know it won't do you any good, but I leave Vietnam in 10 days and I'll send a contribution then. Register me as a member and send me my handbook and all.

Keep up the good work!

Dave Tinker

A1C Danang

[Petition with signatures from DaNang Air Base, Vietnam]

∞

December 16, 1968 — TWO RECON MEN IN NAM SPEAK UP

We are two Infantrymen and also a part of the Big Green War Machine over here in the Senseless War.

Being in a Recon Platoon we are out in the field a majority of the time and we don't get beautiful publications such as The Bond because of the Big Brass and REMF's (Rear Echelon Mother Fxxxers). We would like to submit our application to the ASU because we both feel the War Machine has to be stopped before it gets out of hand and kills us all.

Groovy & Bill

January 21, 1969 — 'THE ARMY TAKES CARE OF ITS OWN' — LIKE HELL

Just finished reading a copy of The BOND, and I agree with you on almost all your major contentions against the military. It is very sad when men are forced into a war they don't like and at the same time are harassed.

The military shows no concern for the lives of any of its smaller people. They couldn't care less when a lousy SP4 or PFC is killed. As you know, there's thousands more to replace them.

As a medical corpsman I realize life is more valuable than lifer bull and having a shave before some cat with a bar.

I'm from San Francisco. My old lady never taught me to kiss ass in the Army and I find I don't know how. I don't seem to have the desire to, either.

Should you ever choose to print anything I write, please USE MY FULL NAME AND ADDRESS.

SP4 John W. Huddleston

HHC 1/8th Inf. Div., Camp Enari, Vietnam

∞

March 17, 1969 — GI DENIED RIGHT TO SEE WOUNDED COUSIN

A few months ago a friend of mine was court-martialed for refusing to go back to the "bush." He told them it was against his religion and that this was not his war to begin with. He was sentenced to six months in the Danang Brig. I say, "Why?" These goddamned lifers start these wars and get us to fight them. I intend to get everyone I know turned on to what the ASU is doing for us.

They have screwed me out of my pay for a while now, but this payday I am turning some of what I do get into greenbacks so that I may join the ASU and make a contribution. I will try to get all my friends to send support money and stories — the facts! We've got to stop the "pig" (military establishment) from getting us killed in their war.

My cousin was just taken out of country laying on his back with a few bullet holes in him. These lifer bastards wouldn't even let me see him before he left. These swine don't think that things of this sort affect the troops. But it all builds up. One guy I know shot and killed a lieutenant because he had been messed with once too often.

When our day comes and our demands are met, maybe a lot of this bullshit will cease. Till then I will keep trying my best. Thank you.

Blackie Ortiz, Chu Lai, [Vietnam]

March 17, 1969 — TRIED TO BLOW UP FIRST SERGEANT — MISSED

Just a few weeks ago the Field First wanted me to fill 50 sandbags as extra duty because I was washing my hands in the NCO shower room. Of course I didn't do it because of my permanent profile, but I was still accused of leaving my so-called "appointed place of duty" and was given a $46 fine in addition to seven days extra duty.

Oppression seems like the key word in this lousy company. Our First Sergeant is nothing but a two-faced S.O.B. and tries to play the role, if you know what I mean. One attempt has already been made on his life: Someone threw a few grenades at his "hooch," but unfortunately he happened to be somewhere else at the time.

ASU Brother, Vietnam

∞

March 17, 1969 — GIVE BOND TO A BUDDY IN NAM

I have one suggestion to make. Many men make their first contact with the Union back in the states after returning from Vietnam. Why not ask each Vietnam vet and Union member to send the paper (in an envelope, to avoid the prying eyes of the Brass) to one buddy back in his unit. If possible, he should send it to his replacement if he ever knew him. It would be ideal if we could just send one paper to as many units as possible.

SP4 (Ret.), New York

∞

March 17, 1969 — THE BOND GOES TO THE FIELD

Just a line to let you know that I'm receiving The BOND. The only trouble is I just have a chance to read it over once, then it's gone. No, it hasn't gone to the Brass, but to where it will do some good. Yes, that's right — out in the field to the men in my company. And from what I hear it is going over big. So you will probably get a few new members from 196th Light Infantry Brigade. Perhaps with the BOND being out there it may open a few eyes to what is going on — because it won't take much to scare the Brass here.

Infantryman, Vietnam

April 15, 1969 — RETURNS TO STRUGGLE, FINDS HE HAS ALLIES

I am Robert J. Foris, a so-called deserter. I left Vietnam because of a wound that I received there and went to Japan after two months. There a doctor looked at me and said that I was going back to Vietnam. I went to Sweden and now I returned because of personal reasons.

I am at Fort Dix, N.J., and since I am here I had the opportunity to meet a PVT Klug, PVT Brakefield and a PVT North and many others that are in this stockade with just about the same feelings about the Army as I do.

PVT Robert J. Foris, Fort Dix Stockade

∞

April 15, 1969 — FROM A MORTUARY IN NAM

Today I feel as if the Man looked upon me with favor. I came across a copy of The BOND this afternoon. How it got in the hooch is beyond me. It was just there. I finally realized I wasn't alone.

I have been slapping around an organization called the Someday Conspiracy. Its purpose is similar to the ASU with the exception of preferring a communal, utopian life instead of stateside democracy. We are small now. Actually, only two of us are fully dedicated to its purpose, but we talk to the others here and they listen with interest.

I work in a mortuary, U.S. Army type, here in Nam. I see every day the bloodied faces of the GI who died in vain: nothing won; everything (his life) lost. I see his family pictures and choke at the thought of how they feel.

I wish to be a part of your institution as a subsidiary unit in Vietnam under our own name. May we have your support in our pursuit of freedom. I support RITA [Resistance Inside the Army] fully.

SP4, Vietnam

Chapter 13 Pentagon at the Crossroads

Four hundred people hushed as A1C Louis "Buff" Parry announced his act of conscience. He would end his "complicity with the U.S. military and its crimes against humanity"[1] and take sanctuary at Honolulu's Church of the Crossroads.

It was Sunday, August 10, 1969. Parry and I were keynote speakers at the Nagasaki Day anti-war rally at Waikiki Beach Park in Honolulu. Even had it remained an individual act, Parry's stand was powerful. But following the rally at Waikiki Beach Park, seven other service members left the military to take sanctuary. It was becoming a mass action. The Honolulu protest's rapid growth presented an opportunity to stop the Pentagon in its tank tracks.

A1C Louis 'Buff' Parry, the first sanctuary member, here in Waikiki Beach Park and at the Church of the Crossroads. Photos: John Catalinotto

Both Parry and I were wearing leis, a gift of the local anti-war group known as the Hawai'i Resistance. The leis turned out to be a welcome to the struggle where soldiers, sailors, Marines and airmen showed the potential for a movement inside the U.S. military to end the war against Vietnam.

A mile east of Waikiki is Diamond Head Monument, a volcanic crater and symbol of Honolulu with views of all Oahu. Volcanic eruptions gave birth to all the Hawaiian islands, including Oahu.

Waikiki Park was filled with palms and 12-foot-wide Banyan trees whose many trunks, intertwined like great serpents around a central column, support one tree's branches and leaves. GIs and anti-war civilians sought similar mutual support.

We marched parallel to the Pacific beaches along Waikiki and Ala Moana parks, where we held the rally, and then another two miles through Honolulu's city center, quiet on Sunday, to the Church of the Crossroads. That evening, we counted eight service members in the Sanctuary. We all slept at the church.*

The next day, we learned that Black Marines at the nearby Kaneohe Marine Corps Air Station had torn apart the mess hall to protest prejudicial job assignments and racist harassment. This rebellion added another dimension to volcanic movements shaking the military.

I was on Oahu almost by accident. The anti-war movement in Hawai'i, motivated by a language student at the University of Hawai'i named Susan Steinman, had invited Andy Stapp to speak. Stapp's spouse was about to give birth, so he sent me instead.

I had nothing like Stapp's charisma to keep an audience spellbound, nor his skill with media. My realm was the union office, writing letters to GIs on a manual typewriter and working as circulation manager for *The Bond*. Now suddenly I was on point at the front lines and the only ASU organizer on site.

The Hawai'i Resistance, the church elders and the ASU had a tiger by the tail. The tiger was growling. My job as ASU organizer was to make the tiger grow.

To the Marine officers at Kaneohe MCAS, what the Black troops did was a mutinous riot. To the ASU, it was a righteous uprising. The rebellion presented a challenge to the anti-war movement.

Solidarity with Black Marines

Could we unite the military resistance at the Crossroads with this outbreak of the Black Liberation struggle that was sweeping the U.S. in 1969 — in this case at the nearby Marine base?

After a night sleeping on the church floor with some 50 young anti-war people, who might have been at home at the iconic Woodstock, N.Y., concert that took place a week later, I made a proposal: "Let's demonstrate at the gates of Kaneohe in solidarity with the Black Marines." And we did. [2]

What I lacked in charisma, I compensated for in organization. I had with me a small bottle of India ink and a steel brush that I used to make the placards we carried: "Solidarity with the Black Marines" and "Stop the War Against Black America."

The night after this symbolic action, a group of Marines from Kaneohe showed up at the church. They brought three sacks to the kitchen. One said, "Here's sixty pounds of meat we found in the mess hall. We wanted to make a donation to the sanctuary." These Marines donated under the table something we could put on the table at the Crossroads.

After that happened, I started to believe we could take down the military and help the Vietnamese get the U.S. out. I wanted to believe we could stop the napalm bombs from dropping. Maybe I was over-optimistic, but the seeds of a widespread rebellion were there. To conceive of it forty-seven years later, you have to recreate the mood of August 1969 and know what a military center Oahu was.

As early as January 1968, the Tet Offensive of the Vietnamese National Liberation Front had inflicted heavy casualties on U.S. troops, demoralized U.S. government leaders, and turned the U.S. population against the war. President Lyndon Johnson, closely identified with the war, was forced to withdraw from the 1968 election.

Richard Nixon, the new Republican president, promised to end the war. Yet he still increased the number of U.S. troops in Vietnam until it peaked at 543,400 on April 30, 1969. Up to that time, 33,641 U.S. troops had been killed there.

In June 1969, Nixon announced plans to gradually remove U.S. troops. The U.S. forces were to be replaced by expanding the puppet army of South Vietnam in a plan known as "Vietnamization."

Meanwhile, the majority of the U.S. population had turned against the war, and the anti-war movement had grown both broader and more combative. To the anti-war movement and the GIs, Nixon's steps were too little, too slow and too easily reversed.

Anti-war resistance also grew within the military. For the GIs, the war was an immediate life-and-death issue. The troops' hostility mounted year by year. Some Pentagon officers worried the war machine would fall apart.

That same month a mass mutiny of a combat unit took place in Vietnam, reported in a big headline in the August 26, 1919 New York Daily News of the 196th Light Infantry Brigade: "Sir, My Men Refuse to Go," the first of many. According to historian Dave Cortright:

> The latter stages of the Vietnam War produced no fewer than ten major incidents of mutiny.[3]

Hawai'i: Pentagon in the Pacific

Since the 1893 planters' uprising led to the U.S.'s illegal annexation of Hawai'i in 1898,[4] the islands have always been a central military base for the U.S. in the Pacific, especially the island of Oahu. An impromptu trip to Haleiwa, north of Honolulu, to pick up leaflets taught me this better than a book could.

On the 30-mile drive my host pointed out the warships in Pearl Harbor, which housed 60,000 sailors, and nearby Hickam Air Force Base. He pointed out the gap in the mountains where the Japanese planes first appeared beyond a cloudbank before bombing Pearl Harbor in December 1941 in the battle of two imperialist powers for the Pacific.

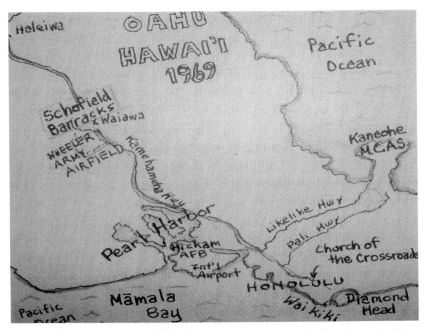

From Haleiwa (upper left) to central Honolulu is 30 miles. Amidst lush tropical forest and superb beaches are five major U.S. military bases. Map: J. Catalinotto

We continued along the Kamehameha Highway past Wheeler Airfield and Schofield Army Barracks, which housed 15,000 Army troops. And then to the east of Honolulu, on the windward coast of Oahu, was the Kaneohe Marine base.

In 1969, tens of thousands of U.S. troops, among the more than half a million doing a year's service in Vietnam, were rotated out for "rest and recreation" in Hawai'i. If you wanted to reach out to U.S. troops, including those in Vietnam, the place to do it was Oahu.

The American Servicemen's Union had a friendly working relationship with the anti-war movement in Honolulu, known as the Hawai'i Resistance. We shipped them hundreds of copies of *The Bond* each month to distribute to the troops.[5]

The Church of the Crossroads congregation itself resolved to "provide moral support and such other assistance as may be appropriate to persons whose conscience is in conflict with requirements of the state," including "sanctuary for those who engage in nonviolent forms of resistance as a matter of conscience."[6]

PENTAGON AT THE CROSSROADS

'Break Chains of Military Injustice'

Hawai'i Resistance announced and promoted the GI-Civilian Walk for Peace set for Sunday, August 10, 1969, to commemorate the atomic massacres of Hiroshima and Nagasaki. The American Servicemen's Union co-sponsored the action.

> Leaflets urging men to 'Break the Chains of Military Injustice' were distributed on bases and in Waikiki and emphasized the ASU's demands, focused on winning a bill of rights for GIs, especially the right to refuse orders to participate in the illegal war in Vietnam.[7]

As the sanctuary movement grew, the ASU approach was to define the gathering of GIs at the church as a "union meeting." In the vision of ASU organizers, none of the actions of the rebellious GIs should be considered illegal. It was the war that was illegal, unconstitutional, had never been declared, and its prosecution meant further Pentagon war crimes against the Vietnamese people.

For the ASU, the GIs were workers who had the right to come to the Church of the Crossroads simply to form their own organization.

∞

Despite my optimism, I was frustrated by having to work "alone," that is, without other party members or ASU organizers I knew I could count on. There were plenty of good people there, but no disciplined working organization to rely on. Nevertheless, I was ready to stay, even if it meant leaving my job in New York. I'd take a chance with whatever happened in Hawai'i.

Based on my reports of the initial few days, the ASU office in New York, with the support of Workers World Party, sent a delegation of four organizers to Honolulu, including two AWOL soldiers who joined the GIs in sanctuary. I was disappointed when they asked me to return to less dramatic support tasks with *The Bond*.

I had confidence our political leadership would find a way to keep us in this struggle. As I expected, the ASU sent civilian and GI organizers, first Maryann Weissman and retired SP5 Bob Lemay, and later, two active-duty GIs who were already AWOL: PFC Greg Laxer and PVT John Lewis.

Because of the rapid and revolutionary developments in Hawai'i, a meeting in New York had quickly raised enough funds to pay for travel expenses. Weissman and Lemay held a meeting with me at the Seattle airport on Sunday, August 17, where I briefed them for ninety minutes just before we continued in opposite directions.

In New York, I discovered that while I was away, my six-year-old daughter had been rushed to emergency care with a high fever. That was a major reason I was asked to return. The fever turned out to be caused by a bad case of tonsillitis.

Internal Differences in Sanctuary

That August 17 weekend, the first political differences surfaced in the movement in Honolulu. The main forces involved in supporting the sanctuary movement and the GIs were, on the one hand, the young, somewhat anarchist and certainly disorganized crowd of people spending most of their days and nights at the Church of the Crossroads. Even though the young people at the Sanctuary were committed to taking action to oppose the war, there was an atmosphere of "love community" that precluded disciplined organization.

The famous Woodstock, N.Y., rock concert took place August 15-17, and the mood among the youth at the Church of the Crossroads reflected the same youthful rebellion. They hated the war, but few were thinking of joining a party of revolutionaries who devoted their lives to fighting U.S. imperialism.

The church elders, on the other hand, complained about what they called the "carnival nature" of the Sanctuary and the role of the Hawai'i Resistance.

One of the members of Resistance, John Witeck, said this at the time about the Church elders, who had spoken out against drug use and sexual relations at the Sanctuary:

> They're more concerned with the order of things than they are with really making some changes in the society that is going to go somewhere. ... I want them to move in. But I want them to move in as part of us.[8]

The church board was comfortable taking a moral position against the war and giving material support to a symbolic refusal from Parry and a few others. But the sanctuary movement had grown much faster than anyone expected. The church elders seemed frightened by the scope of the struggle.

On Sunday morning, August 17, the eighteen GIs in Sanctuary received a standing ovation from the 350 people at the church. To keep the growth of the movement at the church under control, an

> ultimatum from the Executive Board of the Church establishing limits on the support community and declaring a three-day moratorium [on any new GIs joining the Sanctuary] created a crisis situation, with the Church and the Resistance support community at odds.[9]

This meant that the outreach the Resistance people were doing at Waikiki to GIs had to stop, no new GIs could join and the momentum of the struggle would be interrupted.

Along with media publicity, what spread this struggle were Resistance members who distributed leaflets on Waikiki Beach and other gathering points, bringing the story of the Sanctuary to GIs. This had the potential of reaching hundreds of GIs. Many were ready to seek a sanctuary or a union meeting to stop them from going to or returning to Vietnam.

While rapid growth would bring logistical problems, it would also bring more support from the anti-war civilians. The Sanctuary soon got support from the Unitarian Church, which relieved some of the crowding at the Crossroads.

∞

Meanwhile, the Armed Forces were preparing to crack down on this new movement. This was easier ordered than obeyed. The broad support for the Sanctuary from the church community and the strong anti-war movement in Hawai'i meant that a violent state crackdown could spread the struggle and make it more radical.

TURN THE GUNS AROUND

The military police and military intelligence bided their time, keeping a close watch on the movement, while trying to catch and arrest individual GIs. They hovered about, picking off GIs where they could, apparently hoping the movement's energy would decline.

Sanctuary Grows Despite Moratorium

Despite the moratorium on recruiting, the number of GIs at the sanctuary continued to grow, reaching more than thirty, including some GIs who first joined and then left. ASU member PVT Greg Laxer, who had already been AWOL over 30 days, arrived on August 21. According to Laxer's account, he had used a typewriter like the ones on Army bases and cut himself orders to Hawai'i to make the trip from New York "on Uncle Sam's dime."[10]

On August 22, ASU organizer John Lewis arrived. Lewis had spent some time in the Fort Dix stockade and was then AWOL. That same day the Unitarian Church opened its doors. The two ASU organizers did their best to provide political education for the members of the Sanctuary. But their outreach was limited, as they could not leave the Sanctuary without risking arrest, so their contact was restricted to the thirty GIs already there.

By the end of August, some ASU members thought they could play a more effective role by leaving the Sanctuary and visiting military bases. On August 31-September 1, five AWOL GIs left the Sanctuary in three cars. Lewis was in one, followed by Military Intelligence to the Oahu airport. His car was stopped and he was arrested. Another of the cars, noticing what happened to Lewis, turned around and made it back to the church. In the third car, a VW Beetle driven by a Resistance activist, were Greg Laxer and Resistance organizer Susan Steinman.

Laxer wrote later in an unpublished memoir:

> I immediately hunkered down on the floor in the back. We took off and a government car immediately came in pursuit. The personnel in the pursuit car, presumably Army CID (Criminal Investigations Division) guys, decidedly did **not** know the local streets. The young man driving

our getaway car didn't even have to drive at a reckless speed; he shook off our pursuers simply by making a lot of turns onto side streets.[11]

After some nervous hours at the airport, Laxer and Steinman flew to San Francisco and Laxer made his way back to New York City. He was arrested at an anti-war demonstration on September 18 and wound up back at the Fort Dix stockade to continue organizing there. Lewis took a more circuitous route, also reaching the Fort Dix stockade.

∞

On September 2, Navy Lithographer Roy Andrews had been the thirtieth GI to join the Sanctuary. Two leaders, Buff Parry and Lou Jones, went to the General Convention of the Episcopal Church of the United States of America held at Notre Dame University in South Bend, Indiana, to appeal for support. On September 5, the FBI raided the Episcopal Convention, but Parry and Jones had already left to seek asylum in Canada.

The struggle was winding down at the Church of the Crossroads, but there was another high point: On September 6, Lucy Hashizume and Resistance leader John Witeck were married with about thirty GIs all serving as the "best man."[12]

On September 12, about "forty MPs stormed the grounds at Crossroads, kicking in all locked doors including those to the church." They only found and arrested eight of the men, but the police action ended the Sanctuary.[13]

Throughout the five weeks of the Sanctuary, the approach of the ASU delegation was focused on "How can we continue to expand this movement until it affects the entire Armed Forces from Western Europe to Vietnam?" To move in that direction one needed to have the attitude and the ideology that looked at the collapse of the U.S. Armed Forces as both positive and possible.

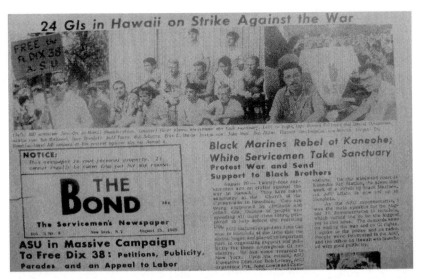

The Bond, August 25, 1969. Author top left holding ASU sign. Photo: J. Catalinotto

The Crossroads became another chapter in this struggle, even if it fell short of its early potential. The Hawai'i Resistance continued to work with GIs into the mid-1970s, helping to organize some successful struggles and in 1971 began publishing an impressive GI newspaper, *Liberated Barracks*.

Louis "Buff" Parry moved to Edmonton, Alberta, in Canada, where he is still living in 2016. In an email Parry told me he was a founder of the Edmonton Coalition Against War and Racism (ECAWAR), which held large anti-war demonstrations in that city in the build-up to the March 2003 U.S.-British invasion of Iraq.[14]

Privates Lewis and Laxer avoided being sent to Vietnam and continued organizing at Fort Dix. When they finally left the Army, they became ASU organizers in the New York office. Susan Steinman never finished her degree in languages, but after becoming the Hawai'i organizer for the ASU, she later became a national field organizer working out of the ASU office.

Chapter Notes

* "Army Spec. 4 Dan Overstreet, AWOL from R & R leave from Vietnam, rose to state his determination not to return to the war zone and his intent to join the sanctuary. Marine Pvt. Vince Ventimiglia, military police undercover agent assigned by the military to undermine the march and apprehend the AWOLs, instead announced his decision to join them in sanctuary. Navy Airman Eric Harms, foregoing the crime of continued silence, declared his intent to join the sanctuary. Navy Seaman John Veal, Army Pfc. Bob Schultz and Navy Seaman Howard Pallaske also announced their active 'retirement' from the Armed Services and their entry into sanctuary. Seaman Apprentice Bob Matheson joined these seven back at Crossroads Church later that night and brought the total to eight men in sanctuary."

That was on Sunday, August 10. By the next day another three had joined: Marine CPL Lou Jones Jr., Marine PFCs Curt Trendell and Ron Allen, stationed with the Army in Vietnam. On August 12, PVT Jim Morris "retired" from the Marines to join.

On August 15, Bryan Bohannon from the Army and Oscar Kelley and Art Parker from the Navy joined the sanctuary, which also drew support from peace and other progressive groups at the University of Hawai'i. By week's end eighteen GIs had joined the sanctuary and more were coming.[15]

Chapter 14 The Great Slaughter

"No war is any longer possible for Prussia-Germany except a world war and a world war indeed of an extension and violence hitherto undreamt of. Eight to ten millions of soldiers will mutually massacre one another and in doing so devour the whole of Europe until they have stripped it barer than any swarm of locusts has ever done." Frederick Engels wrote this in in a preface to a pamphlet in 1887.[1]

On June 28, 1914, Gavrilo Princip, a 19-year-old patriot from the oppressed nation of Bosnia-Herzegovina, assassinated Archduke Ferdinand of Austria. Ferdinand was the symbol of the tyrannical rule of the decadent Habsburg Empire over Princip's country. The militarist rulers in Vienna, the capital of the empire, seized on the assassination in Sarajevo as a pretext to declare war on Serbia.

This decree essentially launched what became World War I. That terrible slaughter killed 20 million people, mostly European workers and farmers, but included thousands of young men conscripted from the colonies held by France, Britain and Germany.

The war would wreak even more havoc than Engels foresaw in his prophetic preface to that pamphlet. Along with the misery imposed on the masses of Europe, however, it would swing open the door to revolutions as never seen before on the Eurasian land mass. And playing a leading role in these revolutions would be the very soldiers and sailors whom the ruling classes had armed and turned into warriors.

No one who supports the self-determination of oppressed nations would fault Princip for wanting to strike a blow at a member of the ruling royal family of the oppressive empire. But whatever one thinks of the effectiveness of his deed, it is patently ridiculous to cite this individual act as the basic cause of a global conflagration.

The war had been in the making since the turn of the century. Some regional wars had already broken out in the Balkans. In 1905 the Russo-Japanese war saw Japan's rising capitalist power defeat the semi-feudal Czarist Empire. German, French and British imperialism had skirmished over the building of the Baghdad railroad.

The major states on both sides of the 1914 war were all oppressor nations. There was no "good side." British imperialism ruled over an enormous empire that included Australia, Canada, Ireland, Egypt, all of South Asia, some Caribbean islands and much of sub-Saharan Africa. Its previous wars had all been one-sided battles where heavily armed colonial troops slaughtered heroic Indigenous peoples armed with spears.

Imperialist France's empire was half as large as the British, but still stretched from Indochina to the Caribbean and included large tracts in West and North Africa. Even "tiny" Belgium controlled and exploited the vast Congo, squeezing the last drop of blood from the Congolese. And that was the side considered the capitalist "democracies." Their ally, the Russian czar, ruled over 12 time zones and hundreds of different nations and peoples with an iron hand.

Germany, more militarist and authoritative at home than Britain and France, and its allies — the Austro-Hungarian Empire and the Ottoman Empire — were just as brutal toward their subject colonies, but the territories and populations they controlled were smaller. Still, they included Southwest Africa (Namibia), German East Africa (Tanganyika) and parts of Poland for Germany; Czechoslovakia and much of the Balkans for Austria-Hungary; and the Ottoman Empire dominated the mostly Arab countries in Southwest Asia.

Washington did not enter World War I until 1917. It had joined in imperialist competition with a bang in 1898 by seizing Hawai'i and the Philippines in the Pacific and Cuba and Puerto Rico in the Caribbean. A relative newcomer to European battles, U.S. capitalists expanded their industry selling weapons to the British-French-Russian alliance, which Washington finally joined.

Though a fledgling imperialist power at the time, U.S. rulers were equally brutal to the Indigenous population in North America, to their Mexican neighbor from which they seized half its territory, to the Asian laborers who built its railroads, to their internal Black colony and to the newly conquered nations that Spain had ruled.

In 1881, many of the European powers met in Berlin, in what can only be described as outrageous arrogance, to divide up Africa — without consulting the Africans. Russian revolutionary leader V. I. Lenin pointed out in his seminal work, *Imperialism, the Highest Stage of Capitalism*, written in January-June 1916, that these colonial powers had split up the entire world among themselves by 1900. The pecking order — how much colonial plunder each got — was based roughly on their industrial, financial and military power at that moment. Since from month to month their relative strengths were changing, the agreement was unstable and prone to conflict.

Germany's industry grew much more rapidly than that of Britain and France after 1900, as did its military power. German capitalism had gone through a late but rapid industrialization, surpassing Britain and France in steel and iron production. But Germany's global empire was far less extensive than that of its two main rivals, which exploited and oppressed a larger part of the world's colonized peoples and vastly greater territory.

Uneven Development Led to War

To find markets, the powerful German industrial machine needed room to expand: The militarists called it *"Lebensraum."* German economic expansion, however, was restricted by British and French control of territories, resources and markets. Something had to give. How could rising imperialist powers redistribute the colonial territories in their favor? Only by war. This war was not to be restricted to the colonial areas, but exploded among the imperialist countries in Europe itself.

This sharp competition among the capitalist classes of the different powers also expressed itself in ideology: National chauvinism and vicious hostility to other nations and peoples ruled the day. The capitalist ruling-class ideologists and propagandists imposed this chauvinism on their respective populations. Their goal was to line up each population to support the war and supply its cannon fodder.

THE GREAT SLAUGHTER

Chapter 5 illustrated how the French capitalists had been willing to concede territory to the German capitalists in 1871 after losing the Franco-Prussian war. The French made this deal with the German rulers because it allowed them to crush the first workers' government, the Paris Commune. But in 1914, the hypocritical French capitalists insisted that the French workers must hate the German workers. The German ruling class mirrored this chauvinism.

The workers' movement in Europe, and especially its most revolutionary wing, attempted to combat this increasingly dangerous national chauvinism. At earlier gatherings of socialists, and for the last time in 1912 in Basel, Switzerland, meetings of the workers' parties of the Second International issued a manifesto on the war question. The Basel Manifesto shows that two years before the assassination at Sarajevo, there was a growing war danger and the massive workers' movement was aware of it:

> If a war threatens to break out, it is the duty of the working classes and their parliamentary representatives in the countries involved supported by the coordinating activity of the International Socialist Bureau to exert every effort in order to prevent the outbreak of war by the means they consider most effective, which naturally vary according to the sharpening of the class struggle and the sharpening of the general political situation.
>
> In case war should break out anyway it is their duty to intervene **in favor of its speedy termination** and with all their powers to utilize the **economic and political crisis created by the war to arouse the people and thereby to hasten the downfall of capitalist class rule.** [Emphasis in the original][2]

This manifesto clearly called for working-class solidarity and for workers' refusal to side with what could be called "their own" ruling class against the foreign workers. It also meant taking the opportunity caused by the horrors of war to overthrow their own capitalist class. Throughout the manifesto there was urgency in the call on the working class in all the countries to take any actions they could, from the parliament to the streets, to prevent the impending war.

The capitalist parties ruling the European imperialist democracies, France and Britain, as well as the monarchies in Germany, Austria-Hungary and Russia, entered the war without hesitation, even with enthusiasm. Each believed their state would win a quick victory. They salivated at the thought of conquered territory and new colonies — as shown later when Russia's successful workers' revolution revealed and published treaties that the rulers had kept secret.

Whether or not the Social Democratic parties could have stopped the war before it started, it was a severe blow to the world and to revolutionaries throughout Europe that most of their leaders failed to follow the Basel Manifesto that they had signed onto. Under enormous pressure from "their own" ruling classes, most Social Democratic parties and leaders lined up with the war drive.

This betrayal was a sobering lesson on the need for revolutionary parties to train themselves under all situations to stand up against all forms of national chauvinism and racism and to resist imperialist war. Once again it showed that the main enemy of the workers and the oppressed is "their own" capitalist class.

Even the Social Democratic Party of Germany, which was the largest of the socialist-oriented parties in the major European countries, abandoned its position of internationalism. Only one Social Democratic member of the German Reichstag (Parliament) — Karl Liebknecht — voted against funding the war in December 1914. Following his speech at a May 1, 1916, anti-war demonstration in Berlin, Liebknecht was imprisoned. He and revolutionary leader Rosa Luxemburg, who was imprisoned later, led the Spartacist group that, while part of the Social Democrat Party, actively opposed the war.

Lenin and the other leaders of his party, the Russian Bolsheviks, held firmly to the program of the Basel Manifesto as the war began. Lenin went further in September 1915 by gathering the revolutionary wing of the Social Democratic movement in a meeting in Zimmerwald, Switzerland. The Zimmerwald Manifesto clearly called on the masses to turn the great imperialist slaughter into a war against each country's ruling class:

> Since the outbreak of the war, you have placed your energy, your courage, your endurance at the service of the ruling classes. Now you

must stand up for your own cause, for the sacred aims of Socialism, for the emancipation of the oppressed nations as well as of the enslaved classes, by means of the irreconcilable proletarian class struggle."[3]

And this is exactly what Lenin's Bolsheviks did in Russia.

It is unnecessary here to review the entire course of the great slaughter known as World War I. A description of one major battle should be enough: the first Battle of the Somme River in 1916 on the Western Front in France. The British generals thought they had a foolproof plan: A week of unbridled British artillery fire would soften the German lines. But this artillery barrage, begun the last week of June, killed few German troops, disarmed few machine guns and destroyed little of their barbed-wire obstacles.

Oblivious to this failure, on July 1, 1916, the British generals ordered their planned offensive to proceed against the German army. Following orders, British troops, laden with equipment, walked clumsily and slowly toward the German lines. They were quickly mowed down by German rifle and cannon fire. The first day ended with 58,000 British troops killed or wounded. The front had moved just two kilometers, a little over one mile.

The battle of the Somme ground on for months. Until snow brought it to a halt in November 1916, the fighting killed or wounded 420,000 British, 200,000 French and 500,000 German troops. To move seven miles cost 1.1 million casualties.

By November 1918, when the war ended, major rebellions and mutinies had broken out in nearly all the imperialist armed forces. In most cases, the ruling classes and their general staff were able to crush these uprisings. However, these rebellions overthrew the ruling monarchies in the defeated powers of Germany and Austria-Hungary and led to a world-changing social revolution in Russia.

Chapter 15 Russia: February and October 1917

On February 23, 1917, by the Julian calendar used in Russia at that time — March 8 in the rest of Europe — a 25-year-old revolutionary sailor named Fyodor Fyodorovich Ilyin, whose party name was Raskolnikov, looked out his window in Petrograd, Russia's industrial center and capital.

This city, like many revolutionary individuals in Russia, had another name. The Russian rulers had decided to stop calling it Saint Petersburg so it would sound less German, as they were at war with Germany. Raskolnikov thought, "Today is Women's Day. Will something happen in the streets today?" Something did happen. Some 128,000 workers were on strike. The whole city was seething.

As things turned out, "Women's Day" was fated to be the first day of the revolution. Working women, driven to despair by their hard conditions and prey to the torments of hunger, were the first to come out onto the streets demanding 'bread, freedom and peace.' The crowds were facing down police mounted on horses, who would push the people around or smack them with the flat side of their swords. Wrote one observer: "... [A]s soon as the mounted policemen had returned to the roadway, the crowd would close up again into a solid mass. In some of the groups we could see men, but the overwhelming majority consisted of working women and workers' wives."[1]

Eight weeks earlier, as 1917 was beginning, Vladimir Ilyich Ulyanov, whose party name was Lenin, was in exile in Zürich, Switzerland, where he had been organizing and speaking against the great imperialist war. In a talk to young students, he remarked that Russians as old as he was — forty-six at the time — would likely never see a revolution overthrow the Russian czar, but that the youth would. Thus even this most revolutionary leader of the working class was surprised by the explosive speed of change.

One can imagine how oblivious Czar Nicholas II was at that time to his imminent fate. The February revolution was to soon remove him from power and end the Russian monarchy, but leave a weak capitalist class in power. This class was trying to keep Russia fighting in the imperialist war, which would undermine its rule.

This unstable situation led to the second Russian Revolution of 1917, which was to determine the political history of the twentieth century. It created the Union of Soviet Socialist Republics, the first state put in power by the working class. The existence of this workers' state impelled a series of revolutions in East Asia, national liberation struggles in colonies around the world and workers' struggles in Europe and North America.

With almost unbelievable sacrifices and as many as twenty-six million people killed, the USSR would defeat Nazi Germany's imperialist war machine during World War II. This all occurred between 1917 and 1989-91, when a counterrevolution finally overthrew the Soviet workers' state.

The 1917 workers' revolution created an overwhelming challenge to all owners of land, industry and wealth. All these exploiters of labor who ruled the rest of the world outside Russia thus dedicated enormous amounts of energy and wealth during those seven decades to destroy that revolution. Their efforts included plans for a nuclear war that might have exterminated life on Earth. They also waged a complete ideological and propaganda war against the Soviet Union and against socialism and communism.

Since 1991, those same ruling classes have used every resource at their command to distort, ridicule, minimize, demonize and if possible destroy the collective memory of the 1917 revolutions' enormous accomplishments.

This chapter will present only a synopsis of how the 1917 revolutions unfolded, with special attention to the role of mutinies and rebellions in the Russian armed forces during World War I and the revolutionary role of the sailors in the Baltic Fleet and at the Kronstadt naval base near Petrograd (see map on page 131). It will show how, under pressure from the ongoing imperialist war, the rank and file in the military shifted their allegiance decisively away from the capitalist-led government that succeeded the czar in March 1917 and attached themselves to the Soviets of Workers, Peasants and Soldiers — which laid the basis for building socialism in Russia.

This chapter also shows, in brief, another essential lesson of this revolution: The key role of a political party, trained in combat of all forms, is to act with iron determination to carry out the class struggle to its end. That party was the Bolshevik (majority) faction, the left wing of the old Russian Social Democratic Workers Party, and Lenin was its leader.

∞

As Raskolnikov wrote, the first of the two 1917 revolutions in Russia began on February 23 with a strike of women workers on International Women's Day. In one week it grew into a general strike and mass political revolution in the capital city. The week ended with the overthrow of the czarist monarchy that had ruled Russia since 1547.

The second revolution in October led to the seizure of power by the oppressed and exploited masses, led by the modern proletariat in Marxist terminology — those who lived by selling their labor power. The workers' party took the reins of power on October 25 (November 7 on the Western calendar) of the largest geographic state in the world, one made up of many nations and peoples, and wielded that power for more than seven decades. The attitude and actions of low-ranking soldiers and sailors were a determining factor in the success of both phases of this revolution.

The czarist empire had ruled over many subject peoples — Finns, Lithuanians and Estonians in the Northwest; Poles and Ukrainians in the West; Georgians, Armenians and many Turkic and mostly Muslim peoples in the Caucasus and South; plus Indigenous peoples throughout the Arctic and Siberian regions; and Jews and other minorities throughout its vast territory.

124

February Revolution

Czarist Russia was far less developed economically than the major imperialist powers in Western Europe — Germany, France and Britain. Some five-sixths of Russia's 185 million people were peasants, who had been liberated from legal serfdom in 1861, but were still in the thrall of the landlords and the nobility. About twenty-six million of its people were wage laborers in 1917, including 6.5 million farm laborers and another six million in private and state-owned industry. [2]

Although a smaller part of the total population than in Germany, Britain and the United States, the workers in Russian industry were more concentrated, toiling in recently established giant factories that employed thousands and even tens of thousands of workers.

Russia was by far the poorest of the major countries, yet some fifteen million men, mainly peasants, were mobilized by conscription and thrown into the battles of World War I, with little training or equipment. They were cannon fodder. By 1917, more than two million had died and another four million were wounded. [3]

With so many men under arms, a large number of women were employed in heavy industry in Petrograd; women made up about one-third of the workforce there. [4] More than 100,000 of these women went out on strike on February 23, defying the czarist state, defying the cautions of their political parties, defying everyone.

That first day, the striking women escaped clashes with the police generally unscathed. Encouraged by this success, male workers joined the women the following day, and in all more than 200,000, or half of the city's workers, were in the streets. General Sergei Khabalov, who commanded the Petrograd army garrison, was responsible for controlling the demonstration.

But the workers, and especially the women, many of whom were soldiers' wives, were talking with the garrison troops. They were even approaching the Cossacks, who were mounted troops often used in punitive actions against crowds, but who showed the workers they were weary of this unpleasant duty. On the other hand, the workers were hostile toward both the regular police and the secret police; the latter especially were enemies of the people and staunch defenders of the czar.

A political intellectual named N. N. Sukhanov, who was in the internationalist wing of the Menshevik Party (the right wing of the old Russian Social Democratic Labor Party), wrote a detailed eyewitness account of the 1917 Revolution. In this book, he described one telling moment when a Cossack became so riled up seeing a police inspector attack one of the demonstrators with his sword that he "flew at the inspector and slashed off his hand."[5]

On February 26, as ever-friendlier fraternization between the workers and the troops was going on, something special happened. Something like this has probably taken place in every successful revolution in urban society. Soldiers from the Pavlovsky regiment, a major military unit of the Petrograd Garrison, witnessed a police unit on one side of a river fire on the people protesting on the other. Sukhanov wrote:

> Seeing this shooting at unarmed people and the wounded falling around them, and finding themselves in the zone of fire, **the Pavlovskys opened fire at the police across the canal.**[6]

When a regiment as big as the Pavlovsky breaks with tyranny, its soldiers have only one road forward: Spread the rebellion — or die. The revolution demanded this activity, and so did the soldiers' own self-defense. That same day representatives of the workers and peasants' parties — the Mensheviks, the Bolsheviks and the Social Revolutionaries — gathered to form the Petrograd Soviet, the Russian word for "council."* This political leadership of the revolution, for its part, had to help spread the soldiers' rebellion.

That evening, the Provisional Executive Committee of the Petrograd Soviet, elected from the Soviet, convened, declaring that the Soviet was now open. Its first task was to begin organizing emergency rations for the garrison troops that had come over to the revolution. The mutinous soldiers knew they were still a minority of the garrison, and their lives were on the line if the revolution were not carried through to the end. They needed to act.

To act meant to arrest members of the ordinary police, still loyal to the czar, and of the hated secret police. One by one a dozen other regiments met and decided to pledge their allegiance to the Petrograd Soviet of Workers' Deputies. Their representatives went to the Petrograd Soviet and reported from the regiments' assemblies:

> They told us to say that we refuse to serve against the people any more, we're going to join with our brother workers, all united, to defend the people's cause. ... We would lay down our lives for that. Long live the revolution![7]

At this point the political leaders changed the name of the Soviet of Workers' Deputies to the Soviet of Workers' **and Soldiers'** Deputies, thus fusing the spontaneous rank-and-file soldier organizations to the workers' councils.

The Soviet received a report that a regiment loyal to the czarist regime was arriving, which caused some nervousness, but Sukhanov ended his text with this description that showed how much the population and all of the army had turned against Czar Nicholas and the war:

> Later we [Soviet members] became persuaded that any attempt to dispatch troops for the pacification of Petersburg was fruitless. All the "loyal" troops preserved their loyalty and obeyed their commanders only as far as the railway stations, then immediately went over to the side of the revolution, and the commanders obeyed them.[8]

The Bolsheviks, Lenin's party, may have been as surprised as everyone else with how quickly the revolutionary movement was developing, but they were the first to adapt to the new situation. Groups of Bolshevik workers raided police stations, took weapons and passed them out to their supporters. The soldiers, who as a whole were still wavering, could then see there were armed, determined and well-organized contingents of workers who were ready to see the revolution to its end.

With tens of thousands of troops already in a state of mutiny and facing deadly punishment if the revolt were to end before overthrowing the czar, the troops who had already mutinied had no option but to reach out to their brother soldiers and win them over to the revolution. It was no difficult task, as the rank-and-file soldiers were completely fed up with the hated czar and the rest of the nobility, and most were anxious to return to their farms. In the next few days the entire Petrograd garrison joined the Revolution.

Pressured by the bourgeois parties in a new government, on March 1 Czar Nicholas II attempted to abdicate in favor of his brother Mikhail, but Mikhail refused to take over the sinking ship. The czarist ministers were arrested. Armed soldiers answering to the Soviet arrested any police who were still on the streets interfering with the masses, who were in turn tearing down the symbols of czarist rule. On March 3, the Executive Committee of the Petrograd Soviet ordered the arrest of the czar, who attempted to flee. He was captured, along with the rest of the royal family. The empire had ended.

Two Centers of Power

Two separate centers of power thus replaced the Russian monarchy in March 1917. One was the Provisional Government, where the pro-capitalist parties took the lead and collaborated with the remnants of the old czarist state — the bureaucracy, the police and courts and the regular army generals. The Provisional Government acted as the center of capitalist power.

The other center was the Petrograd Soviet, where the main parties were the ones representing the peasants, workers and soldiers. As of the beginning of March, none of these poor-people parties, not even the Bolsheviks, had plans to make a socialist revolution in Russia. They did, however, plan steps to prevent the czarist monarchy from making any kind of comeback — that is, they defended the new regime against counterrevolution.

As part of this defense, the first Joint Plenum of the Soviet of Workers' and Soldiers' Deputies issued Order No. 1 of the Petrograd Soviet on March 1 (14), 1917,[9] which we publish in Appendix D-I.

Had Order No. 1 applied only to the units in Petrograd, it would have helped safeguard the revolution. Applied to the entire army, it would open the way to making the Petrograd Soviet the center of state power for all of Russia. During those next eight months, the loyalty of the troops, and thus real power, shifted from the Provisional Government to the Soviet.

The order insisted that rank-and-file soldiers elect representatives to the Soviet. That meant setting up a de-facto second authority within the military. This new authority challenged the old chain of command that kept the troops serving the privileged classes through their representatives in the caste of officers. Although the order did not explicitly call for the rank-and-file troops to elect their own officers, it led toward this step in many military units. By insisting that no movements could be made without the go-ahead from the Soviet, the order made this new authority explicit.

The Provisional Government was formed from the Duma — the old parliament that was powerless when the monarchy existed. Its leader was Alexander Kerensky, a lawyer who became Russia's war minister. Kerensky faced a great dilemma: Either he must break with the masses — who wanted to end the war — or he must break with the capitalists and Russia's imperialist allies — who wanted Russia to keep fighting Germany.

Russia was tied by secret agreements to its French and British allies. These agreements were to award Russia, following their victory over the so-called Central Powers, with a warm-water port in the southwest, cut out of Turkey, among other territorial advantages for the Russian capitalists. There was constant pressure from London and Paris on Russia throughout 1917 to stay in the war and to open a new offensive against Germany and its allies. Thus, to maintain its ties to its imperialist allies, the Russian Provisional Government had to keep spilling the blood of the poorly armed and equipped peasant army that wanted nothing more than to go home to their farms. Some 700,000 Russian soldiers deserted in 1917.[10]

As the two centers of power were beginning to face off, Lenin returned to Petrograd from Switzerland in April. The German government gave him a sealed railway car. The German rulers hoped Lenin would cause trouble for their Russian enemy. It did. It also led to a workers' revolution that shook the German rulers' world.

According to their previous political orientation, the Bolsheviks expected that the czar's overthrow would lead to establishing a more democratic but capitalist phase of society in Russia. They did not expect to immediately open a struggle for a socialist society without further development. From his analysis of the class struggle in Russia and the inability of the capitalists to end Russia's role in the war, however, Lenin had come to the conclusion that it was time to open a struggle for socialism. He thus had to win over his party to the goal of immediately fighting for Soviet rule, not to simply support an elected capitalist government, no matter how democratic.

Leon Trotsky (born Lev Davidovich Bronstein) arrived a few weeks after Lenin from exile in the United States. Though he had split from Lenin for fourteen years, Trotsky too oriented his political group — the Interdistrict Organization — toward a socialist revolution and merged his group with the larger Bolshevik Party, which was a combat party of trained and disciplined revolutionaries. From March onwards the Bolsheviks organized and agitated in the factories, found weapons for units of workers and built their organization in the army, especially among the sailors in the Baltic Fleet where they were particularly strong.

The sailor referred to earlier, Raskolnikov — he was a junior officer in the Navy and a Bolshevik — wrote a running account of the party's conscious work winning over the armed forces to the revolution. Raskolnikov was stationed at the Kronstadt naval base, a concentrated center of industrial workers and sailors on a small island in the Gulf of Finland, about 30 miles from central Petrograd. During the uprising that overthrew the czar and from the first days following the February revolution, Kronstadt was the hot center of armed Bolshevism in Russia.

In the eyes of the Russian capitalist class, wrote Raskolnikov:

> Kronstadt was a symbol of savage horror, the devil incarnate, a terrifying specter of anarchy, a nightmare rebirth of the Paris Commune

on Russian soil, [while for the workers, soldiers and peasants] Kronstadt in 1917 was the impregnable citadel of the revolution ... the vanguard of the revolution.[11]

Even after Lenin won over his own Bolshevik Party in April to the immediate necessity of overthrowing capitalism in Russia — and he had to win them over; it was not automatic — the Kronstadt Soviet was ahead of the rest of the country in wanting to push the Soviets to take power. The Bolshevik central leadership was often in the unenviable position of having to hold back the Kronstadt sailors until the rest of the country — or the rest of Petrograd — caught up.

Raskolnikov attributed Kronstadt's revolutionary fervor to the concentration of the working class there, both in the factories and on the big ships, which were similar to factories. The sailors were mainly workers conscripted to operate the equipment used on the battleships, destroyers, cruisers and submarines. He would often board a ship to speak with the crew, and even before April when the Bolsheviks became a majority in the Kronstadt Soviet, he found that of the 1,500 personnel on board a battleship, 600 had already joined the Bolshevik Party. He wrote, referring to his co-leader of the Kronstadt Bolsheviks:

> When Comrade [Semyon] Roshal went round the ships, there were occasions when entire crews asked to join the Party. According to Roshal, the total number of sympathizers with our Party reached at that time the colossal figure of 35,000, although formally the number of party members did not exceed three thousand.[12]

In April, the Kronstadt Soviet tried to break with the Kerensky government in Petrograd. Those who were anti-Bolshevik in the government tried to demonize the Kronstadt sailors before their attitude could spread to the rest of the fleet.

In May Raskolnikov went with a delegation from Kronstadt to speak with other sailors in the Baltic Sea Fleet who were stationed at Vyborg in Russia, Reval (Talinn) in Estonia and at Helsinki (Helsingfors) in Finland (see map). The delegation's task was first to expose the charges against Kronstadt as slander and then win over support from the rest of the sailors. It was also to gauge the support for the Bolsheviks and for Soviet rule within the Navy. If the sailors'

Gulf of Finland. It's about 190 miles from Helsinki to Petrograd. Raskolnikov visited the port cities where the Russian fleet was in harbor. Map: J. Catalinotto

delegation went on a ship where the Bolsheviks were a small minority, they were often able to neutralize the influence of the officers. On a ship where the Bolsheviks were already strong, they won over nearly all the rank-and-file sailors to the Bolsheviks, and a few of the officers, too. It was a successful trip.

∞

On June 18 (July 1), 1917, Kerensky ordered Russian troops on an offensive to capture the city of Lvov in what is now (2016) western Ukraine. The Russians attacked along a 40-mile front, but the offensive disintegrated within five days, eventually collapsing before a German counteroffensive. The disaster of this offensive won even more support within the army for the Bolsheviks, as it was the only party in the Soviets that promised over and over that it would end Russia's participation in the war.[13]

Anger over that offensive and its collapse set off workers' demonstrations in July in Petrograd that called for an end to Kerensky's Provisional Government. The demonstrations nearly erupted into an insurrection. The Kerensky regime and the capitalist parties blamed the Bolsheviks, who, even though they didn't call for the insurrection, were in the streets in solidarity with the workers and troops who were rebelling.

When the uprising fell short, many Bolsheviks were arrested, including leaders Kamenev, Zinoviev and Trotsky. Lenin went under-

132

ground over the border in Finland, and while in hiding, he wrote the pamphlet, *The State and Revolution*, quoted in Appendix B.

October Revolution

Then came another turnaround. In late August word came that the old czarist regime was sending troops loyal to it from the provinces under the command of a General Lavr Kornilov. Faced with this danger the government formed the Military Revolutionary Committee to defend Petrograd and freed some of the Bolshevik leaders to participate in it.

The parties in the government that feared a czarist counterrevolution absolutely needed the Bolsheviks to organize a defense because the revolutionary workers and sailors would only follow orders from the Bolsheviks. In return, the Bolsheviks would only work in the Military Revolutionary Committee if the government would supply them with arms for the workers. By mid-October the Bolsheviks were a majority of the Petrograd Soviet and directed the Military Revolutionary Committee.

The soldiers were determined not to keep fighting the war against Germany. Sukhanov wrote how representatives of regiments came in one by one to tell the Military Revolutionary Committee that they did not trust the Kerensky government and they would rise up at the first call to overthrow it. By October 21 this included the Petersburg garrison. Petrograd and Russia were inexorably moving toward a second revolution.

∞

Then a new crisis came up in the Soviet. The Army commandant of the Peter-Paul Fortress, most likely a pro-czarist officer, refused to recognize the commissar assigned to the Peter-Paul Fortress from the Military Revolutionary Committee and threatened him with arrest. This strategically important fortress inside Petrograd was essential to the victory of the uprising that was planned. But to attempt to take it by force was risky, an act of war. Sukhanov wrote:

> Trotsky had another proposal, namely, that he, Trotsky, go to the Fortress, hold a meeting there, and capture not the body but the spirit of the garrison. ... Trotsky set off at once, together with Lashevich. Their harangues were enthusiastically received. The garrison, almost unanimously, passed a resolution about the Soviet regime and its own readiness to rise up, weapons in hand, against the bourgeois government. ... A hundred thousand extra rifles were in the hands of the Bolsheviks.[14]

The national Congress of Soviets had been set for October 25 (November 7) in Petrograd. It would be a perfect time for this body to deliberate about taking state power. But the Provisional Government could still surround the congress with reactionary troops and arrest the Soviet. The Bolshevik leaders considered it more prudent to move first. No street clashes were necessary. All the street fighting had already happened in February (March). And it was no secret coup. The mainly Bolshevik leaders of the Military Revolutionary Committee openly declared their intention to protect the Congress of Soviets.

The sailors of the Baltic Fleet, the workers who controlled the bridges, the Petrograd garrison, the soldiers at the Peter-Paul Fortress — all had already joined the revolution. Under orders of the Soviet's Military Revolutionary Committee on the night of October 24-25 (November 6-7), armed workers known as Red Guards and revolutionary sailors seized postal and telegraph offices, electric works, railroad stations and the state bank.

That night at 9:45 p.m. a blank cannon shot rang out from the Cruiser Aurora, whose sailors were loyal to the Bolsheviks, anchored nearby in the Neva River. At this signal, thousands of sailors and Red Guards stormed the Winter Palace. The Provisional Government collapsed.

Exhausted workers, soldiers and Bolshevik leaders crowded the Congress of Soviets. After word came that the Winter Palace was taken, people rose, filling the hall with shouts and cheers. Lenin came to the podium and proclaimed, "We shall now proceed to construct the socialist order."

This was just the beginning. To sign a peace with Germany took months. There followed a long struggle and civil war before the Soviet Union could even be established. The Baltic Fleet sailors and armed workers of Petrograd became the shock troops of the Red Army, and many of these heroes, who were the driving force of the Russian Revolution, lost their lives in the costly civil war and invasion by Japan, Czechoslovakia, Britain, France, the United States and other capitalist countries that followed until 1922. Nevertheless, the experience of 1917 in Russia showed that the interaction between the revolutionary workers and the soldiers of the Petrograd garrison as well as the decisive actions of the sailors of the Baltic Fleet made the success of the revolution possible.

Chapter Note

* Soviets had first formed during the 1905 revolution that attempted but failed to overthrow the czarist empire. They were popular organizations that were elected by workers and peasants. That's where the left parties gathered. The capitalist and rightist parties gravitated to the Duma, the old parliament.

Chapter 16   The Kaiser's Blue Youths

Otto, a sailor in the North Sea Fleet, on November 2, 1918, wrote to his father, a Social Democratic representative in the German Reichstag: "We shook each others' hands heartily with the words, 'Victory down the whole line.' ... I must share this with you, that if the armistice isn't signed soon, that the most awesome military revolt will break out here and we will be forced to make our way back to our homeland with weapons."[1]

When Germany declared what was to become World War I, its rulers promised that the war would last only a few months. Kaiser Wilhelm II and the German General Staff said that the army's rapid and glorious victory would allow Germany to annex parts of Belgium and France and increase its colonial rule in Africa and the Middle East. They told this to the ruling class — the industrialists, bankers and landowning nobility — and they told it to the masses of workers and farmers.

Germany lacked access to the resources that would allow it to maintain the living standards of its population and field a mass army during a long war of attrition. It needed a quick victory. The German rulers may even have believed that their promised rapid results would come true. This self-deceit left their politicians and generals unprepared for what became four years of grinding slaughter.

Without organized opposition to the war as in Russia (see Chapter 15) from Germany's powerful Social Democrats, the German workers offered little resistance to the ruling class's enthusiasm for conquest as the war began. Many Germans were caught up in a chauvinistic war fever in the summer of 1914 that was mirrored in France and Britain. Millions of young German men volunteered not only to join the military but to go to the front. They imagined war would be an ennobling opportunity to exhibit one's courage and skill in battle.

Ernst Toller, a socialist leader and writer, provided his personal experience to illustrate how the mood of large sections of the German population changed between 1914 and 1918 as the German war effort collapsed. Toller was a German Jew who grew up in East

Prussia in a town whose working class was mostly of Polish origin. Like nearly all his contemporaries, he volunteered for the army and for the front. He aimed to prove his heroism in battle. [2]

At the front, all it took was one morning spent in a ditch in a French town in the company of some uniformed German cadavers to erode Toller's patriotic fantasies. He was not the only German, French or British soldier to have his fairy tales laid to rest after a few weeks in the trenches on the Western Front.

Instead of glorious contests of skill and courage, what they experienced was the overbearing damp, cold, hunger and boredom of trench warfare, broken only by the occasional thud of artillery and the fear of a sudden or, worse, a lingering death. Any glory-seeking commander who ordered his troops forward out of the trenches saw them mowed down by withering gunfire or poison gas.

Meanwhile, life at home grew steadily more miserable for most Germans. The British fleet imposed a tight blockade, which cut the German population's access to food and warmth. According to German war propaganda, a glorious victory was near. Always. Each year it was harder for the German population to believe in victory, and this lie fell apart completely in the summer of 1918.

Ralph Haswell Lutz, a member of the American Military Commission in Berlin in 1919 and a historian, wrote about how the German Army attempted a last-ditch offensive on the Marne River in April 1918 that collapsed and then succumbed to a French counteroffensive in July: "The failure of the Germans in the second battle of the Marne is the first cause of the German revolution." [3]

Lutz described the organized political opposition to the war:

> More important than the enemy propaganda was the attempt of certain groups of Independent Socialists to undermine the fighting power of the army. Since the failure of the general strike in Germany in January 1918, these groups worked systematically for the overthrow of German militarism. Thousands of strikers who were sent to the fighting lines helped to spread this propaganda among the troops. [4]

The German state sent the unionized workers to the front to punish them, but the workers struck back by organizing inside the army.

Germany's allies began to desert and sign separate peace agreements; Bulgaria signed on September 30, 1918. By the first week of November, Germany's Austria-Hungarian ally had signed a peace treaty with Italy and Austria's Kaiser had abdicated.

By this time, according to Toller:

> Want in Germany is growing, the bread gets worse, the milk thinner, the farmers chase the city dwellers from the fields, the city food gatherers come home with their pockets empty, the soldiers at the front, bitter about the debauchery and indulgence of the officer staff, about the misery at home, are tired of the war. "With equal food and equal pay, the war'd not last another day," sing the soldiers.[5]

One might expect that the rebellion would hit first among the vast infantry forces that had suffered so much and with little recognition or glory. On the contrary, it was the cream of the Kaiser's forces, the sailors, who were to lead the way. They had first rebelled in 1917,[6] but the final revolution began at the end of October in 1918. Toller continues:

> The sailors of the fleet, the Kaiser's blue youths, are the first to rebel. The High Seas Fleet is set to sail on a suicidal mission; the officers would rather "die with honor than accept a shameful peace." The sailors, who were in 1917 already pioneers of the revolution, refuse; they put out the fires powering the ships. Six hundred men are arrested. The sailors leave the ships, storm the prisons, take over the city of Kiel, then the shipyard workers team up with them, and the German revolution has begun.[7]

Erich Kuttner, an anti-war Social Democratic Party member and organizer who had been wounded at the front and, like Toller, a writer, described the sailors' rebellion. By November 20, just three weeks after the rebellion had broken out, Kuttner, a sympathetic participant, had written a thirty-page pamphlet about the spread of the revolt and the heroism of the mutinous sailors. Kuttner's facts were verified in another pamphlet that described the same events, but one that was written by a naval officer. Lieutenant Commander

Baron Georg von Forstner was a submarine commander whose description was hostile to the rebellious sailors, excoriating them for "cowardice."[8] These two contrary evaluations of the Kiel sailors' rebellion nevertheless corroborate the external facts described here.

Unlike the infantry, which recruited heavily from among the millions of German farmers, the navy needed able sailors with experience using modern machinery. For this reason it recruited from the working class in the industrial cities. Because they had been workers who were often active trade union members, this meant they had the habits of unionists and often had contact with the Social Democratic Party. While this party's majority leadership was still cooperating with the war effort, many members had turned against the war.

Also, work on ships was difficult, exhausting and stressful. Combat was deadly. There were fourteen-hour shifts where a sailor's whole life was surrounded by steel floors and gates. As Kuttner describes it, the big warships were a cross between factories and prisons. There was little human contact between the overworked sailors and the privileged officers, who, like civilian bosses, ate separately with much better food. Officers' orders allowed no questioning; they only demanded obedience.

On October 28, the admiralty issued orders to Admiral von Hipper to proceed with the fleet to the Belgian coast. This move was allegedly an attempt to use the fleet to relieve German land troops in a battle in Flanders. But the sailors didn't trust the naval command. The admiralty was a hotbed of ultra-patriotic "Pan-German" officers. This group had always been the most aggressive, pushing for war. They also refused to admit Germany's defeat.

Whether these ultra-right officers really had ordered a suicide mission on October 28 was unclear. Von Forstner denied it. Kuttner wasn't sure. Whatever the reality, the sailors knew their super-patriotic officers were intransigent and believed them capable of sending the fleet on a suicide mission. And the sailors had no wish to commit suicide.

Kuttner printed the letter that sailor Otto had written to his father, an elected Social Democratic representative in the national parliament, cited at the beginning of this chapter. Otto also wrote that the sailors believed this was an order for a suicide mission. Rejecting suicide, the sailors refused to hoist the anchors on some ships. On others, the stokers put out the fires that created the steam that drove the ships.

When sailors on Otto's ship heard of these refusals, his crew decided to act in solidarity with their fellow sailors and join the movement. Faced with growing insubordination, the officers kept postponing the hour for the ships' sailing: first, from 3 a.m. to 7 a.m., then, to 8:15 a.m. In the end, no ships sailed toward Flanders.

When the ships all returned to German ports, some to Kiel on the Baltic Sea in Schleswig-Holstein, others to Wilhelmshaven on the North Sea in Lower Saxony, the naval authorities in Wilhelmshaven arrested 600 of the sailors who had taken part in the work stoppage, with focus on the leaders, calling the rebellion a mutiny. Von Forstner called all the rebellious sailors "cowards" whose fear of dying stopped the ships. More to the point than their physical courage, however, was their political consciousness. Kuttner wrote:

> But the first experience of struggling together successfully had made the sailors aware of their strength and their feeling of solidarity grew extraordinarily. The sailors of the Third Squadron in Kiel demanded the release of their imprisoned comrades, and, when this was refused, they called for a protest assembly on Saturday, November 2, at the union hall. By now this would not only make demands for a release of the comrades, but would protest the entire system of bad treatment on board the ships and the inadequate food and accommodation.[9]

The authorities ordered sailors taking part in the protest to go nowhere near the union hall. This order only got the sailors angrier. They called a mass demonstration that reached beyond the fleet to Kiel's working class. Each step the officers took to stop the protest — like ringing alarms — made more sailors aware of the revolt and forced them to choose sides. Some 3,000 began to march through the barracks, calling on more sailors to join them. Then they ran into a roadblock of naval officers — forty-eight mates and trainees — on the way to the military prison. The mates fired on the demonstrators, first a salvo of blanks and then lead. They killed eight demonstrators and wounded twenty-nine, including some from worker families.

Some sailors, too, were armed. They fired back, severely wounding the lieutenant commanding the mates. Kuttner:

> Taking their cue from the Russian Revolution, the troops elected a soldiers' council, which ordered and carried out the general arming on the morning of November 4, when 20,000 rifles with sixty cartridges each were distributed.[10]

That same morning, the ships of the fleet flew red flags, wrote Von Forstner, "their officers surprised and pushed overboard."[11]

∞

The military command then sent four infantry companies from the Kiel battalion against the sailors. Instead of shooting at the sailors, the infantry companies negotiated with their leaders. Three infantry companies joined the rebellion. The other allowed itself to be disarmed. Kiel's organized working class joined the general strike. Without another shot being fired, the city was in the hands of the workers' and soldiers' council, elected by the sailors, infantry and organized workers.

The workers and sailors grew confident; the top officers grew anxious. The *Schleswig-Holstein Folks' Newspaper* wrote:

> The cold sweat of fear glowed on the white foreheads of the admirals and captains as they negotiated with the fresh young sailors, whose eyes gleamed with the happiness of a better future.[12]

The sailors knew the only way they could escape severe punishment was to spread the rebellion far beyond Kiel. Commandeering the ships in the fleet, they moved the struggle along Germany's northern coast. Wherever the sailors landed, organized workers went on strike and joined them.

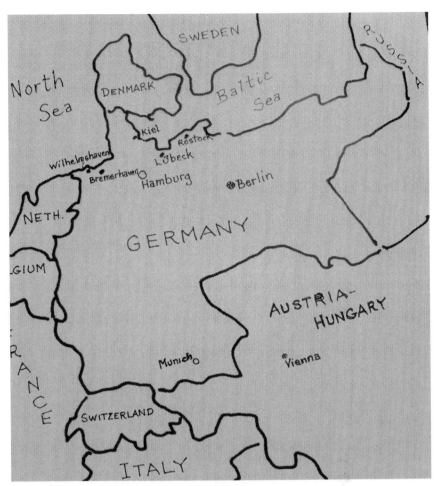

Central Europe, November 1918. It took only nine days for the North Sea Fleet sailors' revolt to reach Berlin and end Kaiser Wilhelm II's rule. Map: J. Catalinotto

The generals sent the army out to crush this movement of sailors and workers. Before shooting, however, the army troops held discussions with the sailors — and then joined the movement:

> It was revealed how rotten the old system had become. Often all it took was the landing of a small unit of armed sailors to bring large and important cities into the hands of the revolution within a few hours.[13]

By November 6, the harbor cities of Cuxhafen, Rendsburg, Brussbüttel and Warnemünde-Rostock, among others, were in the control of workers and soldiers' councils. On the same day, the movement won an outstanding victory. In Hamburg, the second-largest city of

KAISER'S BLUE YOUTHS

the German Empire, which happened to be near the coast, workers laid down their tools on the docks and in many factories. Ships in the harbor raised the red flag. On the streets patrols stopped the officers and disarmed them.

The rebellious sailors presented an ultimatum on November 6 to the military authorities with the following fourteen points:

1. The release of all those arrested and all political prisoners.
2. Complete freedom of speech and press.
3. Abolition of censorship of sailors' letters.
4. Appropriate treatment of the sailors by their officers.
5. Sailors return to ships and barracks without punishment.
6. Prohibition under all conditions that the fleet should set sail.
7. Take all preventive steps to avoid bloodletting.
8. Withdrawal from Kiel of all troops not in the Kiel garrison.
9. Sailors' Council has the authority to protect private (personal) property.
10. When off-duty there is no recognition of superior officers (no saluting, saying "sir").
11. Unlimited personal freedom for all enlisted men off duty.
12. Officers who accept the authority of the sailors' Council are welcomed; the others are dismissed without claim to compensation.
13. Members of the Council are exempt from any service.
14. All future orders must be countersigned by the Council.

All these demands must be recognized as general military orders.[14]

On the same day, Wilhelmshaven, where the rebellion began, joined the movement when more than 60,000 sailors and shipyard workers demonstrated. What was now called the Soldiers' Council negotiated the takeover of Wilhelmshaven with the station chief. The revolt spread to the smaller coastal towns and naval stations nearby. By that time the naval uprising to stop the fleet from sailing to war had turned against the Kaiser and any remnants of the German monarchy. What had begun as a sailors' revolt turned into a political revolution.

Military historian Lutz wrote:

> Although the Independent Socialists had in many instances planned uprisings for later dates, the sudden arrival of armed revolutionary soldiers and sailors furnished the leaders and the dramatic moment so essential to any revolt. It was the navy [to be precise, the rank-and-file sailors' revolt – JC], which destroyed the imperial rule in North Germany.[15]

∞

The revolt leaped over central Germany to Bavaria in Germany's South. Although it was part of the German Reich, Bavaria had the structure of a separate kingdom. There, as early as November 3, a mass demonstration in Munich, the capital, against continuing the war freed political prisoners from Stadelheim prison.

On November 5, at a mass anti-war demonstration in Munich, both the Social Democratic Party and the more leftist Independent Socialists called for a meeting of the entire population two days later, on November 7, the one-year anniversary of the Bolshevik Revolution in Russia. The meeting would be to demand an end to the Kaiser's rule. That November 7 afternoon, 100,000 people cheered the twelve speakers who demanded that the Kaiser abdicate.

The soldiers in Munich at the November 7 demonstration moved in military formation to release their comrades, who had been confined to quarters by their officers. Thus, the opening of the military revolt in Munich began with the freeing of 250 soldiers who had been confined in the military prison for their "revolutionary acts," as their officers judged them. Soldiers in trucks with red flags patrolled the streets, and Bavaria's capital was in the hands of the soldiers and workers.

By the morning of November 9, the southern region of Germany was controlled by the Councils of Workers, Soldiers and Peasants of the Free State of Bavaria.[16] Bavaria's King Louis III put up no resistance. On November 13 he abdicated and fled to his estate in Hungary.

The main target of the North Sea Fleet uprising was Berlin, the capital of the empire, which was the seat of power of the Hohenzollern family monarchy, of which Kaiser Wilhelm was the last ruling member. Germany's old noble ruling class was ready by this point to try to set up a constitutional monarchy led by Prince Max of Baden if, by pushing out Wilhelm, they could save some of the old ruling structure, along with their privileges. This old structure had prepared its defense. Since 1916 the German General Staff had made plans for an elaborate defense of Berlin and the Kaiser should the masses revolt, which they apparently expected was likely as war sacrifices continued.[17]

The General Staff prepared a chain of command and set out the key points of the city to be held, from the railroad station and post office to the Kaiser's palace. On paper, it was a perfect plan. It had only one problem: It needed obedient troops to carry it out. There were none to be found. Berlin's population did not need Facebook or even cell phones for word to travel that the troops would not shoot down the workers.

On November 6, Prussian General Alexander von Linsingen, who was in charge of this repressive machinery without gears, still had the arrogance to forbid a demonstration set for November 7. The workers wanted to celebrate the first anniversary of the Russian Revolution. And they did. As each hour passed, even Von Linsingen was beginning to get the message. His troops were in place at key points throughout the city, but he began to doubt they would fire on the workers.

Instead of waiting to find out, Von Linsingen said goodbye to Berlin on the evening of November 8 without ever giving an order to fight. The next morning, Saturday, November 9, 1918, workers spontaneously began a general strike, shutting every factory in Berlin. There was no resistance from the old government.[18]

With the empire vanished, two diverse political leaders each declared a republic — really two different kinds of republic. Karl Liebknecht, recently released from prison for his anti-war agitation and a co-leader, with the still imprisoned Rosa Luxemburg, of the Spartacist League, declared a socialist republic in the afternoon.

Friedrich Ebert, who had rushed to beat Liebknecht to the punch, had declared a democratic (capitalist) republic two hours earlier. The two declarations signaled the struggle that was to take place between these two political tendencies.

On one side, Ebert and the conservative Majority Social Democrats defended the rule of the capitalist ruling class of Germany, but without the Kaiser and eventually without any trace of the monarchy. On the other side was the Spartacist League, which was to develop into the Communist Party of Germany. The Independent Social Democrats, whom Lutz referred to as playing a role in the November revolution, held an intermediate position.

Over the next two months the Majority Social Democrats did all they could to restrain the revolutionary workers from taking over the government. In mid-January 1919, they made a desperate and brutal move. They collaborated with the military officers of the Freikorps – the officer-led organization of military reactionaries – to execute the leaders of the Spartacist League. The Spartacist group was too small and weak to seize power on its own, as the Bolsheviks had done in Russia. The Independent Socialists vacillated and refused to challenge the Majority Social Democrats. Consequently, the German working class was unable to take advantage of the revolt in the military, seize power in its own name and smash the old state.

∞

Lieutenant Commander Von Forstner made an important assertion in his pamphlet: that the rebellion came not from within the fleet but was brought in from the outside by social-democratic organizers. Von Forstner refused to believe the impulse came from the sailors themselves. Perhaps, since he was a submarine captain, he imagined the relations within the entire fleet mirrored those on his submarine, where a handful of officers, mates and ordinary sailors worked closely together, shared conditions and dangers, and depended on each other to survive in combat. Even then, Von Forstner might have overestimated the loyalty of the sailors on his vessel. Still, the hierarchical relationship on a big battleship, with much greater privilege and comfort for the officers, was more likely to accentuate class differences and antagonisms.

Kuttner argued, on the contrary, that the revolutionary impulse came more from the sailors than from the worker-organizers. This is believable. For the sailors, everything was an immediate question of life and death. Also, the sailors' living conditions on the fleet mirrored that of workers in factories, only under more repressive conditions.

Is it really possible, though, to separate the political changes taking place in the working class and the population as a whole from those within the fleet? The sailors were from the working class in the major cities and had family members who were Social Democrats. Some were themselves workers and union members as civilians. Could the officers possibly isolate the sailors from these political changes among the workers? Could they isolate the workers from the revolutionary sentiments of the fleet?

There is another important point: Once the sailors began to revolt, it was almost impossible for them to safely retreat without first upending the monarchy. Leaving the monarchy intact left all the sailors at risk. They had mutinied. At a minimum they faced long terms in military prisons, at a maximum, execution. From the sailors' point of view, the struggle had to be seen through to its conclusion: political revolution.

In addition — and this is essential — the sailors were armed. After the first repression in Kiel, they distributed tens of thousands of weapons and ammunition. This meant they could march into city after city, connect with striking workers and place a tacit ultimatum before the military authorities and, more importantly, before the rank-and-file soldiers: Either join us or we fight! Once discussions began, the troops on land could see that if they joined with the sailors and workers in solidarity, they would represent the new power in that city and could reach out city to city until they took Berlin.

Again in history, the collapse of the capitalist military forces — albeit a temporary collapse — opened the door to a successful political revolution by dissolving the prior-existing structure and opening the path to a possible social revolution. Unlike in Russia a year earlier, however, the German working class and its disparate parties were unprepared to seize this opportunity to take power and wield it in their own class interests. The class battle continued for fourteen more years of the Weimar Republic and ended in the defeat of the workers in 1933, when Adolph Hitler's Nazis took power. An analysis of that struggle is beyond the scope of this book.

This failure to seize power eventually had tragic results for humanity. But this does not negate the historic lessons of the heroic revolt of the sailors of Germany's North Sea Fleet.

TURN THE GUNS AROUND

Chapter 17 Dear Andy
Letters From Around the World

June 11, 1968 - BRASS & NON-COMS MAKE RULES BUT DON'T OBEY
THEM

Since I last wrote you there have been some changes made here (all bad!). We now have to report for work five minutes ahead of time and anyone who doesn't report is sent to the Squadron Commander. They have cut our lunch break from one hour to 45 minutes. We now work an extra half hour, six days a week.

And all of this was thought up by our Chief Master Sergeant who never comes to work on time and when he does he usually gets the day off to sleep his hangover off. Everyone including all our training NCOs hate the SOB but there's nothing we can do. I guess once you join the service you can kiss your freedom good-bye.

The thing that really pisses me off is that the Chief Master Sergeant makes the rules but he doesn't go by them. And our Captain is just as bad. He walks in the office anytime he feels like going to work.

Yours with a union,

A1C, Philippines

∞

July 16, 1968 - I AM A FREE MAN

I want to subscribe to the Bond. Officially I am still in the Army. To my way of thinking I'm not. But I have no income, no money at all. Could you consider me a serviceman stationed in Montreal, Quebec? I'm doing what I like best: Writing poetry. That and war resistance is all I want to do for a very long time. I am a free man. Canada is a great place. No extradition because of being a deserter. I will have landed immigrant status soon. Please write and let me know how you are and of anything I might be able to do here or there if necessary.

Jeffrey Arnold, PVT E-2,

Montreal, Quebec

August/September 15, 1968 - REPORT FROM HONOLULU

Just a few lines to let you know that the Honolulu arm is still alive and moving. The enclosed note was put into various areas where the guys at NCS Hono could read the Union's aims. The part above "Subj" was added by the Brass — "Mr." Rueb is the officer in charge of 31A, 31B, 31C.

My objective of saturating the base with Bonds is starting to pay off.

Yours for the ASU, Hawaii

∞

(Following is an excerpt from the bulletin put out by the Brass in Hawaii)

To: All Watch Chiefs/Crew Supervisors:

The below 'subj' info is to be published at qtrs, and at completion, the men are to be informed of the following:

1. It is not an 'accepted' organ., military-wise;

2. They are liable for 'action' if found to be 'involved.'

3. Any having any info, such as contact or pressure made by members, is to bring the info to Mr. Rueb's attn. V/R

Subj: AMERICAN SERVICEMEN'S UNION, Room 633, 156 Fifth Ave., New York, New York 10010

1. The AMERICAN SERVICEMEN'S UNION, organized during the early months of 1968, is a project of a group known as the COMMITTEE FOR GI RIGHTS. It has been publicized in THE BOND, and anti-Vietnam war, anti-military monthly publication sent gratis and unsolicited to enlisted personnel in the armed forces. The Editor in Chief of the BOND and Chairman of the Provision Organizing Committee of the AMERICAN SERVICEMEN'S UNION is Andrew STAPP, a former Army enlisted man, who was given an undesirable discharge for refusal to obey a direct order on 19 April 1968.

The union's membership fee is $1.00 and all who join receive copies of THE GI'S HANDBOOK ON MILITARY INJUSTICE, a 40-page pamphlet that attacks the Uniform Code of Military Justice and attempts to undermine discipline in the military service and to make a mockery of officer-enlisted relationship.

October 16, 1968 - AUSTRALIANS TO PASS OUT BONDS

Thanks for the sample copy of your magnificent newspaper.

We shall be very interested in distributing the BOND among GIs on R & R here.

We have a big demo here on September 20 which will end at the CHEVRON HILTON here where many R & R people stay. We shall be handing out a statement which shall include material from this sample issue of the BOND and also some RITA material from France.

The BOND sets an example of what should be done in our own Army — I hope some will take up the example.

Fraternal greetings, and the best for your vital work,

Denis Freney,

Harbord, Australia

∞

January 21, 1969 - THE THAI PEOPLE ARE VICTIMS LIKE YOU AND I

I'm in Thailand now and really feel cut off from the movement. I will truly welcome receiving the BOND again because, as you know, the truth never reaches a GI — only propaganda.

The Thai people are victims like you and I, the Afro-Americans and the poor. Americans are degrading the Thai people, making the women prostitutes and in general showing little respect for the Thai culture and customs. Korat AFB is continguous with Camp Friendship (Army) and is used for bombing raids on the Democratic People's Republic of North Vietnam. Even the money the U.S. pumps into the Thai economy merely increases their dependence upon and subordination to the U.S. government. "We" have three major Army only bases here, nine minor and possibly more, plus of course several AFBs. From the structures at Camp Friendship it's obvious "we" are here to stay.

Yours in the struggle, Thailand

June 17, 1969 - REPORT FROM FASCIST SPAIN

I was very glad to hear from you, and those orange ASU stickers — what a
gas they were! The lifers and Brass really got uptight! They ran around
like ants ripping them off. Even though they did this they (stickers) were
noticed by many of the EM.
Not too much is interesting about Moron AB. It just sits here. It's about 40
miles from Sevilla. Half of the base is occupied by Spanish and the other
half by the U.S. Hardly any planes or anything. Like I said it just sits there.
And rots. Northern Spain looks like an occupied country because of this
group of people called Basques. The students here are also raising hell
against Franco's fascist oppression.
If you've never seen a Spanish soldier, let me fill you in. You won't believe
it but they wear WW II Nazi helmets! Very suitable. Didn't believe my eyes
when I first saw it. There is definitely a revolutionary environment being
created here and I'd say before a few years have gone by Spain will have a
revolution. As will the U.S. People can only be put down for so long.

Chuck Thompson, Spain

∞

August 25, 1969 - HEADS WILL ROLL IN MISAWA, JAPAN

Our chapter has vowed to develop our previously independent sorties
against the Brass into a cohesive unit of action, united under one cause —
the downfall of Big Brotherism. So far we have forced our commanders
over here into obviously illegal actions designed to punish us for having
the audacity to challenge their redoubtable perches. However, instead of
punishing us, this illegal harassment has filled our ranks with dedicated
men burning for revenge.

Although our chapter is still in the embryo stage (around 50 members), we
plan to create such an uproar that the Brass pigs will take even more dras-
tic steps against us until we can finally "hand their asses" for some illegal
usurpation of military rights (what few we now have). We in Misawa plan
to have an additional 20 to 40 names to add each month until every enlisted man here is united in our cause. Some heads are going to roll when we
finally succeed! Support the Fort Dix 38 and keep the faith, baby.

Founder, ASU of Misawa, Japan

August 25, 1969 - OUR ICELAND RADIO STATION STILL BROADCASTING

Things are really happening here. Peace signs and ASU initials are appearing all over the base — on barracks walls and mess hall doors. Two weeks ago some lifer in my department turned in 26 ASU stickers he had taken down from our barracks. It never ceases to maze me how far the movement is spreading.

Every day a collection is taken to help spread the word. We are planning to have a newspaper and a radio. The radio has operated in the past.

I see in the BOND that you have already heard of our problem concerning organizing. I have talked to many members about this. We have decided the best way is just to talk among ourselves a lot and to pass out info.

The Brass here on base are getting pretty scared with all these things going on. They already know about the radio but can't find our source (since we move it all the time) and all the ASU stickers, etc. They're looking to hang somebody's ass for it too. But so far they haven't caught anyone.

The Brass fascists may destroy our group, our newspaper or radio, or even me, physically — but they can never destroy the truth. The truth will destroy them and their ugly wars and racism.

U.S. Navy, Keflavik, Iceland

∞

August 25, 1969 - SOUTHERN WHITE FOR BLACK JUSTICE - KOREA

I am a "cracker" GI (drafted) who has, since my early teenage years, supported the struggle Black people are going through to receive all this freedom our government professes they have been given.

Recently a group of us were playing cards in the barracks. There were four whites, including myself, and a mutual friend of all of us who happened to be a soul brother. We played five or six hours that night, and our Black friend never left the barracks. But around midnight the MP(ig)s showed up with a lieutenant who swore that our Black friend had been involved in an attempted theft in the mess hall.

Having seen the MP truck drive up, I was curious to see what was going on. I walked over and was told that this Black friend of ours was suspected of being in the mess hall — during the time he was right there with us. I said to the Louie: "There will be four witnesses who will make statements that he was with them all night and during that period."

The Louie replied: "And they're all soul brothers, aren't they?" I answered: "No sir, they're all white."

Ex-PFC, S. Korea

October 20, 1969 - AIRMAN SPREADS THE TRUTH AT GUANTANAMO

It's hard to explain, but I have become the center of a lot of information about our government, world problems and our People's Revolution. I feel that with your material I can finally tell the true information.

I found your address in the Washington Free Press and through a friend in the U.S.S. Forrestal. He inquired recently and now has most of his people forming into a non-violent group who only ask for their rights from the Brass on the ship. At least they are recognizing themselves. I shall do the same here at Guantanamo Bay, Cuba.

AMN, USNAS, FPO, N.Y.

∞

December 16, 1969 - IT'S DIFFERENT IF THE BRASS DO IT

I am at the Arctic Test Center in Alaska. A few weeks ago a friend of mine was taken to the stockade near Fairbanks. It hurts me to tell you why. On the second National Moratorium Day he donned a black armband to silently show his opinion of the blood-soaked fields of Vietnam. Here in a place so very far away, and a place where the Brass make up their own rules, to even wear a peace medal is putting yourself into the "commie" category. (We were told at one time that to wear a peace medal is carrying a concealed weapon.)

My friend is off crushing rocks now. I will never see or hear from him again, because he is a "criminal," a "revolting instigator." And all because he wore his feelings of the war to work one day. Our company commander has his feelings pasted to the back bumper of his car: "WIN IN VIETNAM." That's his prerogative, to win that next higher rank off GI sweat and blood. Sure, he was in Vietnam, and made a small fortune too, just like the steak-eaters in Washington are.

SP5, Alaska

Chapter 18 Stockades: Prisoners Rebel

"The month of August 1968 witnessed two of the largest prison rebellions of the Vietnam War period, both led by Black GIs," wrote GI historian Dave Cortright.[1] These rebellions took place among troops in Vietnam at the Da Nang Marine brig and in the military prison known as Long Binh Jail. The GIs called the latter prison LBJ, after then U.S. President Lyndon Baines Johnson. GIs in these prisons who were members of the American Servicemen's Union wrote letters to *The Bond* and other GI publications about the rebellions, providing eyewitness accounts. Here are excerpts from an article in *The Bond* dated September 18, 1968, based on some of those letters and from other articles on the prison revolts:

Jailed Men in Nam Rebel Against Brass

The anger of EMs imprisoned in Vietnam by the Brass has exploded. Men fed up with military oppression have rebelled at both the Marine brig at Danang and at the Army stockade at Long Binh, twelve miles north of Saigon.

On the night of August 16, [1968,] Marine prisoners at the Danang brig tore the place apart and burned a cellblock. Angry at the humiliating requirement that they call the guards "sir" and at the poor food, the overcrowding and the long delay before trials, they decided to stand up and fight back. It took a force of MPs firing shotguns to crush the rebellion among the 228 unarmed men. Seven prisoners and an MP were reported wounded. And it still wasn't over.

Two days later a second rebellion broke out when the officer in charge of the brig, Lieutenant Colonel Joseph Gambardella, ordered some of the prisoners moved out. This time MPs had to use tear gas to stop the uprising.

Chairman of the American Servicemen's Union Andy Stapp immediately called the Pentagon and demanded names of the men involved. Speaking to ASU Chairman Stapp, Lt. Col. Ludvig, director of Marine Public Relations, refused to release any information to the ASU or to the American people.

Stapp said in a press release, "The Brass does not want brought to light the rotten and abusive conditions that they have foisted upon the enlisted personnel in the Armed Forces."

In a statement to the New York Post of August 20, Stapp said, "We have nineteen union members in Danang and we suspect that at least some of them are involved in the uprising."

Less than two weeks later, GI prisoners in Long Binh, the Army's biggest stockade in Vietnam, broke out in rebellion. Long Binh Jail (known to GIs as the "LBJ") was also overcrowded — there were 719 men where there were supposed to be only 550 — with angry GIs whose grievances were probably much like those of their brothers at Danang.

Shortly before midnight on August 20, an apparent fight among the prisoners in a barbed-wire enclosed medium security section brought three guards running inside to quell it. They didn't come out. The GIs inside had grabbed them and their keys. When the three guards didn't come out, an outside guard blew his whistle. At the same time, a band of prisoners rushed the gate between the medium security section and the recreation and administration area in the main part of the compound. They broke through. They then proceeded to burn down the building, which contained all their records, and nine other large buildings.

When the Brass, commanded by Colonel William Brandenburg of Elloree, S.C., sent in MPs armed with M-16 assault rifles, bayonets and tear gas grenades, the unarmed GIs inside fought back. They wounded five MPs and put the acting warden of the jail in the hospital. One GI prisoner gave his life in the brief but bitter struggle and fifty-nine were listed as wounded.[2]

A group of prisoners at LBJ sent a collective letter to *The Bond* after reading the above article. Publication and dissemination inside the prison of both articles spread solidarity and strengthened those rebelling.

Report from Long Binh Jail

Today my man from New York managed to smuggle into the compound your September 18 issue of your dynamite thing, *The Bond*. Your paper was thoroughly ready by most of my fellow prisoners; speaking for those who read it, including myself, we would all like to say thanks for everything you are doing to further the ASU and bring to the attention of GIs all over the world the many injustices, inhumanities perpetrated on servicemen by the U.S. Government Armed Forces judicial system — particularly the Army.

TURN THE GUNS AROUND

Cited here are a few case histories of prisoners that I think would be of interest to men in the Armed Forces everywhere.

Case 1 — An infantryman just out of the field was caught stealing a peanut butter and jelly sandwich from his base-camp mess hall. First offense — sentenced to six months hard labor in LBJ.

Case 2 — An infantryman after serving ten months of his twelve-month tour was given an order by a second lieutenant for him and the 17 other men in his element to assault a 250-man fortified North Vietnamese Army force, and was severely wounded in his right leg, right arm and kidney while the rest of his element was completely eliminated. After recuperation in Japan his medical record was lost by the U.S. Army and he was refused further medical therapy and was returned to the Republic of Vietnam without a profile for further combat duty.

Upon reassignment this man was charged with missing three formations and the misuse of a government vehicle (a 15-minute trip to the PX). This was a first offense. He is now on a pre-trial confinement in LBJ awaiting a special court-martial.

Case 3 — (my own case) — I am an infantryman, not by choice but by force of the U.S. Army. My own political and personal beliefs will not allow me to carry a weapon in the field. My company was going to a heavily VC-infested area on a three-day operation. Being that I don't carry a weapon I refused to go.

My company commander ordered two fellow GIs to hold me while he tried to bind my legs and arms with ropes and to forcefully take me on the operation. Not being a fool and with no other course to take, I went AWOL. After being apprehended I was threatened by the Brass in my unit that I would be killed. I am now in LBJ on pre-trial confinement awaiting a general court-martial for this act, which I know was right.

We could go on forever with many similar cases but the Brass here at LBJ will not afford us with ample stationery. We feel a great need and desire for this to be published in your next issue of *The Bond*. If this is possible it would be deeply appreciated by everyone in the Long Binh Stockade both Black and white.

We would like to do more to further the cause of the ASU but at this time our hands are tied by the Brass in LBJ.

[Signed] The inmates, Mike Rouch, Tommy McDonnel, R.C. Brown, Brien M. Schulik, Marcy Schuman, Dave Landry, J.A. Epriam.

News reports as late as September 24, a month after the big Long Binh Stockade rebellion, tell of a group of a dozen Black GIs still bravely holding out against the Brass in part of the prison.[3]

'Mutiny' in the Presidio in San Francisco

One of the most dramatic and publicized actions in a stockade took place in the Presidio in San Francisco in the fall of 1968. The Presidio case became a central event for the anti-war movement nationally and especially in the Bay Area, where the anti-war movement was strong. A similar mobilization of the movement on the East Coast took place supporting the rebellion in the Fort Dix Stockade of June 1969, where the ASU played a central role.

The Presidio case highlighted how many anti-war GIs were concentrated in military prisons and jails. It also stood out because the Army handed out especially onerous sentences in the first courts-martial of GI prisoners — fourteen years and more for a non-violent, symbolic action. The sentences the Presidio defendants received shocked the anti-war movement. Remember, this is long before changes in civilian sentencing, such as mandatory long sentences for possession and selling of illegal substances, put so many people behind bars for long periods of time.[4]

Civilians protested in the streets against the long sentences for the Presidio GIs until, a few months later, the Army was forced to greatly reduce them to less than two years. The following, from an article in *Workers World*, describes the Presidio case:

The Story of the Presidio 'Mutiny'

On October 11, 1968, a guard in the stockade killed PVT Richard Bunch. The private was known to be emotionally unstable and suicidal, and had practically begged the guard to kill him. Three days later, 27 GIs sat down in the Presidio, chanting and singing in protest. Walter Pawlowski read their demands that guards be changed every 30 days, prospective guards be given psychiatric examinations, shotgun work details be ended and racist treatment of Black prisoners be stopped.

During the preliminary hearings into the case, attorney Terrence Hallinan, who was representing 14 of the GIs, was able to expose some of the atrocious conditions prevailing in the stockade. Up to 146 men were jammed into the stockade built to hold only 76 prisoners; armed guards were often drunk or high on drugs while on duty; two prisoners in addition to Bunch have been shot on work details; 30 attempted suicides by 21 prisoners had been reported recently; "segregation cells" for so-called troublemakers consisted of black iron cages, 4.5 by 5.5 by 8 feet, where men were fed lettuce, celery and water; Afro-American GIs are held in isolation cells without beds, tables or toilets; rats, mice and roaches abound in the cells and mess hall.

For protesting these conditions, the first three defendants got fourteen, fifteen and sixteen years in prison. ... The harsh sentences handed down began a wave of protests across the country. In San Francisco about 6,000 civilians staged a demonstration in March 1969 outside of the Presidio walls demanding freedom for the heroic Presidio 27. And on Feb. 16, some 3,000 marchers in Seattle, including 275 GIs, listened to speeches condemning the vicious prosecution of the men.

Meanwhile, three of the defendants escaped from the stockade to Canada. Among them was Walter Pawlowski, who had read the demands of the 27 aloud to the Brass.[5]

Andy Stapp was able to meet in Vancouver, British Columbia, with two of the escaped Presidio prisoners. Stapp wrote then:

Escaped Presidio 'Mutineers' Tell Their Story

Two of the 27 GIs charged with "mutiny" at the Presidio in California escaped shortly after their action. Recently I met with the two, Keith Mather and Walter Pawlowski.

Walter and Keith were among the Presidio GI prisoners.

On Xmas Eve, Keith Mather and Walter Pawlowski escaped. Both, working as carpenters, were escorted to a tool house outside the stockade and then to work. As their hammers continued to pound in work-like rhythm, they pried open an unguarded window and disappeared. Because of typical Army bumbling and a change of guards their absence was not discovered until later, and the two made good their escape to freedom.

The heavy sentences given out by the 6th Army Brass in these Presidio "mutiny" show trials so far brutally testifies to the Pentagon's fear of rank-and-file GIs fighting for rights. ...

I spoke at an anti-war rally in Seattle just two days after the first three of the Presidio "mutineers" had been sentenced to fourteen [to] sixteen years in Leavenworth. Among the 3,000 antiwar activists who roared their anger as I described the hideous mistreatment [at] the Presidio by General Collins and his flunkies stood 275 servicemen from Ft. Lewis and Fairchild Air Force Base. These are 275 defiant GIs and airmen, who by this demonstration of solidarity with the 27 blasted the Brass' dream of an army of obedient slaves.[6]

The Pentagon officers were discovering that the usual punishments aroused more anger and resistance. Inside the stockades and brigs was fertile soil for growing revolutionaries.

Chapter 19 Special Processing

Fort Dix, New Jersey, was the major military base used for basic training closest to New York City — and closest to the national office of the American Servicemen's Union. GIs on passes or AWOL would often come to New York and stop by the union office; some would stay overnight at union organizers' apartments.

Nearly all GIs returning to base from New York would be at the Port Authority Bus Terminal on Sunday nights, where we handed them a copy of *The Bond*.

The Fort Dix stockade was also home, starting in early 1969, to ASU key organizers, Terry Klug and John Lewis, and to Henry Mills and others. The stockade and the related Special Processing Detachment, which was sort of a halfway house between the stockade and regular army duty, concentrated dissident GIs in an ever-narrower space. The Brass's rotten treatment, the concentration of rebellious and angry GIs, and the presence of a kernel of resolute organizers made resistance inevitable.

Soviet filmmaker Sergei Eisenstein first used the innovative techniques that made him famous[1] in his 1925 film, *Battleship Potemkin,* about the role of sailors on this ship in the 1905 Revolution, which was the first serious attempt to overthrow the Russian czar.[2] Driving the sailors' mutiny was the overall political situation and the czar's oppression of the peasants and workers. But the final slap in the face that set off the revolt was the sailors' revulsion over being served rancid, wormy meat at mess.

Compare with the first-hand accounts from *The Bond of January 21, 1969* of how the pressure built up at the Fort Dix Stockade:

Dix Prisoners Rebel Over Lousy Food

By Eugene A. Sylvester (prisoner of the state — time of confinement: Sept. 4, 1968 to Oct. 23, 1968)

I had been in the Fort Dix Stockade about a month when a food riot broke out in the mess hall. It seemed like there was never enough; and if you were the last compound to eat you waited on line for what seemed like hours. On this particular day, supper consisted of cold, dehydrated potatoes covered with something closely resembling gravy but tasting like stale water. As one cell block came to eat, one prisoner blew up. Having had all he could take, he let his tray fall to the floor, exclaiming, "I won't eat this shit!" That was all that was needed.

All the other prisoners began dropping their trays, some even throwing them, they were so disgusted. Panic-stricken, the guards cleared the mess hall. From then on the cellblocks that had yet to eat refused to even enter the mess hall. The word out: hunger strike until something is done to improve the food.

Just because we were prisoners didn't mean that we should be treated like animals. We were human beings and deserved to be treated as such. After all, going AWOL because the military machine was too much to endure any longer (which was why most of the men were there) did not make you a hardened criminal.

In order to strike fear into the men and make them willing slaves once more, one of the MP officers, a man who prided himself on being able to scare prisoners, entered the hall block and began screaming that he wasn't going to "put up with this type of nonsense." Then he made his all-time threat. He said that all those prisoners who didn't want to be charged with mutiny should step outside.

NO ONE MOVED!

The big, bad officer suddenly realized that the men facing him were just that — MEN — and that they were no longer afraid and that they were going to stand up to someone they considered no better than a petty tyrant. His power gone, he had no other choice but to back down. You can't threaten men who refuse to be threatened and who aren't afraid to stand up for their rights. There was no charge of mutiny against anyone and the food began to improve — for the time being at least.[3]

Vietnam editor Bill Smith wrote this in *The Bond* for the March 17, 1969 issue:

The Fort Dix Stockade

I walked under the sign and into the Fort Dix stockade on Sunday, Feb. 2, [1969,] with approximately 200 friends and relatives of the GI prisoners who were being victimized by Pentagon laws within the stockade. I was there to visit and extend Union support and solidarity to SP4 John Lewis, a brave Union member who was stopped on the Jersey Turnpike by State pigs while he was on his way to Fort Polk, Louisiana, where he was to refuse orders for Vietnam. He was brought to Dix and charged under article 86 (AWOL).

Once inside the stockade reception building we visitors were told by the NCO in charge that nothing was to be given to or accepted from the prisoners. ...

When I met John Lewis he told me that he and the men in his cellblock (C-B 83) had successfully staged a strike only two weeks before. Thirty-two of the men were told on Jan. 18 that they would have to pull eighteen hours of KP the following day from 5 a.m. to 11 p.m. All of the men reported to work but by 7:15 in the evening, 27 of them had gotten together and refused to work any longer. The mess sergeant ran over to them and screamed, "What is this? Get back to work; this is mutiny!"

Five minutes later, ten MPs came rushing in and the men were told by an officer that if they didn't go back to work in three seconds they would all be charged with mutiny. Nobody budged. The men were then brought back to their barracks — but one of them (a quiet Puerto Rican) was taken by the MPs and accused on the scene as being a leader and an instigator. John said, "He was just one of the guys. They were looking for somebody to crucify." ...

Lectures on "military justice" have become a joke. Fifteen to twenty men are court-martialed a day and at the end of the week at least sixty-five percent have been given the maximum.

A conversation began among the Union GIs. One man asked: "What's the union local number outside the stockade?"

"We could have a meeting right now in the yard," another man proposed.

Another commented, "I don't think we'd have much success right now. I think we should talk privately with each other and try to come closer to the Black and Puerto Rican guys."

At the moment it didn't seem to matter which one was right — a discussion of tactics had started.[4]

The next excerpts are from different reports in *The Bond* on the developing struggle the following month inside the Dix Stockade and on the GIs involved.

On 3 February in a training class on the Code of Conduct in the Fort Dix Stockade two men were put in maximum security because they believed what the history books told them: that America was a freedom-loving country and that they had the right to openly discuss points brought up in the Training Class. They were mistaken, of course. The two men were Bob North and John Lewis.

The class instructor told us how bad Communism was. How if we weren't watchful it would "get" us. How the communists were trying to take our freedom away — we had to laugh at that one. How if we were captured by the "enemy" we would be brainwashed and beaten and degraded.

At this point John Lewis stood up and asked the instructor what he was trying to do to us except brainwash us into believing the lies he was telling us?

Lewis asked him and the other prisoners who had captured them and put them behind the wire? The communists? Who had sent them to the jungles of Vietnam? The communists? Who was trying to brainwash them right now? The communists? Who spent hours harassing and degrading them? The communists? No, to all those questions. The enemy of the prisoners in the Fort Dix Stockade is the Army and the Government of the United States. ...

To the instructor Lewis said, "You are my enemy. You talk about how free this country was after the Revolution in 1776. You tell this to the 50 or 75 black men in this room and knowing that their forefathers and mothers were slaves in 1776.

"You talk to us of freedom. We are not free. We are prisoners of war. We are in a concentration camp. We are deprived of our human rights and our civil rights."

Lewis pointed his finger at the instructor and said, "You're a liar! Everything you have said today is a lie!"

John Lewis was ordered to leave the training room. All during his rap the guys in the room applauded and yelled their approval. Now they yelled their demand he be allowed to remain in the training room.

John Lewis was held in a cage called a bullpen for twelve hours before he was finally sent to maximum security. His friend and supporter Bob North was asleep when guards came for him in the night.

On February 5 John Lewis and North were put on bread and water simply because Lewis exercised his right of free speech.[5]

PFC Terry Klug, whose story is described in Chapter 9, wrote the following while he was held in the Fort Dix Stockade awaiting trial on desertion charges.

On the 1st of March 1969 at approximately 1:00 pm in segregation cell block 71, Sgt. Wicklow, then on duty as segregation shift leader, conveyed to me the reason that I was placed behind bars in maximum security and not committed to the Pound along with the majority of the prisoners. The reason is, as he put it, because I am a "trouble-maker and instigator." He went on to explain that Maj. Cashman could not possibly afford to release me into the Pound because I would undoubtedly speak to the other men of my political ideas and convictions and that the majority of them would probably listen to me and adhere to my ideas, not because what I have to say to those men would be the truth, but "because most of them are stupid!" ...

Witness to what Sgt. Wicklow said to me is prisoner John Lewis who at this time is in the cell immediately next to mine.

— Terry Klug, ASU member and organizer[6]

∞

Through much of 1969, PVT Henry Mills was a key organizer in the Fort Dix Stockade, working together with John Lewis to win unity in struggle in the Special Processing Detachment/Battalion. The following excerpts are from an interview with Mills by *Muhammad Speaks* New York editor Joe Walker. The article ran Feb, 21, 1969.

'The Black Liberation Army Is the Only Army I'm Interested in'

NEW YORK — "Hell no, I won't go" is becoming a more frequent response from Black youth facing the draft and an increasing number of Afro-American GIs who get orders for Vietnam. One such man in the latter category is 20-year-old PVT Henry Mills of New York City.

"I don't see no sense in my doing to the Vietnamese people what the United States has done to us and still continues to do," declared Mills to this MS reporter before he surrendered to Army authorities earlier this month after being AWOL (absent without leave) since last November. He was due to report to Oakland, California, and embark for Vietnam.

After receiving 16 weeks of intensive infantry training, Mills' whole company received orders for Vietnam duty. Almost to a man, his unit, which was about half Black and Puerto Rican, opposed the Vietnam War and their involvement in it. So when they got leave before their shipment date, a couple headed for Sweden, a few braced themselves to face courts-martial and confinements and others prepared to stick it out and hope for the best.

Mills went AWOL and has returned to face the music. He doesn't consider his act brave but a necessary one. He believes it will take revolution to resolve the Black man's predicament in the United States and "the Black Liberation army is the only army I'm interested in," he said.

He speaks deliberately and chooses his words carefully. "Before I was drafted I had made up my mind that I wouldn't go to Vietnam," he said. ...

At an anti-war coffee house outside the Fort Jackson, South Carolina post, he read copies of The Bond, organ of the American Servicemen's Union. He has subsequently joined the ASU and the union has arranged for legal counsel to defend him in his inevitable court-martial for refusing to go to Vietnam.[7]

∞

Lewis wrote the following article in *The Bond* of October 20, 1969, which describes the nuts and bolts of the work he, Mills and other ASU members did at Fort Dix through much of that year in the Special Processing Detachment/Battalion.

TURN THE GUNS AROUND

Rebellion In SPB at Fort Dix

A sister organization of the stockade is the Special Processing Battalion. The men here are also some of the militant and active GIs. All the guys here also have voiced their stand against the fascist U.S. Army by going AWOL. At this time there are about 700 men in the Dix stockade and about 400 men in SPB — altogether about one thousand militants at Fort Dix alone — there are about 32,000 troops at Dix.

Back in April of this year [1969], Henry Mills and I and some more union brothers in SPD — it was called the Special Processing Detachment before it expanded to a battalion — (all just having been released from the pound) began to put out a newspaper called *SPD NEWS*. This paper was the newspaper of the ASU chapter in SPD.

When we arrived in SPD, we saw that it was just about like the stockade except there was no fence around it. The harassment and other bullshit were just like the pound. There was a guard platoon in SPD to control us and put down rebellions. There were very few passes. No one got paid. And there wasn't enough food in the mess hall. The mess hall draws rations for 150 men and over 400 are there. The permanent party are fed first and SPDers got what was left.

For our own survival and human dignity we had to get ourselves together. The union organizers began at once to organize. We passed out *Bonds* and other union literature. We got a number of other SPDers to join the ASU. Then as we began to be suppressed by the Brass, we had to go underground. Sort of. We began to publish our own unit paper — *SPD NEWS*. ...

Things went very well for about six weeks. The cadre of union guys organizing for the ASU grew and strengthened itself. The organization grew and we saw some changes come about in SPD. We began to get passes. We began to be paid. And harassment began to slacken off. But the pigs that ran SPD were furious; and a mad pig is a very dangerous animal. Many of the union guys got hit with trumped up charges — of AWOL (when they weren't), disrespect to NCOs and the Brass, etc. Some were shipped to other units. Some got orders for Vietnam and went AWOL again. And then some of us got thrown into the stockade again. Our organization was temporarily busted up.

But one note of the strength that ASU organizers had built in SPD was that while Henry and I were back in the Pound, issues six and seven of the SPD news came out.

SPECIAL PROCESSING

And, now today in SPB? Henry was sent to Fort Riley, but the ASU Organization at Dix SPD is as strong as ever, maybe stronger. *SPD News* is coming out again. And while the pigs are back trying to do their job of union-busting, the struggle goes on.[8]

PVT Henry Mills (left) and PVT John Lewis organized in the Fort Dix Special Processing Battalion in 1969.
Photos: ASU collection

Henry Mills received an Undesirable Discharge at Fort Riley a year before his scheduled time to leave the military; for Mills this was a victory. Lewis got out in 1970 and began working at the national ASU office as a field organizer. But before all that happened, the Fort Dix Stockade erupted.

Chapter 20 Fort Dix Burns

Like the Presidio "mutiny" in San Francisco, the Fort Dix Stockade rebellion grabbed the attention of the anti-war movement. It was a rebellion with leadership from the American Servicemen's Union. The movement's response was a demonstration of thousands of people, led by women, which invaded Fort Dix, New Jersey.

To add to the stockade's infamy, the military Brass put up a sign hanging over the entrance to the Fort Dix Stockade that reminded some people of the slogans Nazis posted over concentration camps: "Obedience to the law is freedom."

Some of the most effective anti-war soldier organizers were being held in the Fort Dix Stockade during the first half of 1969: Henry Mills, Terry Klug, John Lewis, Bill Brakefield, Tom Tuck, Tom Catlow, Jeffrey Russell and Robert North. Lewis, Mills and North had organized meal strikes and other mass actions in the stockade in early 1969.

The stockade commanders considered the whole prisoner body to be a pack of trouble, and accordingly, they inflicted whole groups with collective punishment. For weeks building up to June 5, the anger of the GIs had been growing. Their issues: inadequate food, long confinements without trial, racism in the stockade system against Black and Puerto Rican GIs, and interference with their mail.[1] On that day, with temperatures in the sun over 90°F, the guards ordered the GIs housed in prison blocks 66 and 67 to stand in formation for hours that afternoon.

To this kind of provocation, the men's reaction was destined to go beyond refusing to eat a meal. That evening, hundreds of prisoners smashed windows, threw beds and footlockers out of the barracks, and some set buildings afire. The stockade authorities sent in 250 troops armed with riot guns and tear gas. They beat ASU member Bill Brakefield until he was unconscious.

As soon as the union learned of the rebellion and of the brutal repression of our members and other GIs, Andy Stapp got to work building support for the prisoners and for any of the GIs facing new charges. The first step was to put the Army on the defensive for systematic, brutal treatment of the prisoners, most of whom were facing charges for the very low-level offence of AWOL. The next step was to demand the right to investigate conditions in the stockade. This article appeared in *The Bond* that July:

On June 20, the Army answered the ASU. In a letter written for the Secretary of the Army by Col. James C. Shoultz, Jr. ("Acting the Provost Marshal General"), the Brass denied that GIs in the Dix stockade had been abused, denied overcrowding, denied that MPs used "physical contact" with the prisoners (but admitted that nine prisoners had been hurt), denied that tear gas was used, and refused to allow the ASU to investigate the stockade or see medical records.

In addition to imprisoning and then further mistreating these citizen soldiers, the Army now proposes to try them for their resistance. Of the 150 involved in the rebellion, 38 have now been charged as a result of this resistance. Ten have been singled out for special charges of riot, inciting to riot, conspiracy to riot, arson, etc. Four of these are ASU organizers. One is Terry Klug who returned from Europe several months ago, where he worked with RITA — GI resisters.

Another is Tom Tuck, a Black GI who earlier led the "Dirty Dozen" at Fort Knox, Ky. Bill Brakefield received sanctuary at City College in New York last fall when he refused orders for Vietnam. Jeff Russell joined the Union while confined in the stockade.

It should be made perfectly clear that the Army has no right to try them. It has no more right to try them than General Motors has a right to try workers who go on strike against them.

The ASU is not only busy publicizing the vicious injustice of this Brass attack, it is rallying support among civilians as well as GIs to fight back.[2]

If Mills and Lewis escaped being arrested and charged, it was only because they weren't housed in Cell Blocks 66 and 67. The two had been organizing effective mass actions against the stockade authorities, but none had turned into a spontaneous general rebellion.

The charges against the thirty-eight, and especially against the five GIs singled out for general courts-martial and possible heavy sentences — including the ASU organizers and their closest allies — were extremely serious. Klug faced more than 56 years in prison. And long sentences had recently been handed out to GIs for their symbolic "mutiny" in the Presidio stockade in San Francisco, which was really a sit-down demonstration to protest the murder of a fellow prisoner by the guards.

The first three Presidio GIs to be tried received sentences of 14 to 18 years, which were later reversed. But even so, the Presidio GIs, most of whom had served in Vietnam for a year, were imprisoned for six to fifteen months. For the 21-year-olds at Fort Dix, it was mind-boggling to think they were facing decades in prison merely for rebelling against injustice.

For us in the ASU office, there was only one guilty party: the U.S. Army. Sure, someone set the stockade on fire, but it was a building that shouldn't have been there in the first place. And it was holding the wrong prisoners. The Pentagon officers were dropping napalm bombs on villages all over Vietnam and setting people on fire every day. The GIs knew that, and you could tell from their letters that many of them hated it. The ASU members especially hated it, and some took direct action to express their feelings.

We started to organize defense for the Fort Dix 38 just as we had for the Fort Hood GIs the prior summer. We decided to first build solidarity among other GIs and with the civilian anti-war movement. Then get publicity out to all the anti-war media to build support and break the story into the corporate media.

We had an advantage now: By 1969 a majority of the population had turned against the war, with an even larger majority in the Northeast. Also, Fort Dix was only thirty-six miles from Philadelphia and seventy-two miles from New York City. Unlike Fort Hood, Fort Dix was not in rural Texas where the anti-war and anti-racist GIs could be isolated from their supporters.

The government still had its repressive state power right there at Fort Dix, but there were thousands of young revolutionaries and hundreds of thousands of sympathizers who would, when they heard the truth about the stockade, support the Fort Dix 38.

FORT DIX BURNS

During that summer of 1969, when the Richard Nixon admin- istration was making the first tentative moves to pull U.S. troops out of Vietnam, the ASU published a special message from the GIs among the Fort Dix 38 who were closest to the union and faced general courts-martial and the most consequential charges. Here are excerpts from some of their statements published in a special flyer by the ASU:

Jeffrey Russell: "On June 5, the prisoners were made to stand at at- tention for four hours in the boiling sun. The same day two prisoners were beaten by guards. Twice that day the people's personal items had been torn through and scattered. After lunch cellblocks 66 and 67 were uprooted and the people were forced to change cellblocks. The people stood in the sun for three hours before they were moved. ... Other guards said that this was part of a plan to force the people to riot. ... The riot that came on June 5 was a glorious retaliation, by the people, against the Nazi repression and the mercenary Army... . The people chanted, 'Vietnam, we won't go.'"

Carlos Rodriguez Torres "The next thing I tell you is absolutely true and I can use the person's name because it was me. ... Sgt. Himan put his hands on me and I tried to protect myself. SP4 Miller started punching. Next thing I know all six are trying to put me down and tie my hands behind my back and begin to put on pressure. More punches on my back, sides, head and, next thing I know, SGT Himan, to prove he is the man he isn't, puts my head on the floor, left side up, and leaves an imprint of his boot and bump on the other side. They kicked me in the back of my head and put a foot on the back of my neck and applied pressure."

William Brakefield: "What we want as a union has been said before. We want the rights afforded human beings, and not what being slaves of capitalist exploiters forces us to accept; we don't want 'yes-sir-ing' or any more 'sir-ing' of officers, which is equal to 'yes mista bossman' and 'nosa mista charlie'... . We want freedom for those of us who wish not to serve the nation in times of unjust wars or in any war the United States wages if we choose not to serve. ... We want the plague against the Black man removed from the army forever, especially against the Black Panthers and the Black Muslims."

Terry Klug: "We as 38 GIs who have already served much time in Pig concentration camps for crimes against nature and mankind — such as going home to be with our wives, girlfriends and families, for refusing to go to Vietnam and participating as human beings in an imperialistic and inhuman war against brave men and women fighting for their own freedom, for speaking out against the fascism that presides in our military and, indeed, throughout our entire governmental system, and for the crime of being Black or Puerto Rican. ... May our many comrades who are presently and fortunately on the outside take up the fight with us so that we together, as one strength, as one righteous force, may bring an end to the evil that is warping our country and bringing destruction and suffering on our brothers of the world."

Klug's supporters outside got his message. The ASU, the Fort Dix anti-war coffeehouse, Students for a Democratic Society, YAWF and the Rainbow Coalition — which included the Black Panther Party, the Young Lords Organization, the Young Patriots, the Resistance and the Committee to Free the Ft. Dix 38 — all began to start organizing for a mass demonstration on October 12.

As the popular mood was turning decisively against the war, organizing the Fort Dix demonstration proceeded during the summer of 1969. Then something happened that gave it a special direction. The movement for women's liberation had been developing in the population as a whole, along with the overall rebellious sentiments of 1968 and 1969, led by the Black Liberation Movement. The drive for women's liberation was even more intense among women in the anti-war and other movements, women who considered themselves revolutionaries, than it was in the general population.

In an organization like the American Servicemen's Union, where 98 percent of its members were men, it was difficult for a woman, let alone a civilian woman, to play a leading role. Most of the women who worked with the ASU helped with the technical work of producing *The Bond*.

On the other hand, there was nothing stopping the women from leading the demonstration of civilians at Fort Dix except tradition. The women working with the ASU, especially if they were in Workers World Party — who at that time included Susan Davis, Laurie Fierstein and Maryann Weissman — were quite ready to break tradition's chains. Naomi Goldstein wrote this account in *Workers World*:

FORT DIX BURNS

Three hundred determined women showed that they could give both tactical and political leadership to a mass march. We broke out of our prescribed roles as passive supporters on demonstrations and took the lead, while the men marched behind us, some accepting our leadership reluctantly.

The idea for a women's brigade had been brought up at a planning meeting for the demonstration by Maryann Weissman, National Coordinator of Youth Against War & Fascism, who pointed out that in Vietnam, NLF [National Liberation Front] women are leaders in the struggle for liberation.

The idea was enthusiastically supported by women from SDS, MDS and various women's liberation groups. What began as a tactical move, to confront the GIs with their own male chauvinism, developed into a well-organized effort by a women's caucus to give the most militant and effective leadership possible to the Fort Dix demonstration.[3]

Just as on the first day of the Paris Commune and the first day of the February Revolution in 1917 Russia, women led the invasion of Fort Dix. According to *The Bond*:

People's Army Invades Dix, Demands Freedom for GIs

The marchers moved forward eight abreast and the line stretched back as far as you could see. It was October 12, 70 miles south of New York City at Fort Dix, NJ. There were maybe 10,000 people, men and women.

They marched past the gas stations, houses and hamburger stands of Wrightstown toward Fort Dix, chanting in an angry roar their demands for freeing jailed GIs and ending the war.

It was a people's army — as yet unarmed. Banners carried by the American Servicemen's Union stood out in a forward section. Marching with the ASU contingent were ASU leaders, ex-GIs and active duty GIs on leave or AWOL.

But leading the huge march were young women. Women determined to show the world that they were in the front of the battle to free their brothers from the military dictatorship.

October 12, 1969. Women lead march backing Fort Dix 38. Photo: David Felton

The column marched past abandoned barracks and signs barring demonstrations, as MPs scurried to eject stray photographers who ran onto the base from the road. Then suddenly the front of the column swerved left, off the road and entered the base in a mass. The thousands of marchers followed, stirring dust from the grassy field.

Then the Brass sent hundreds of MPs running across the field with clubs, bayonets and gas masks to intercept the marchers.

But the marchers continued to advance defiantly until they were face to face with the lines of MPs. Then the two forces stood still, holding their ground as the young men and women appealed to the MPs to act as GI brothers and not as cops. But these were for the most part special MP pigs flown in from Fort Meade, Maryland.

The Brass had feared to use Dix GIs as MPs because of their great sympathy with the marchers. The Brass also had shown their fear of this unity of feeling between the thousands of young people and the GIs by sending some 375 stockade prisoners to other base stockades just before the march and also granting passes to nearly all SPD [Special Processing Detachment] inmates to get these militant guys out of the area.

FORT DIX BURNS

As the marchers faced the MPs, a plump colonel alighted from his car behind the MPs and hurriedly consulted with another well-fed officer.

An order was given.

MPs carrying special gassing guns opened up and a cloud of tear gas enveloped a large section of the demonstrators.†

The marchers put on plastic gas masks and retreated slowly, prodded by the now advancing MPs, to the roadway. At first there was confusion; then the march reassembled and continued with the Brass sending MPs to stand in a solid line along the road which forms the perimeter of the base, barring any further entry by the marchers.

But the marchers continued to express their demands and continued to appeal to these MPs to act as GI brothers, not as pigs for the Brass.

And throughout the base the 32,000 GIs heard the story of the march. In particular the point came in loud and clear to those courageous men imprisoned in the Dix pound and facing trial for the rebellion of June 5th.[4]

Judging by how they treated most of the Fort Dix 38, the Army knew it was facing trouble if it came down too hard on the soldiers. But they still could single out those they suspected of being leaders. The struggle to free the GIs had to continue both by organizing their legal defense and with actions supporting the guys. The Workers Defense League and the National Emergency Civil Liberties Committee handled most of the cases. Even before the demonstration, twenty-six of the defendants had received special courts-martial. Twenty-two were acquitted. The other four received sentences between four and six months. Three of the men somehow escaped and disappeared.

Five of the soldiers most closely associated with the ASU faced general courts-martial with potentially much heavier charges. Their sentences had little to do with actual proof of guilt. Jeff Russell was found guilty of rioting and received a sentence of three years in prison. Tom Catlow was found guilty, but was sentenced only to an undesirable discharge. William Brakefield got three years at hard labor and Carlos Rodriguez Torres two years.

In Klug's case, the prosecution strategy depended on frightening the defendants with very heavy charges and getting them to give testimony against each other as the way to reduce the charges. The prosecution would lie, saying, "So and so ratted you out already. Why should you take the whole rap? Give evidence against him." Klug once told me he had to spend an afternoon convincing one of the defendants that he hadn't given testimony against him, that the pigs had lied once again. He succeeded.

As one witness testified, the prosecutors kept hounding him to give evidence against Klug. They targeted Klug because of his history as a political organizer, his conviction for desertion and his role in the ASU. Sometimes these prosecution tricks work. In this case, however, the solidarity of the GIs remained strong. Besides, no one in the stockade wanted to be known as a rat.

On December 8, 1969, five of the GIs who had given depositions against Klug under pressure from the guards and officers testified. Under oath they all repudiated their earlier statements.

The court-martial board acquitted Klug on all charges. His statement called attention to the recent exposure of massacres of villages in Vietnam and condemned the murder four days earlier of Black Panther Party leader Fred Hampton in Chicago.

Klug added, "My acquittal was due to the solidarity of the men, the offensive legal defense put up by my counsel, Henry di Suvero, and the political struggle waged by the anti-war movement."[5]

This struggle had its casualties, but the anti-war movement and the ASU came out stronger than before the Fort Dix stockade rebellion. Klug was transferred to the federal prison at Leavenworth, Kansas, to serve his conviction for desertion. But in September 1970 he won an appeal. After twenty months behind bars and barbed wire, he was out of prison and out of the Army without having to go to Vietnam. He went to New York and immediately started working with the ASU national office, organizing GIs and veterans.

Chapter Notes

* The protest at Fort Dix was part of a wave of anti-war demonstrations in the fall of 1969. On October 15, an action called The Moratorium was held in cities all over the country. No longer isolated in New York, Washington and San Francisco, the movement was reaching the interior. More than a million people around the country walked away from their workplaces, mostly during lunch hour or before closing time, wearing black armbands to show their opposition to the war in Vietnam. The action gave people who had been fighting against the war for years an opportunity to "come out" on the job and talk to all their co-workers and neighbors. This happened despite the heavy burden of Cold War anti-communism that the media, schools and universities had imposed on the population for decades.

A month later, on November 15, in Washington, D.C., between a quarter million and a half million people gathered for what was the largest single action against the war up to that time. Within that massive crowd, there was a more revolutionary contingent of maybe 10,000 mainly young people, who left the main group to surround the Justice Department, where, according to later reports, they terrified Attorney General John Mitchell.

The night was filled with hundreds of tear-gas cannisters that police lobbed like mortar shells into the crowd. They exploded, covering all of downtown Washington with noxious fumes. In the outside air, we in the Youth Against War & Fascism contingent failed to notice how much tear gas had remained on our coats. Back together in a hotel room for a meeting, we found we couldn't breathe once we took off our coats and lay them on the bed — we had brought the tear gas inside.

† Andy Stapp's spouse, Deirdre Griswold, who had given birth to their daughter just seven weeks earlier, was among those tear-gassed as the women faced the line of MPs at Fort Dix. She had absorbed enough tear gas into her system that her daughter refused to be nursed later that night.

Chapter 21 The Sum of Its Parts

In mathematics, the whole is equal to the sum of its parts. In organizations, it depends. With mutual trust and shared goals, with free and sensitive discussion while combating all privilege, the whole can be much greater. Even without reaching this ideal, people working together can go further than individuals, no matter how talented and hard working, can on their own.

An organizer welds the group together, averts unnecessary conflict and keeps the group functioning so it never falls into bickering and becomes less than the sum of its parts — or even falls apart.

From 1967 to 1970, I was the most experienced party organizer working day-to-day with the GIs in the American Servicemen's Union. My strength was administration. Andy Stapp was no administrator, but he provided the personal glue, camaraderie and political education to hold the ASU staff together.

Stapp might reach the office any time from noon to three, but just as when he was in the barracks, his political discussions both fascinated and educated the rest of the staff. He helped make the ASU office a place in which people wanted to work.

Richard Wheaton added grease to the organization's gears. He was everyone's boy next door, whose army experience, transformed by the war, had turned him into a committed revolutionary. He knew how to put the needs of the group high on his list of priorities.

Bob Lemay's steady work discipline and even temperament kept the office functional. Bill Smith had his ups and downs, but he was a creative writer whose work spiced up *The Bond*. Richie Richardson, the old man in this young group, kept *The Bond* on time and under budget for its first three years with the ASU.

180

My strengths complemented Stapp's. Typing, work discipline, planning routines, making a division of labor and then doing whatever was left over — not leaving until everything was done was my forte. Public speaking made me nervous, and it was better anyway for the "retired" GIs to do the speaking and reaching out on campuses, at anti-war demonstrations and to the media. There was plenty else to do answering correspondence or mailing *The Bond*.

One veteran ASU organizer, Greg Laxer, sent me an email in 2016 calling me "Herr Kommissar." This referred to the political organizer the Soviet party sent into a military unit to make sure the soldiers knew their politics and pointed their guns at the class enemy. Terry Klug once said on video camera, "Damn, Cat, you were straight. Revolutionary, but very straight." I considered both statements compliments.

By the summer of 1970, I was spending about sixty hours a week doing volunteer work at the ASU, and that conflicted with the thirty-seven hours at the insurance company. Finally, my supervisors had enough and told me — in those days they had to warn you — "Catalinotto, either shape up or you'll be fired."

I could live with being fired. But the Workers World Party leadership recommended I try to keep the job, so I began to work rather than just show up. It surprised my bosses that I could turn out well-written, intelligent reports, since they had seen nothing like that from me for two years. All my energy and thought had been going into the ASU.

The harder part was to transition off the ASU to other political work. I was addicted to the idea that we might collapse the Army. The party was growing fast, so I shifted my ASU experience to help coordinate the party's national organization — using snail mail.

Few organizers are indispensable. The ASU continued to thrive without me and the staff grew. By the fall of 1970, PVT John Lewis was out and Leavenworth had released PVT Terry Klug. Greg Laxer joined them in 1971. We called them "retired."

Other GIs and ex-GIs became available to work at the union center as they either finished their stint in the Army or received an early discharge. Gene Weixel, who was stationed at a small military base right in the city, Fort Hamilton in Brooklyn, started helping to edit *The Bond*. So did Laxer. Wheaton eventually took over as managing editor when Richardson stopped. Mitch Smith was discharged for punching his superior officer and started doing ASU radio broadcasts to U.S. troops in South Korea.

I still saw the GI organizers regularly. We would often be at the same political meetings. Many of us lived near the Brooklyn Museum and Prospect Park in its pre-gentrified days, when most apartments were rent-controlled and, by present standards, dirt cheap.

Throughout 1970 the ASU was expanding its work beyond Vietnam and anti-racism. When the Richard Nixon administration called out the military to do the work of the striking postal workers,[1] the ASU agitated against soldiers being used as strikebreakers.[2] Of course this was the Army, and the soldiers were likely misplacing more letters than they sorted correctly.

Without giving up plans to control south Vietnam, the U.S. had nevertheless slowly begun withdrawing troops. The Nixon administration relied on building up the puppet army in the southern part of the country. Even with 150,000 fewer U.S. troops in Vietnam in 1970 from the high point of March 1969, GI revolts continued and spread. Meanwhile huge anti-war demonstrations erupted coast-to-coast in the spring of 1970 when Nixon ordered new military invasions into Cambodia.

Troops rotated home after their year "in country" were often given an early out. Otherwise they would be waiting impatiently for the end of their service and spreading their anger against the war to the troops just finishing basic training.

Dave Cortright, in *Soldiers in Revolt*, summarized the problems the military had with desertions:

> During the five peak years of Vietnam involvement, the Army desertion rate increased from ... 14.9 incidents per thousand in 1966 to

73.5 in 1971. Army desertion and AWOL rates in 1971 were the highest in modern history.[3]

Not all deserters made it to Canada or Sweden, and only a few actually fought for the other side. Many were just AWOL for more than thirty days, but even that created big problems for the Brass.

Cortright discussed the troops' use of illegal drugs, such as marijuana — which young civilians were also using at that time — and heroin, which was easier and cheaper to obtain in Vietnam than in the United States. According to letters to *The Bond*, lifer sergeants from an older generation did their own self-medication with alcohol, a legal but equally debilitating and addictive drug. The soldiers said booze made the sergeants even nastier.

Cortright also wrote that troops were not reenlisting:

> First-term reenlistment rates declined steadily during the Vietnam War, plunging in 1970 to 12 percent–the lowest year figure on record.[4]

The total of those in the U.S. Armed Forces, including the Navy and the Air Force, reached a peak of about 3.5 million members in 1968-69.[5] While armed with much more destructive weapons than their "enemy," the U.S. Armed Forces showed signs of falling apart.

Though the ASU staff had to find day jobs to sustain themselves while volunteering twenty to forty hours a week for the union, they were more of a unit than the troops inside the Army. The masthead of *The Bond* from 1970 to 1972 shows that most of the original core of GIs from 1968 stayed active. The list grew from six to fifteen people. My name was off by the end of 1970, but nearly all the others stayed on the masthead through that period. They were the whole that was much greater than the sum of its parts.

Chapter 22 The Camp McCoy 3

From left, Dannie Kreps, Steve Geden and Tom Chase. Photo: ASU

We are charged with "bombing." We do not believe that a government which has dropped over a billion tons of bombs and poisonous chemicals on the people of Indochina has the right to charge anyone with "bombing."[1]   ~ SP4 Tom Chase (ret.)

*This chapter was contributed by Joyce Chediac.**

In the wee hours of July 26, 1970, three bombs went off at Camp McCoy, Wisconsin. Rank-and-file Army soldiers had been sent there for the summer and ordered to train members of the National Guard. Many of the trainees were angry Vietnam returnees, some now strongly opposed to the war. For many this training mission was especially infuriating as the assignment came just two months after the Guard in Ohio had killed four anti-war protesters at Kent State University.

Three ASU organizers — Tom Chase from Glen Rock, New Jersey; Steve Geden from Milton, Massachusetts; and Dannie Kreps from Torrence, California — were arrested and charged with the bombing. They became known as the Camp McCoy 3.

My Lai, Cambodia Bombing; Kent, Jackson State Murders

To understand the militancy of the soldiers' statement and the urgency felt in 1970 by many anti-war activists, soldiers and civilians alike, it is important to see how the war was unfolding. The My Lai massacre of March 16, 1968, had been reported for the first time in November 1969 in the *St. Louis Post-Dispatch* by journalist Seymour Hersh, pictures included. Here, under direct orders, U.S. troops had systematically murdered hundreds of Vietnamese villagers, mostly women, old people and children.

Also revealed to the public by 1970 was President Richard Nixon's "secret" carpet bombing of Cambodia, which began on March 18, 1969, in Washington's unsuccessful attempt to cut the supply lines of Vietnamese liberation fighters, which extended into Cambodia. This indiscriminate bombing of villages, crops, animals and the environment as a whole was begun without congressional approval or public knowledge, and lasted four years. Then, on April 30, 1970, shortly after air-war revelations hit the press, President Richard Nixon announced the beginning of a U.S. ground invasion of Cambodia.

The war brought casualties at home, too. The mostly U.S.-based state National Guard units had been used throughout the 1960s to put down justified rebellions in African-American communities against racism, police repression and economic inequalities. However, 1970 saw Guard guns aimed at the anti-war movement, too. On May 4, 1970, Ohio National Guard shot into a crowd of mostly white, unarmed students protesting the invasion of Cambodia at Kent State, killing four and wounding nine.

Days after Kent State, on the night of May 14-15, Mississippi state and city police shot into unarmed students protesting the invasion at Jackson State, a traditionally Black university. Two were killed and twelve injured.

The response was increased mass outrage, more anti-war protests and a deepening of anti-war sentiment in the population as a whole.

Nearly 2.7 million U.S. troops did tours in Vietnam during the period of the U.S. occupation. Most were from the working class, either drafted or pushed to enlist in the military by the threat of conscription.[2] From 1969 to 1972, there were some nine hundred[3] documented or suspected incidents of low-ranking U.S. troops in Vietnam killing or "fragging" their officers or sergeants.

By 1970, more than half those who had been stationed in Vietnam had returned to the U.S., already discharged from the military or about to be discharged. Hundreds of thousands of troops returned home disgusted and disillusioned, having seen for themselves what the war was really about. Many joined the anti-war movement, where they were welcomed with open arms, often marching in their own contingents. By April 19-23, 1971, in a giant week-long national anti-war protest in Washington, D.C., soldiers who had been to Vietnam threw away 700 medals they had received in the service.

By 1970 U.S. bases were already filled with tens of thousands of "short-timers," U.S. soldiers who had served most of their time and were waiting for their discharge. Fort Carson, an Army base located in Colorado Springs, had 26,000 service personnel at that time, more than 80 percent of them short-timers, many of them angry and disgusted with the military.

I was an anti-war activist at the time. I had come from New York City to volunteer at Home Front, a GI coffeehouse in Colorado Springs, close to the Ft. Carson Army base. The coffeehouse was a place where GIs could come after work, hang out, discuss with us and with each other timely issues, especially those concerning the war, and hear occasional speakers.

Together with the most active servicemen, Home Front staff organized and provided the backup for anti-war demonstrations in which GIs participated. These demonstrations often targeted escalations in the war. They usually took place on the side of the road near the entrance to Ft. Carson at those heavy traffic times when soldier were entering or leaving the base and the cars were backed up for ID check.

Civilian support always meant being ready with legal representation. Soldiers in the U.S. Army were subject to the Uniform Code of Military Justice. They knew that participation in an anti-war protest meant they were risking arrest when they got back to base.

It was at Home Front that I met a tall, handsome and soft-spoken Vietnam returnee named Tom Chase, an anti-war soldier who told me he was a member of the American Servicemen's Union. We soon were a couple.

Chase, Dannie Kreps and Steve Geden were all Vietnam returnees and short-timers, that is, they only had months remaining in the Army and were waiting to be released. Strongly against the war and fed up with the mindless rules and contradictions of military life, they organized for the ASU. All three were sent from Fort Carson to Camp McCoy, in Monroe County, Wisconsin, in the summer of 1970 and ordered to train National Guard and Army Reserve troops. The response of the three men was to organize for the union, oppose the illegal war in Vietnam and fight for the rights of rank-and-file GIs, especially those of color.

ASU Organizers Ordered to Train National Guard

Tom Chase wrote about the situation at Camp McCoy:

At that time, the Guard and Reserves were composed almost entirely of whites. These units were being trained in all the skills necessary to crush just rebellions everywhere; occupying Black, Latin and other Third World communities, setting up concentration camps, etc. In fact, only a month before, National Guard troops had fired into unarmed students at Kent State University in Ohio, murdering four.

At Camp McCoy, there was widespread discontent among the lower-ranking enlisted men. The problem that faced the three of us was that of changing low-level grumbling into strong resistance to the dictatorship of the Brass.

As soon as we arrived, we started distributing copies of *The Bond* and rapping to the guys. We found that racism was rampant on and off the post. The barracks were in a state of disrepair — drafty and leaky.

Many of the men had jumped at the chance for this shit duty in order to avoid — they hoped — levies for Vietnam from Forts Carson, Riley and Leonard Wood. As we talked to the guys we were asked many questions about our union, the ASU."[4]

SP4 Steve Geden (ret.) wrote:

One of the strongest Union members at Camp McCoy was PFC George Doakes, a Black GI who didn't take any shit from the Brass. He was especially angry because he knew that, of all the menial jobs at Camp McCoy, he had been given the most degrading for a Black man — that of personal chauffeur for the racist Headquarters Brass.

I met George in a GI bar in La Crosse, and it wasn't long before he was telling me about his job and his firsthand knowledge of the racist policies and harassment the Brass would dream up. These pigs would openly discuss and laugh about their latest acts of racist oppression as he drove them to their air-conditioned officers' club!

George made his feelings very clear. "Someday soon we'll have a trial. We'll try these pigs and sentence them to death!" When I told him about our union and what we stand for, he joined immediately, to make that day come sooner.[5]

188

Anti-War Explosions Rock Camp McCoy

Then on July 26, the anniversary of the Cuban Revolution, explosions rocked Camp McCoy's electrical station, telephone exchange and waterworks. No person was hurt or injured. The only injury was the war effort. While many soldiers at Camp McCoy had the skills and were angry enough at the military to have set the explosions, the Brass responded by coming down hard on the budding ASU chapter.

Chase wrote:

> The explosion of July 26 saw the beginning of a frantic attempt by the Brass to smash the union at Camp McCoy. Steve, Dannie and myself were immediately placed on restriction to our barracks. After many illegal searches and much questioning and harassment, the Brass were forced through legal pressure to release us and sent us all back to Fort Carson.[6]

Geden added:

> The resulting fascist terror unleashed by the Brass against every EM, especially ASU members, effectively broke up our chapter, and most of us were sent back to our permanent bases. George [Doakes]† went back to Ft. Leonard Wood, not far from his home in Trenton, Tennessee.[7]

On February 21, 1971, Chase, Geden and Kreps were charged by a federal grand jury in Madison, Wisconsin, with destruction of government property, conspiracy and two other counts of bombing at Camp McCoy. They faced thirty-five years each in prison if convicted and fines of $30,000 each. The FBI moved the three from Colorado to Madison, Wisconsin, where the trial would take place.

With hundreds of instances of fragging underway in Vietnam, and with the anti-war movement going into fever pitch, the U.S. government sought to make an example of the Camp McCoy 3. The indictments themselves were announced by the highest government source, U.S Attorney General John Mitchell. The government threw the book at the GIs, whose litany of charges could have put them away for the rest of their lives. In addition, they were to be tried in civilian court, a first for active-duty ASU organizers.

This writer moved from Colorado Springs to Madison in order to work on the case of the three men. Peggy Geden, Sandi Kreps and their two toddlers accompanied me. Together we formed the core of the Camp McCoy Defense Committee.

The military may have thought that by trying the men in civilian court they were removing them from their base of support in the military. At this time, the ASU was at its height, with *The Bond* being read by 10,000 active-duty soldiers. The ASU was not intimidated.

Madison had a significant anti-war movement. This became our first base of support. With help from the ASU office in New York City, we formed strong and lasting ties with this movement. Right from the beginning, we made clear to the three men that they had support and were never alone. Chase described their first court appearance before they were released on bond:

> The courtroom was packed with people who were on our side. They gave us a standing ovation when the pig brought us in from our cells... . People demonstrated outside the courthouse, carrying signs that said, "Whose law?" "Free the Camp McCoy 3!" "ASU Power" "Stop union busting in the military![8]

The Defense Committee vowed to make the case of the Camp McCoy 3 a household word. For the many months between the indictment and the trial date, every time there was a scheduled court appearance for these anti-war GIs, we would plaster the town with posters and do mass leaflet distributions explaining the issues of the case and calling for freedom for the men.

Assisted by Youth Against War & Fascism, the ASU organized nationally to expose this indictment as an attack on the soldiers' union. The case was brought up and explained at anti-war activities around the country.

The defendants and their closest supporters decided to use their case as an opportunity to put the Army on trial. As Chase explained:

> We charge the military and the federal government with conspiring to murder over a million people in Indochina and over 55,000 GIs, with conspiracy to take all rights away from GIs so that they are forced to do

the killing and be killed for something they don't believe, and with conspiracy to destroy the ASU and all attempts of GIs to organize.

Chase continued:

> We are charged with "bombing." We do not believe that a government which has dropped over a billion tons of bombs and poisonous chemicals on the people of Indochina has the right to charge anyone with 'bombing.'[9]

Chase, Geden and Kreps were also able to reach rank-and-file GIs with the details of their case. They and other ASU organizers gave updates on the case on Radio ASU, a weekly program recorded in New York City and broadcast to GIs in Korea, Japan and Southeast Asia with the cooperation of the Democratic People's Republic of Korea. The U.S. government saw that for close to two years the vigorous defense of the Camp McCoy 3 did not waver. Additionally, the men remained determined to use a trial to indict and try the Pentagon for war crimes.

At the same time, greater numbers in the U.S. ruling class sought to end the Vietnam War, which they had lost, and keep it off the front pages. The U.S. government no longer saw it in its interest to bring Chase, Geden and Kreps to trial. Originally facing thirty-five years, the three men were offered a plea bargain. If they pled "guilty" to lesser charges, they would end up serving a year in jail. After discussing this with the ASU leadership, Chase, Geden and Kreps accepted the deal.

The ASU attitude in cases when its members were charged with, for example, fragging or destruction of property as an expression against the Vietnam War or against racism, was to defend its members and consider them not guilty of any crime. The ASU considered the Pentagon, the U.S. government leaders and their agents to be war criminals and mass murderers. Pleading "guilty" in this case was tactical recognition that the Army had a high probability of proving "guilt" in a stacked court-martial, and it was a decision the union was forced to take.

Chapter Notes

* Joyce Chediac was a volunteer at Home Front, a GI coffee house located in Colorado Springs, Colorado. She became a leader in the Camp McCoy 3 Defense Committee and later, as a civilian organizer for the American Servicemen's Union, expanded union demands to speak to the needs of the wives and families of rank-and-file soldiers and to oppose the sexual exploitation of Vietnamese women by the U.S. military (discussed in Chapter 24 on Women's Liberation).

† In an example of the racism the three men and their union fought, Doakes was shot and killed a few months later. While on leave, Doakes, having taken a wrong turn, drove his car into a driveway in a wealthy, all-white area of Humboldt, Tennessee, in order to turn around. Jesse Hill Ford, who had written books defending racism, considered this appearance of a Black man on his block to be a crime, ran out of his home with a gun and shot Doakes in the head.

Chapter 23 **Dear Andy**

Bond Letters from WACs, WAVEs, Spouses and Dependents

June 16, 1968 — WIFE OF DRAFTEE WOULD AID IN OPPOSING ARMY

I recently read an article about your organization in Kaleidoscope-Milwaukee. I am firmly anti-draft and am becoming more anti-Army all the time.

My husband was drafted five weeks ago. I will be joining him at the end of July. If there is anything I can possibly do, I'm willing to help. Please send me any information you can.

Wife of draftee,

Milwaukee, Wisconsin

∞

June 16, 1968 — POVERTY AT HOME

I got a letter from my wife stating that she'll have to find another place to stay after our baby is born or the welfare will cut my mother-in-law's check. My father-in-law is in the penitentiary two ten-year turns and my mother-in-law only gets $99.00 for herself and her two daughters ages 12 and 14 to live on (each month). She's got to pay $40.00 rent with this and $44 a month for $66 worth of food stamps. My wife cannot help her mother because we already have to pay our bill exceeding her monthly allotment. There's nowhere else for her to go.

I'd like to know if there's any act I could take if they would deny my hardship discharge. I'd also like to know what they will do to me when I refuse to go to Vietnam because I don't believe in the war.

Any help would be greatly appreciated, not only by me but by my wife also.

Thank you,

PVT John Seaux

February 17, 1969 — SO ARE THE WIVES

My husband is serving in Vietnam now, but since he's only been there a few days I have no permanent address for him as yet. However, I'll be sending him his issue of the BOND every month. I myself am happy to receive the BOND, as I can read it and let the others read it before sending it to him.

In your recent letter, you asked what military experience pissed him off the most at the armed forces. My husband could tell you of many, but I myself have one story. There have been many, but I remember this one especially well.

While attending school at Fort Lee, Va., the men in his class received orders to report to Atlanta Army Depot on a certain date. All was fine until they were informed that they were all traveling on a bus together and that the wives had to find their own way down!

All protested, naturally, because many of the wives were between three and seven months pregnant and could not drive from Virginia to Georgia. The answer to their protests was, and I quote: "If the Army wanted you to have a wife, the Army would have issued you a wife!"

As it worked out, everyone made it safely, no thanks to the Army.

If I had my way, the Army would go straight to... .

Mrs. F., Pt. Orchard, Washington

∞

February 17, 1969 — BLISS GI MAKES BOND AND NLF BENEFICIARIES

I'm fed up with the way the Brass and lifers are screwing over us. So I've decided to make out my insurance policy to the ASU, which would receive one half, or $5,000, and to the National Liberation Front, because it can be put to good use if I should die or be sent to fight an illegal war and get killed. I encourage more of you who feel as I do to do this also. You can get the addresses of these groups by writing to the BOND.

Ft. Bliss, Texas

May 20, 1969 — PIG LIFER HARASSES EM'S WIFE

I am an enlisted man's wife at Fort Knox, Kentucky. The EMs are not the only ones to receive harassment at the hands of the Brass, lifers and MPs (Military Pigs) here at Knox. We have been here since the middle of December and I'd like to turn you on to what happens to wives of EMs (excluding lifers' wives).

The first week we were here I had just received a shot against bubonic plague (there are a good many rats in Kentucky). Since we had just come from Los Angeles, I had no winter coat, so I wore a field jacket with no tags on it. I was making a phone call and an E-7 sergeant walked up and told me that I looked disgraceful and elaborated for about five minutes.

I thanked him and the ten or so people around were rather shocked at his piglike manners. That wasn't enough for him, though. He called the MPs, who were on the scene in about 30 seconds. They harassed me and told me it was illegal for me to wear the jacket (many civilian employees here wear them) but since it was raining and the jacket had no tags they were going to allow me to go (how generous of them).

On a serviceman's pay it is all a family can do to pay rent and eat, much less dress in 1940 styles to go with the 1940 "Action Army" which persists today. I could write a book, and we've only been here three and a half months.

Your future, your decision, choose Sweden; Peace.

Fort Knox, Kentucky

May 20, 1969 — ARMY WIFE IS ON OUR SIDE

I hope an Army wife has a right to say a few words.

Interestingly enough, my husband is career Army and was sent to Vietnam just last week; which would not be so funny if his father and brother hadn't been in the Nazi Army killing Americans during World War II.

On Good Friday I was ejected from Ft. Lewis, Wash., where we went to pass out leaflets, because my friend had a beard and is a Conscientious Objector. He was manhandled by the MPs and they were also searching cars of civilians without the owners' knowledge or presence, the legality of which I question.

I recently returned from three years of being stationed in Germany. The Germans do not want us there any more than the Vietnamese do in Vietnam.

I am completely and totally on the side of all you people who are too smart to be brainwashed by our social system, our government, lifers, and all the other people who believe it is right to kill or be killed by other innocent people who also don't want to do the same.

All I can really add is that my husband has left me because of my anti-Army, anti-war views, which can only show you how complete the brainwashing is.

I'll help all I can!

Wilma C. Saager, Seattle, Washington

∞

April 22, 1970 — GI SISTERS REACH FOR THE REAL NEWS

Recently, I got ahold of Fort Benning's underground newspaper, Rap. It suggested your newspaper along with a few others, as to the type of paper we can read without wondering if it's been censored ahead of time.

We GIs (yes, I guess we're called that too) are confined to these various reservations, and not that much national or international news (the kind we want to hear) is broadcast over military radio or television.

May I please start a subscription? It would boost my morale, as well as the other girls', who would surely be picking it up and reading it. We sisters really dig Rap. Looking forward to your newspaper. I am sending four more names along with mine. I'm sure they would enjoy it too.

Martin Army Hospital, Fort Benning, Georgia

September 21, 1970 — JUST AS BAD AS SHE THOUGHT

I have just finished reading your book "Up Against the Brass," and I feel I must congratulate you on an excellent job of telling the public what's going on today in our Armed Forces.

As the almost-fiancée of a recently inducted 1A-O, currently taking basic at Fort Houston, Texas, I am making every effort to learn his rights within the service, and to understand the issues behind our current involvement in Southeast Asia. Your book has provided many answers and aroused all the fears and discontent I've begun to feel within the past year toward our military system and its "kill" credo.

Pam

∞

December 16, 1970 — CHANUTE AFB — ON-BASE MEETINGS

Sisters and Brothers,

I am enclosing four new applications for membership in the ASU. Since I joined ASU on the first of this month, our chapter has grown quite a bit. It has been great seeing our numbers increase.

Last Tuesday a number of ASU members gathered in the bowling alley on base. The idea was to show our unity to the Brass who have a league there on Tuesdays. Last Tuesday they had a dine-in so we are going to meet again tomorrow. Major Hess, Chief of Security Pigs, will be there.

Right now many Airmen are really uptight about the condition of the plumbing system on base. Many student squadrons have only one commode in a building that works. They are constantly backing up. With typical A.F. efficiency — you can imagine how long it takes to get this fixed. Obviously, since this is a problem all over the base, it is the whole sewage system that is fucked up. But the A.F. is "broke" so it can't afford to fix it. More shit to shovel through than usual.

All power to the people!

Your Sister, Kathy Christian, Chanute ASU (Illinois)

Chapter 24 Women's Liberation

This chapter was contributed by Joyce Chediac.

Even before the Camp McCoy 3 made bail, the significant women in their lives had organized a committee in their defense. Only days after the three were arrested, Peggy Geden, Steve Geden's wife, and I grabbed all our possessions and Peggy's two-year-old daughter Michelle, loaded up her VW bus, and drove the thousand miles from Colorado Springs to Madison, Wisconsin, where the men were jailed and would be tried. Sandi Kreps, Dannie's wife, and their toddler daughter Shawnee joined us shortly.

In Madison the women hit the ground running. Consulting with the ASU national office in New York, we contacted the Madison anti-war movement and Milwaukee Youth Against War & Fascism, who were key supporters in that nearby city. By the time Tom, Steve and Dannie were released pending trial, we had already organized a public meeting and several informational leaflet distributions in Madison on the case. The three men were always the public spokesmen for their case. As Vietnam returnees, they also discussed the Pentagon role in Vietnam. However, Peggy and I remained the main organizers for their defense.

It took a while for the ASU staff, a thousand miles away, to understand the women's central role. The first ASU organizer who arrived from New York strategized with and solicited the opinions only of the three defendants. The women were doing most of the work, and had all the organizational strings, yet we felt invisible. Excluding the women from leadership hurt the defense work.

Peggy and Steve and Sandi and Dannie had small children. Since the women were the main organizers, and our loved ones were the defendants and the main speakers, sometimes the best way an ASU organizer from New York could help was to take a shift on child care, so the rest of us were free to organize.

All the ASU organizers from New York were heroes. Many had put their lives on the line to oppose the Vietnam War from within the military and to organize for the union. They respected that women were participating in the struggles they knew. For example, all of the men were passionately supportive of Black WACS (Women's Army Corps) who stood side-by-side with Black GIs in a rebellion against racism at Fort McClellan, Alabama, in 1971.

So were we. However, child care and household chores, burdens that fall mainly to women, were also political issues. ASU organizers who came to Madison did not yet understand that. They resisted taking a shift on child care or doing the dishes after dinner. They did not yet see that leaving the women to carry the bulk of these burdens hampered the work of the defense committee.

They were not alone. These were new realizations that women's liberation activists brought to progressive struggles and to society. Family issues, like chore divisions and child care, were not "just personal." They were political. They involved oppression of women and inequities in workload and needed to be addressed. The work in question, often trivialized, was important because it was the daily hard work of life.

Women in anti-war organizations challenged discriminatory practice, asserted their rights to be recognized for political and organizational leadership, and raised issues such as chore divisions. In groups where the male leadership was unyielding on these issues, many women sometimes left.

The ASU, however, "got it" when challenged on these issues by the women. Once it was brought to their attention, ASU organizers recognized the crucial and leading role the women played and briefed us and consulted us on everything. It became the ASU's policy that when its organizers came to Madison, they pitched in on child care, domestic chores and whatever else was needed to help the committee.

Our work had won us the ASU's respect. By listening to us and acting on our suggestions, these organizers won our respect as well.

'The Personal Is Political' — from Redstockings to the Home Front

I was to make the American Servicemen's Union my own organization. I become a national field organizer. In addition to Camp McCoy 3 defense work, I was to work with other women to add the perspective of women's rights to the working class, anti-racist view of the GI union.

This was no peripheral issue. Misogyny, racism, anti-gay bigotry and rigid class stratification were fundamental to the U.S. imperialist military. High-ranking officers set a precedent for and established a culture of treating enlisted women and the wives of enlisted men with contempt, ridicule and derision.

In basic training, men were incited against their wives and girlfriends, against women soldiers, and against the women of Vietnam as a way to isolate the men, break them down and get them to do the Pentagon's bidding. These policies hurt men as well as women.

I helped the ASU educate its members on these questions and to develop union demands that represented the issues of women enlistees, the wives of the GIs and the women of Vietnam. This is how it happened:

In 1970 hundreds of thousands of people took to the streets to oppose the U.S. war in Vietnam. But this was not the only movement for social justice at the time. The fight for civil rights for African Americans, begun in the 1950s, had expanded into the Black Power Movement by 1970, with the Black Panther Party electrifying many youth in African-American communities with its message of pride and the right to armed self-defense.

In July 1970 the first gay pride commemorative march took place on the anniversary of the 1969 Stonewall Rebellion. People with disabilities held a national march on Washington in 1970 to demand civil rights, access, legal protections and equal employment.

I was passionate about and supported all these struggles for social justice. For me, however, the Women's Liberation Movement was most personally electrifying. Only a few years old, it was spreading like wildfire.

I was part of a radical feminist group in New York called Red-stockings. The group was known for popularizing the phrase "The personal is political." This phrase meant that what society thought of as only "personal" hid inequities suffered by women. Relations between men and women, starting with the family, masked the oppression of women. The unequal burden placed on women for housework and child care and the power inequities that existed between men and women throughout society cried out for *political* redress.

Redstockings also popularized the phrase "Sisterhood is powerful." We strove to expose and reverse capitalism's pitting of women against each other, competing for the attention of men, and to replace it with solidarity so that all women might fight together for their liberation. We said no woman could be truly free until all women were free, and that we were fighting to liberate all women.

These conclusions were drawn from and reinforced by using a tool called "consciousness raising." In weekly meetings we raised our consciousness on women's oppression by collectively examining the details of our lives to identify and call out sexism. We questioned and reexamined all values, all assumptions, all experiences, all behaviors and all mores.

These weekly sessions brought life-changing revelations to me. I saw how all the women in the room shared some of my deepest shames and insecurities. These were not "personal failings," as we had believed. They were part of women's oppression and the large and small diminishment of living with sexism.

I looked at how this shaped who I was and who I thought I could be. I saw how women's oppression was fundamental to the capitalist system of inequalities.

The encouragement and learning opportunities provided by Red-stockings gave me much-needed confidence in my own ability to think, analyze and act. I wanted to know more. What was important to the working class, women and men? What was important to people of color in the U.S. and around the world?

∞

I left New York and joined a fellow Redstockings member and founder of that group, Ellen Willis, at the Home Front GI Coffee House in Colorado Springs, Colorado.

I volunteered at the Home Front for a year and a half, working as a waitress in that military town to support myself. Colorado Springs was near Fort Carson army base, temporary home to 26,000 soldiers. Most of these men were Vietnam returnees waiting to be discharged. Many were against the Vietnam War. Virtually all were bursting at the seams with anger at the military's petty and oppressive and demeaning treatment of them and couldn't wait to resume civilian life.

For me, the time at Home Front was an opportunity to work politically with working-class men like my brother and his friends who were facing military conscription, the draft. At the same time, I continued to examine and analyze the treatment of and attitudes towards women in all that I encountered. I used what I had learned in Redstockings to explore how women's lives were affected by and regarded by the U.S. military.

My co-workers, neighbors and friends were the wives and families of low-ranking soldiers. I listened to their grievances. I interviewed many rank-and-file soldiers, many of whom came to Home Front, regarding how the military apparatus regarded women. The soldiers, including occasional Air Force women from a nearby air base, willingly gave me details.

This two-pronged approach, helping run the coffee house while learning about women and the military, was how I saw my work in 1971 when Tom Chase, who was my partner, and the other members of the Camp McCoy 3 were arrested and taken from Fort Carson, Colorado, to Madison, Wisconsin. I went to Madison to join Tom and to work on the Camp McCoy 3 Defense Committee.

A Service*men's* Union?

The American Servicemen's Union was the only anti-war organization focusing primarily on active-duty men and women. It affirmed and protected the rights of enlisted men and women. The ASU saw the indictment of Chase, Geden and Kreps as an attack on the union itself and organized a strong defense.

The U.S. military was not all male. Then why was it called the American Service*men*'s Union? The draft targeted only men, the vast majority from the working class. Only men, both draftees and enlisted, were sent to the front lines to fight or be killed, though female nurses weren't far behind.

Most of the struggles taken up by the ASU were related to these men refusing to fight or opposing the racism of the Brass. Calling it the Servicemen's Union was consistent with the level of social consciousness when the union was founded in 1967, a few years before the women's movement gained steam.

One percent of low-ranking enlisted personnel were women. They had some of the very worst jobs and were disparaged and constantly harassed sexually. They had joined the military for the same reasons as male enlistees — promises of a decent job or job training, which often never materialized. However, they were subjected to a steady stream of sexist invective and lesbian baiting instigated by the officer caste.

Women realized that if their boss made a pass at them and his rank was high enough, he actually had life-and-death control over them, according to military law.

Three percent of the officers were women. They were almost all nurses, who entered the military as lieutenants. They also had plenty of grievances against the Brass. Women in the military, however, had not yet spoken up for their rights. The ASU would address these rights.

Other women's lives were affected by the military. Thousands of women were married to or in relationships with GIs. Though Peggy, Sandi and I were in Madison, we were still fuming over the indignities of life in military towns and the Brass's treatment of what they called "military dependents," that is, the families of low-ranking troops.

The U.S. Armed Forces, taking a cue from the Victorian British military, rated women according to their husband's rank: "Officers and their ladies, sergeants and their wives, soldiers and their women." The military ridiculed married enlisted men. Starting in basic training, they were told, "If the army wanted you to have a wife we would have issued you one." This was no joke.

Peggy, Sandi and I filled in the details of how this contempt for working-class families of enlisted men affected us. We gathered much of this material along with information on how the Brass treated women in Vietnam and how the Pentagon used misogyny to isolate men in basic training and published it in a pamphlet entitled, *Army Dependents Speak: Women in the Military.*[1]

Peggy had been a military dependent for three years and Sandi for two. In my year and a half at the Home Front in Colorado Springs, I had lived in the substandard housing available to the families of enlisted personnel. I worked as a waitress making a tiny salary side-by-side with Army wives, and I watched the buying power of my small purse get even smaller as merchants raised prices on military payday.

Soldiers' Families Forced on Welfare

Salaries of enlisted troops of rank SP4 and lower were below poverty level. This forced tens of thousands of enlisted men and their families onto welfare. The army allotment for a PFC's family was a tiny $60 a month.[2] In Steve Geden's first years in the army, the family income totaled $1,024 a month. Soldiers and their wives worked second jobs to survive. Pay in military towns was often at or below minimum wage.

By the early 1970s, GIs were openly rebelling, and many back home from Vietnam and awaiting discharge were anti-war and angry at the military. The Brass made a few reforms to try to keep the GIs quiet. Fort Carson, where we had all been before the three men were indicted, was called a model base for these reforms.

The "model" was that the Brass relieved the soldiers of some of the more odious and demeaning tasks like kitchen cleanup (KP). Instead, the Army hired solders' wives at low wages to clean the pots and pans.

On-base housing, cheaper than off-base, was issued to officers first, leaving most enlisted men and their families to rent off-base. In military towns, many of the landlords were officers, and they all jacked up rents for working-class military families. In Colorado Springs, Sandi Kreps' monthly rent rose by $50 when the landlord found out that her husband was a soldier.

On-base commissaries were supposed to be cheaper, but often weren't. Later exposés showed many supervising officers raised prices and pocketed the difference.

There were separate schools for the children of officers and the children of enlisted men on some bases, including Fort Carson. Officers' children were discouraged from associating with enlisted men's children, who sometimes were expected to salute the children of officers!

Seen frequently in military hospital emergency rooms were children battered by their fathers — soldiers trained to kill who are not helped to transition to civilian life by the military.

GIs and their families used to say that military surgeons asked the rank of their patient (or the patient's husband) before closing operative wounds. If the patient was an officer, then the surgeon made small stitches to limit scarring. If a GI, the stitches were large and haphazard, with no concern for scarring. This story certainly captured the spirit of the military's practice of medical triage by rank.

Officers and their families were regularly seen by doctors before the families of EM, even if the latter had been waiting hours and had more serious health problems. Many of these doctors were indifferent clinicians, just serving their time, said dependents, who often questioned their competency.

Peggy and Sandi, who both gave birth in military hospitals, described the experience as frightening and degrading. Medical personnel regularly belittled wives of GIs. Women were harassed by arbitrary dress codes that frequently changed. For example, one forbid wives wearing sandals, slacks or hair curlers to enter on-base clinics and emergency rooms.

After being impoverished and demeaned and having their lives turned upside down by the Brass, military dependents were often told by officers and lifers that they didn't know anything about the military, because they were not in it. If a low-ranking army wife went to the Brass to raise a legitimate gripe, they called in her husband, scolded him and told him to "keep his wife in line."

At the same time, if a soldier was thrown into the stockade for being active against the war, or for organizing for the ASU, his family lost the Army stipend. This family punishment was meant to pressure wives to get their husbands not to protest.

Peggy, Sandi and I concluded that this divide-and-conquer strategy, which brought discord into the homes of GI families, was meant to get men and women to fight each other instead of uniting to fight the Brass. We felt it would strengthen the ASU to validate what the military did to dependents and to show the guilt of the same officer corps that beat down the GIs. Because of our work, the ASU added the following demand to its basic program that was published every month in *The Bond*:

> Wages for rank-and-file enlisted men and women adequate to maintain them and all dependents at a decent standard of living. Adequate housing for dependents supplied by the military. Free day care centers for dependent children, controlled by their parents. Free and decent medical care for rank-and-file dependents, equal to that of officers' dependents."[3]

WOMEN'S LIBERATION

GIs and their families responded to the new demand with letters to *The Bond* detailing their situations. Even an officer's son offered to distribute *The Bond* on base.

Pentagon Promoted Misogyny

Many wives and significant others found their men edgy and mistrustful of them upon their return to the U.S. and civilian life. This hurt them and their relationships. The interviews I had done with rank-and-file soldiers at the Home Front and the experiences of the Camp McCoy 3 defendants and their families made it clear that the military encouraged misogyny.[4]

We found that the Brass and NCOs used racism, misogyny and anti-gay bigotry to isolate and break men down, so they would be submissive to the Pentagon's bidding. Starting in basic training, hostility toward women was fomented among the recruits. Trainees were sneeringly called "old women" as well as "p—ys" and other words for women's sex organs. In the crudest language, drill sergeants repeatedly asked the men who their wives or girlfriends were having sex with now that they were far away. The men were even forced to sing a cadence song with this theme while they marched until exhausted.

Anti-war and women's activists in the U.S., including Peggy and I, were inspired by the women of Vietnam, who played leading roles in many aspects of the Vietnam people's fightback against the Pentagon. We noted that the U.S. officer caste targeted their hostility toward the women of Vietnam. They even incited GIs to rape Vietnamese women, soldiers told us.

In some cases, low-ranking soldiers claimed NCOs "ordered" their men to do this and, of course, did it themselves. These were war crimes and crimes against humanity.

That the U.S. military had a deliberate policy of using racism and sexism to incite soldiers against Vietnamese men and women, and to desensitize them to war crimes, was corroborated by The Winter Soldier investigation of January-February 1971. More than a hundred

Vietnam veterans and sixteen civilians, organized by Vietnam Veterans Against the War, gave testimony to war crimes they had participated in or witnessed during their combat tours in Vietnam. Described were hundreds of atrocities against innocent civilians in South Vietnam, including rape, arson, torture, murder and the shelling or napalming of entire villages. The witnesses stated that these acts were committed casually and routinely, under orders, as a matter of policy.[5]

During the war, the Pentagon destroyed thousands of Vietnamese villages and poisoned the land with defoliants. Millions of Vietnamese lost their livelihood and were forced into the cities where there were no jobs. The U.S. military killed many more husbands, fathers and sons than women.

As a result, to support themselves and their families, some 400,000 women in South Vietnam were forced to sell sex to U.S. service personnel. The ASU, whose members were active-duty enlisted men and women, was in a better position than other anti-war groups to stop such crimes. Additionally, we did not want our husbands, brothers, fathers and sons influenced by racism and misogyny. It impacted right back upon them, on us and on our families. We wanted the ASU to speak out on these issues.

When we raised these points, the ASU organizers agreed — that the Pentagon's use of misogyny needed to be exposed and that anti-women propaganda was harmful to the women of Vietnam, military dependents, enlisted men and rank-and-file GIs as well.

The ASU used *The Bond* to bring this view before their members and supporters and give them an opportunity to respond. Tom Chase and Steve Geden, who by then understood the issue was important, wanted to educate other GIs. Here are excerpts from the article they wrote using the language every soldier heard:

> Remember in basic training, one of the worst insults that a sergeant could make towards a man involved some kind of reference to women? "You sound like a bunch of old women!" "You're nothing but a bunch of p— —-s!"

WACs [members of the Women's Army Corps] are singled out for special abuse by lifers, especially in basic training. According to the warped officers, a WAC is a woman "who couldn't make it" with men on the outside. ... Lesbian baiting them, and calling them "pigs."

We must reject this trash. ... We have each spent a year in Vietnam, and we know for a fact that in some units, rape, torture and murder of Vietnamese women and children is SOP [standard operating procedure].

We demand an end to all anti-woman propaganda, especially in basic training. We demand that officers and NCOs stop inciting, encouraging and ordering us, rank-and-file GIs, to commit crimes against women.

We must also understand that we, as men, will have to start now to change our attitude and actions.[6] (See Appendix F for full article.)

The response from readers of *The Bond* was thoughtful and positive and showed the ASU could influence the troops.[7]

In 1972 a new demand was added to the ASU's basic program:

An end to the systematic attempt by officers and NCOs to create prejudice against women, both in and out of the military. An end to the prostitution and rape of Vietnamese and all other women, which is conducted and incited by the military. We demand an end to the degradation of women, and their treatment as sexual objects rather than equal human beings.[8]

The ASU, and its women organizers in the Camp McCoy 3 Defense Committee, were the first to describe the many ramifications of the U.S. imperialist military upon women — from women in the military to the families of working-class soldiers to the women of Vietnam. This information and analysis were picked up and used by others in the anti-war movement.

Chapter 25 *The Bond* Gets Around

Veteran Mike Gill, speaking to a meeting in New York in October 2013:

> As I walked into the mess hall one day in July 1969 at Walter Reed Army Medical Center in Washington where I was stationed, this GI handed me a copy of *The Bond*. It was illegal to distribute literature, especially anti-military, anti-war literature on an Army post. I don't know if he was caught or not, but he defied the Brass's rules, and I do know that he changed my life and the newspaper changed my life.
>
> This was a time of gigantic anti-war demonstrations, especially in Washington, and the radical underground newspapers that I and a lot of other GIs and civilians read, were around, but *The Bond* was different. It denounced the military, the Brass, the officers and war. It was electrifying. I immediately joined the American Servicemen's Union.[1]

Gill's story and that of SGT René Imperato illustrate how *The Bond* reached tens of thousands of troops, even during months when no more than 15,000 copies were printed.

Gill, who worked much of his life as a bicycle messenger and who only rarely spoke during political discussions, showed that night that it would have been foolish for anyone to underestimate his understanding of U.S. society or his ability to effectively resist the war machine:

> I was able to use my position delivering mail in the U.S. Army to make a contribution toward ending the war against Vietnam. I was fortunate enough to have a mailroom to run as an Army postal clerk, first at Walter Reed Army Medical Center in Washington, D.C., and later in Vietnam. This gave me access to the mailing addresses of thousands of GIs in the U.S. and in Vietnam. With the help of the American Servicemen's Union organizers in New York, I made sure each one of them received a copy of *The Bond*.
>
> The Brass must have been upset when they realized that thousands of copies of *The Bond* were flowing into those military mailrooms. Whether the Brass had their suspicions about me as the source of those *Bonds*, I don't know. But then one of my sarcastic and scathing

anti-war letters was published on June 4, 1970, in the Washington Post and signed Sgt. Wilton E. Gill, Jr., Walter Reed Army Medical Center, Washington. That was apparently the last straw for the Army. Some 72 hours later, I was handed written orders sending me to Vietnam.

This served to "spread the disease." In Vietnam I was attached to an Army Post Office where I had access to far more military names and addresses than in a mere mailroom, and every one of those GIs received his copy of The Bond. And of course these copies were passed around from hand-to-hand at the various military bases, including the famous Fire Base Pace on the Cambodian border. That's where I regularly flew in a cargo plane to deliver the mail, including copies of The Bond.

I did not always immediately see the impact of this work. However, when I got back to the states and got my discharge and was staying with my parents that first month in October 1971, we all watched the lead story on the CBS Evening News with Walter Cronkite about a mass mutiny at Fire Base Pace, where dozens of GIs refused orders to go out on patrol.[2]

∞

From 1968-1970, when I (John Catalinotto) was circulation manager for The Bond, a long-distance telephone call was a big expense, so we had to find another way to connect with groups working with the ASU far from the office. Near many of the bases anti-war youths were beginning to set up what they called GI coffeehouses, where enlisted troops could gather away from the bases and barracks and feel comfortable. Many of the collectives that ran these meeting places were happy to distribute The Bond and the many other GI and GI-oriented publications.

My employer had installed something called a WATS line, so the company could more cheaply make long-distance calls. So I often stayed late at work, not to solve actuarial problems, but to call Colorado, California, Texas and Washington State — I don't remember if Hawaii was allowed by WATS — to connect with sympathetic coffee house organizers about their shipments of The Bond. We also sent bundles of the newspaper to groups in Europe, Japan and Australia.

Buck SGT René Imperato, who was stationed at Tan Son Nhut Air Base in Vietnam in 1970, flew for R&R into Sydney, Australia. While there, Imperato visited the Third World Liberation Bookstore, which carried *The Bond*. Picking it up to read, and already alienated from the war by experiences at the front, the young soldier was captivated by the in-your-face rebelliousness of its coverage. Imperato shared it with the GIs on the plane ride back to Vietnam. *The Bond* was passed from one to the next until all 175 GIs returning to the war zone had read it.

∞

After returning from Vietnam and being sent to Griffiss AFB near Rome, New York, Imperato became an ASU organizer and participated in a May 1971 demonstration there. In a talk at that protest, Imperato said, in response to repression on the base:

> Three to five years for coming here and speaking against the government? Bullshit! ... I'm speaking out against the government right now."

Imperato's article about the protest in *The Bond* continued:

> Well, the swine Brass were upset. Helicopters were flying over the base. ... SPs [Security Police] who were on alert were hanging around their posts, reading *The Bond* and [anti-war] leaflets. They knew that this was their cause: their freedom, not protecting the interests of the Brass and their lackey lifers. In the chow halls, in the hospital, in the streets, in the barracks, GIs were reading *The Bond* and the leaflet right in front of the pigs. ... One GI refused to work on the B-52s because they bomb the people of Indochina. Another GI told us that he wouldn't obey his orders to go to Vietnam... .

> So the Griffiss ASU chapter is growing stronger and stronger every day as more GIs realize that we have the numbers, that unity is our strength and the ASU is our unity.[3]

Both Gill and Imperato learned about Workers World Party while in the Army and at that time committed their lives to political militancy in New York City. As of the Fall of 2016, both of them, at the age most people like to retire from their day jobs, were still participating in anti-racist and anti-war activities and are organizing support for workers' struggles.

Gill has been taking *Workers World* newspapers with him on his messenger route and getting them around New York City. Imperato is now a transgender activist (whose preferred pronoun is she or they), a member of Paralyzed Veterans of America and a consultant on disabled access for music festivals in New York State.

∞

Andy Stapp said that 10,000 GIs had joined the ASU by the end of the war. However, anecdotal reports from GIs that we received in the mail and when we met them face-to-face told us that the influence of the ASU and *The Bond* was even more widespread. Like Gill and Imperato, many of the troops just had to read one issue of the newspaper to see that they were part of a large group of active political people inside the armed forces, that there was social and political support from outside the military, and that if they put their energy into building this movement, we might win.

Chapter 26 **Dear Andy**

Letters from Vietnam II

April 15, 1969 — BRASS GET RICH, LIFERS GET FAT — AND EM DIE

I am presently stationed at (name deleted) which is about 20 miles south of the DMZ. I am a radio operator and I get a lot of calls through concerning enemy action, etc. Tonight another useless action happened which turned me against the war even more. Here is what happened: It's 1:30 in the morning and I've just taken a call from 3rd Med. about a guy needing blood. I passed the word to our sick bay for people to give O- if they were willing to. I later found out that it was our own guns that had done it to him! His left leg was blown off up to his knee and his right leg was no longer there, including part of his hip.

I have talked to many, many people, and their feelings are the same as mine, which are that this war is only killing off helpless young men in the prime of life, and making the Brass richer. On Sunday, while we have leftovers and cold cuts, the lifers eat steak and get fat on our blood and sweat.

PVT E-2, Vietnam

∞

June 17, 1969 — BRASS CREATE DEATH-TRAP

FOR ENGINEER BATTALION

At present we are securing a firebase up in Dak-To, Central Highlands. We are Engineers. All the infantry and support units have been taken out of Dak-To. We remain the only American forces here, other than advisors from the Special Forces.

We have been reading where the South Vietnamese government is going to rapidly take over the fighting in Vietnam. Well, the army of SVN refuses to secure the airbase we're now defending. So instead of building up this sorry country we are sitting ducks.

We are but one battalion and already have taken heavy casualties, due to heavy artillery bombardments and ground attacks. What we are defending we don't know. We have been put on hold up here in Dak-To, instead of our planned move to the coast. Of course, being peons, the Brass tell us it is none of our business why we are staying in this filthy hole.

Keep up the good work and sign us:

Pissed-off battalion, Dak-To, Vietnam

July 22, 1969 — THEY TREAT THEM THE SAME WAY THEY TREAT US

We have a strike force next to us made up of Montagnard tribesmen. The First Pig has severely beaten up at least three of them so far.

In Vietnam the lifers rule with an iron hand, and if you cross them your shit is OUT.

SP4, Vietnam

∞

July 22, 1969 — GIs WANT IN ON THE MOVEMENT

The Brass showed a special film on the GI Underground Movement back in the world, trying to discourage us from it when we return. Little did they realize that they had defeated their purpose, because instead of becoming discouraged the GIs want IN. Information is being given out on how to join the Union, etc. I'm sure membership will pick up.

You can see it in their eyes — the lifers are scared. They know the movement is on and it's not to be stopped. Fight on for us over here and we'll see you soon stateside.

SP4, Dak-To, Vietnam

∞

August 18, 1969 — NAM UNDERGROUND ORGANIZING

I am a writer, of sorts. I've had prior experience in illustrating literature, advertisements, etc.

I've begun circulating literature against the war, Army, etc. We are utilizing mimeograph equipment at battalion headquarters, printing it on government paper and posting the finished product on bulletin boards in various battery areas. The demand is bigger than the production, so I'm organizing a staff to increase our efficiency and output.

I hope my efforts prove useful in spreading the undeniable truth and create an awareness and a platform for us to unite upon.

SP4 Vietnam

November 18, 1969 — A PETITION FOR PEACE FROM GIs IN NAM

Here is a petition signed by 22 GIs supporting the Vietnam War Moratorium. We hope you will print this in the BOND and let other GIs know they have nothing to fear by standing up and being counted.

The Army can suppress only so much and so many. Our day is coming, and it's the ASU that has helped bring us this far. Keep up the good work.

We, the undersigned, all members of the United States Army serving in Vietnam, wish it to be known that we fully support the Vietnam War Moratorium. We urge all Americans to support this great effort for world peace.

Roger De Vito, Michael A. Allerie, David M. Matsouka, James F. Rusie, William E. Green, James B. Edson, William M. Coleman, Thomas B. Williams, Michael J. Poole, Robert P. Sagen, Hugh E. Ross, Robert G. Lee, John W. Flem, Peter A. Compagnoni, Allan K. Patton, Mark Sanchez, Omus H. Nelson, Lowell W. Kilby, John E. Ford, Jr., Richard P. Farutt, Edward P. Dudeh, Robert Onevira

Long Binh, Vietnam

∞

November 18, 1969 — THE BRASS'S DAYS ARE NUMBERED

I am writing you to inform other Union members of a lifer pig purge taking place. Being active Union members, we have been organizing and discussing our problems not only in our own unit, but others as well. When the lifers heard of our action they thought it was funny, but when they saw the huge reaction among the troops they decided to resort to typical lifer tactics to silence us (a feeble attempt against ones so dedicated).

Last night a drunken lifer stumbled into our hooch and manhandled us. We retaliated, our First Sergeant (Super Lifer Pig) told us he would fix us. The next day was Sunday and everyone was on holiday routine. The pigs told us WE had to help build the Battalion Sergeant Major's hooch. Realizing we have been bowing down to enough of their shit, we refused to build it. As a result we have been threatened, told we would never get promoted (give a shit).

And now as a direct result of our refusal to submit to their bullshit, three guys are facing UA [Unauthorized Absence] charges. The lifers already informed us that we'll burn. We, the Union members in our battery, realize these atrocities are commonplace tactics in the armed forces, and we intend to do something about it! We will keep on organizing and planning until someday our Union demands will be reality.

I have informed the pigs that I am testifying on behalf of my brothers and I told them they could shove their stripes, because their days are numbered (and they are). Keep it rolling, brothers.

1st Marine Division, Vietnam

December 16, 1969 — UNION RANKS SWELL IN VIETNAM

Enclosed you will find eight membership forms and a money order for $50. The potential for membership here is great, but we must first eliminate the sense of separation and aloneness that is felt by those who are forced to serve here. I am confident that once we can show the people that they are not alone in their views, and that the only way we will gain our rights is by presenting a UNITED front, our ranks will swell. Looking towards the day when all men will be free to enjoy life, liberty and the pursuit of happiness.

Marine, Vietnam

∞

March 18, 1971 — ON THE WAR IN LAOS

Concerning the invasion of Laos: There is definitely something happening up here. But the average GI is somewhat confused whether or not we're actually in Laos. Most of us feel strongly against a Laos invasion. It could be the Army's last move, because the GIs over here are sick of carrying out Nixon's pig orders, and we just might refuse to go into Laos. The GI looks at this operation as another imperialist tumor growing inside Congress. GIs are just plain tired of getting killed and wounded protecting the interests of Nixon, Rockefeller and DuPont and the rest of those rich bastards who are making a fortune off this war. ...

AND THE WAR WITHIN AN ARMY

In my last letter I mentioned that I'd like to see my First Sergeant up for Lifer of the Month. I also mentioned that he had been gassed and an attempt was made with a white phosphorus grenade. Well, last night that pig got what he so richly deserved — a fragging! It blew the fuck off his hooch, but the pig came out unhurt! "And nobody knows who did it." He was so scared and shaken up he went over to the reenlistment office and re-upped for five more years to get a change in assignment. He was begging to leave, in fear of his pig life. We won! We're getting rid of him. ... Power to the ASU. All power to the people.

Robert Michener, 2/11 Army, 101st Abn, Camp Eagle, Vietnam

∞

JUNE 30, 1971 — PASS IT ON

Just got your package of fifty BONDs, which will be given out by the time you read this. We tell everyone we give them to that they should treat them like we're told to treat the "Stars and Stripes," that is that when they finish reading it to pass it on to five more people. It would increase the number of available BONDs from 50 to 250, which, if guys cooperate, would be fantastic.

GI, Vietnam

TURN THE GUNS AROUND

Chapter 27 Black, Brown and Red

The original core of ASU organizers at the national office was made up of ex-GIs who were white. We knew this was a problem we had to overcome. So we were all elated in late 1969 through 1970 when Black and Latino troops and veterans started becoming leading organizers as part of the ASU national staff. A sample of their stories illustrates what tens of thousands of GIs went through in those years. Those who came to the ASU took the lessons of the war a few steps further than most. For them it was an impulse to battle the whole capitalist system.

The ASU had strong anti-racist credentials from its work defending Marines Bill Harvey and George Daniels, the Fort Hood 43 and many other individual cases and because its key organizers worked closely with activist Black troops, for example, in the Special Processing Battalion in Fort Dix.

The early white ASU organizers were outspoken against racism. They confronted racist officers and noncoms with words and actions in the military units. They also rejected any manifestation of racism among the low-ranking troops. And they fought racism and discrimination by any means at their disposal. This created a healthy atmosphere to attract a multinational, multi-ethnic staff.

One of the first key organizers was Tom Soto, a Puerto Rican from the South Bronx ghetto. In 1961, as soon as he finished high school, he was informed he would be drafted. Instead, he enlisted in the U.S. Army that November.

Assigned to the Army Security Agency (ASA), Soto was trained in cryptography and analysis at Fort Devens, Massachusetts, northwest of Boston. The ASA monitored and copied communications of the Vietnamese forces and of U.S. forces. That information was used to carry out regular bombings of and attacks against Vietnamese forces and populations.

Soto had a Top Secret security clearance, the highest level, and was in Vietnam through 1963, mostly in Saigon, before the big U.S. troop buildup. He wrote in 2016:

As soon as I arrived in Vietnam, I understood the nature of the imperialist war. I rebelled constantly, did not salute officers — unaware of
the ASU demand [first raised in 1967] — used civilian clothing and carried out other petty protests. I went AWOL for two weeks, pulled a
weapon and threatened a superior. I was sent to the shrink, given an
Article 15 [legal proceeding below a court-martial] and busted to PFC. I
spent thirteen months in Vietnam.

Two days before an early-out discharge, I suffered an accident in
Saigon, fracturing several bones. I spent an additional year in military
and VA hospitals, and another year was spent in a wheelchair and using crutches. ... It was the Vietnam War experience which radicalized
me. I went from opposing the war to becoming a communist.[1]

The Army Security Agency even gave Soto a class in dialectical
materialism, which is an essential part of Marxist theory. Apparently
the Army Security Agency wanted Soto to know how the Vietnamese
Communists approached problems in order to better understand
them. Soto understood all too well. His own life experiences clashed
with Army propaganda. Soto wrote about being in Saigon (now Ho
Chi Minh City) in 1963 when four young Black girls were killed by a
bomb set by racists in a Birmingham, Alabama, church:

There, in the streets of Saigon, Elijah [a fellow anti-war GI] and
myself cried like children. We were sad and ANGRY. Elijah saying to
me: "Tom, what the hell are we doing here bombing and killing people
who have done nothing to us, while our children are being murdered
back home."[2]

∞

Unlike most of the veteran ASU staff, Soto came first to Workers
World Party and then later decided to work with the union, which he
saw as an essential tool in organizing against the war:

Previous to entering the Party, I had been involved in some civil
rights and anti-war struggles, for example, as a member of the leadership of the Black and Puerto Rican Student Community at [City College
of New York], which led the strikes, occupation, battles with white racists and negotiations with the Board of Higher Education that brought
about Open Admission [of all NYC high school graduates] throughout
the [City University of New York] system of public colleges. ...

I attended my first anti-war demo in 1965, while still using crutches after having been injured in Vietnam. By 1969 when I entered Workers World Party, I was a very politicized person, not to mention that my family in Puerto Rico is from Guánica [on the southern coast about 20 miles west of Ponce] where the U.S. invaded [in 1898], and various members of our family, who were supporters of the Nationalist Party, were arrested for opposing U.S. colonial rule.

[I chose to work with the ASU] to build a soldier's union, fighting for the stated demands, and of course a central point was undermining the imperialist war. The ASU was [also] outstanding in its opposition to racism.[3]

PFC Tom Soto (ret.) appeared on the masthead of *The Bond* for the first time at the end of 1970. Within six months Soto was writing the lead article in *The Bond* in an issue that took head-on the issue of racism in the military. His article consisted of interviews with GIs at Fort Meade, Maryland.[4]

The same issue of *The Bond* also introduced two Black airmen on active duty who would play key roles in the ASU staff from 1971 to 1973. One was AMN Calvin T. Bonner Jr., who wrote an anti-racist essay on page 2 pressing for "an active and militantly anti-racist coalition of non-white and white GIs" that he argued was needed so "we can overcome those forces which presently oppress us both."

An addendum to the article noted that Bonner had just received a General Discharge for, as his CO said, "apathy and a defective attitude." The addendum continued:

Cal's military record may not look so good to the pigs, but his record as an ASU member, organizer and recruiter is OUTSTANDING![5]

Within a year Bonner joined those on the masthead as a writer. For years after his ASU experience, Bonner was a regular contributor to *Workers World* newspaper.

The other airman was Bill Roundtree, who on June 24, 1971 was the ASU organizer

... arrested by civilian pigs while marching in a demonstration outside the Champaign (Ill.) city jail. The demonstration was in support of Bobby Rush, a Black Panther who was being arraigned that day. ...

Ever since he and other brothers in the ASU chapter organized a very successful mess hall boycott at P-24, the student mess hall on the base, the pigs have been trying to nail him. ... The Air Force pigs are very upset about Bill being on the base, even if he is locked up in jail, because he is very well-known among the Black Airmen and WAFs on base.[6]

The Black airmen published a list of demands, including freeing Roundtree and other brothers who were being held on the base "concentration camp." Also on the list of demands were Black barbers, transportation to Black-oriented cultural events, etc.

Roundtree had learned of the union from another airman named George at Chanute Air Force Base in Illinois, who handed him a copy of *The Bond*. He knew right away that he and the ASU were meant for each other, and he began a life of organizing. After numerous confrontations with officers, Roundtree spent months on what the Air Force called AWOL and what he called "union business." On a phone call in August 2016, Roundtree told me:

> When I returned they put me in the stockade. I was determined to organize for the ASU, even there, so they put me in solitary confinement for thirty days. The other GIs started to ask why I wasn't processed like the rest of the prisoners, started raising questions and found out I was organizing the ASU. That's how the mess-hall strike was organized.[7]

When Roundtree knew he would face charges, he and the ASU insisted that an ASU representative be present when the officers were discussing any punishment for his organizing activity. Somewhat to the surprise of the ASU, the Air Force officers let PVT John Lewis (ret.) argue Roundtree's case. Remembering that day, Roundtree said:

> We couldn't believe they let me have my union rep. John was fantastic. He wouldn't give them an inch. In the end, [the ASU] got me out of the Air Force, which was OK with me, and I wound up keeping my benefits.[8]

Others added to the masthead of *The Bond* in the 1970-1973 period were Pete Perkins, a recent veteran from Oneonta, New York, who took over the responsibility of distribution, and Hakim Gahtan

Abdullah, a Black veteran from Elmira, New York. They were both active fighting for veterans' rights (see Chapter 28).

Julio Ghigliotti Matos, who was later to become a well-known journalist in Puerto Rico, became active with the ASU in 1972 and 1973, also during struggles for veterans' benefits.

Bill Roundtree and Larry Holmes. Right, Pete Perkins and Hakim Gahtan Abdullah.
Photos: Richard Wheaton

Rounding off the team of top organizers, a young Black man named Larry Holmes – not the boxer – began to connect with the ASU staff. In an August 2015 interview for this book, Holmes told his story, which illustrates clearly how the war was making the Army unworkable:

In 1971 I was a fairly apolitical teenager – more into Jimi Hendrix than radical politics. Then I got drafted into the Army during the Vietnam War. Within weeks that experience transformed me.

While in the Army I learned the existence of a group called the American Servicemen's Union. My first thought was, "I did not know we had a union."

I went AWOL from Fort Dix, N.J., and I found the national office of the ASU in a broken-down tenement on 25th Street near Sixth Avenue

BLACK, BROWN AND RED

in New York City. It looked like the kind of place that subversives would cohabit comfortably. In that office I met Andy Stapp, the ASU chairperson, and Terry Klug, who had served three years in military prison for desertion.

My new ASU family felt that it would be in my best interest to get kicked out of the Army as soon as possible. After being AWOL for about three months, I turned myself in to the authorities at Fort Dix accompanied by a delegation of ASU members and an attorney.

I was thrown into the stockade right away. Actually, it wasn't a real stockade because in 1969 the Fort Dix Stockade had burned down in the middle of a rebellion of imprisoned GIs, including Klug. In 1972 Fort Dix was putting its prisoners in an old abandoned barracks building that had little running water, toilets that didn't work and no air-conditioning.

I stayed in Fort Dix's prison for a little more than a month while my attorney and the Fort Dix Brass negotiated my future. Finally the Brass became convinced that it would not serve the interests of the military to court-martial me and keep me inside the Army; it would be better to kick me out.

And so one day they took me from my cell to some captain's office, and he had me sign an order recognizing that I was barred from ever entering any U.S. military installation, whether on the mainland or around the world, for the remainder of my life under threat of six months immediate imprisonment. I signed the order and was handed an undesirable discharge from the Army.

By that time it was clear to me why the Brass would prefer to kick me and mostly anyone else they figured would be a troublemaker out of the Army. In addition to being a base offering basic training, Fort Dix was also an out-processing base for soldiers spending their final days in the Army. It was not unusual to see a group of disgruntled and alienated Vietnam War vets walking around the base, waiting for their discharge papers.

They were so angry about what they were forced to go through that they showed absolutely no respect for the officers. On the contrary, they were as likely to spit at, throw something at or even physically attack an officer as to salute one. In fact most of the Army at that time was in a complete state of advanced demoralization.

Somewhere in the Pentagon about that time it was decided that the best thing to do was to push almost everyone out and start rebuilding the Armed Forces from scratch. I was fortunate to get in trouble with the Brass at the very time they were making this decision, which is why I got the boot instead of more jail time.[9]

∞

By 1972 the ASU had a solid staff of Black, Puerto Rican and white veterans with a supporting staff of civilians. They met regularly to discuss politics. Most attended political forums at Workers World Party. They did the mailings of *The Bond* each month. One of the WWP founding members, Vince Copeland, would often say at meetings, "The more Black we are, the more Brown we are, the more red we will be," meaning the more revolutionary. This held too for the ASU staff. At this point, the ASU staff not only continued to fight against the war, but opened up militant struggles for veterans' benefits for the millions of GIs who were getting out, including many veterans of Vietnam.

ASU Adds Demand for Veterans' Rights

Full employment for veterans of both sexes; adequate employment benefits to last until such employment is provided. Special measures to provide decent jobs for Black, Puerto Rican and other national minority veterans. Free medical, dental and hospital care, and free education benefits or job training with financial support. Abolition of all "less-than-honorable" discharges.

Chapter 28 Veterans' Benefits

Larry Holmes told me, in the August 2015 interview, about why ASU organizers advised him to get out of the Army rather than staying in and organizing:

> While the U.S. was continuing the air war against the Vietnamese, from the point of view of U.S. Army troops, the war was winding down. Meanwhile, there was a frustrated, angry and growing population of Vietnam War veterans who were coming home after the horrors of war to poverty and unemployment. Some had been poisoned by Agent Orange.* They were facing all sorts of other problems and challenges.

> About the time that I met the ASU, in addition to organizing GIs inside the military against the war, we were at the beginning of organizing Vietnam War veterans to fight for better benefits, for jobs programs. One major demand was for a cash allotment, a bonus, of at least $2,500. That doesn't sound like much today, but it was a tidy sum forty-four years ago. [It's about $14,000 in 2016.]

Once Holmes was discharged, he became an ASU organizer:

> Back in New York as a civilian, I joined the national staff of the ASU and immersed myself in finding and organizing recent Army veterans. They were not difficult to find. You could find them at the Veterans Administration either begging for or demanding help. You could find them on various college campuses, where many of them went because they couldn't find a job — and if they were fortunate, they got a little stipend for going back to school.

> But you could also find them hanging out on the corners of the South Bronx or Bedford-Stuyvesant in Brooklyn or Harlem or any one of a thousand poor communities. Many of them had little to no income, no employment and nothing to do except hang out on corners. After a short while the ASU had as many veteran members across the country as we had active service people.

> The veteran members of the ASU began to organize protests, usually at the VA buildings, either the local one on Seventh Avenue and 24th Street or we traveled to Washington, D.C., to protest at the federal Veterans Administration building. On more than one occasion veterans led by the ASU invaded the buildings and occupied them in order to draw

attention to our demands for better benefits and services for vets, who were in desperate need of them.[1]

Tom Soto verified Holmes' memory of the organizing process in New York

I recall participating in a job fair at the Armory in New York City, where the ASU held a pretty radical rally.

Soto then described the 1972 Chicago Job Fair, where the government's promises — which turned out to be empty — brought thousands of veterans desperate for jobs who grew quite angry when no jobs materialized:

And then there was the Chicago Job Fair, a humongous and politically defining event, where many thousands of mostly Black veterans literally tore the doors off the building in order to find employment — where the ASU fraction was able to articulate a program for preferential hiring of vets and monetary compensation. I remember that John Lewis, Bill Roundtree, René Imperato, Hakim [Gahtan Abdullah] (from Elmira) were all there.[2]

The Bond, May 19, 1972. Photo: J. Catalinotto

The Chicago action was one of the most dramatic ASU protests. The Illinois State Employment Service planned what they touted as

TURN THE GUNS AROUND

the "nation's largest job fair" for unemployed veterans on May 9-10, 1972.[3] Since there were more than 300,000 unemployed veterans, some 25,000 in Chicago alone, the chance of many getting work seemed small. But as the ASU squad that went to Chicago found out, no solid jobs were being offered. The ASU tried negotiating with the organizers of the fair, but were turned down on every point. That was a mistake, reported *The Bond*:

> After an hour and a half of going from booth to booth and filling out endless numbers of applications, the anger and frustration of the vets had reached the bursting point. At this time, ASU organizers commandeered an empty table and began handing out our survey sheets. "Did anyone here get a job, or have we been getting the runaround?" shouted the organizers. "Anyone who got a job, raise your hands." No hands.
>
> Our table was surrounded in a matter of minutes by hundreds of angry, fed-up vets, many of whom took our survey sheets and helped us pass them out. It became so crowded that ASU organizers had to get up on the table to rap and distribute the survey sheets. By this time, the crowd had swelled to over a thousand... .[4]

The meeting turned into a militant rally. Some vets suggested they take to the streets and go to Mayor Daley's house. To the corporate hacks staffing the tables, the vets looked so ferocious that before long the suits were heading for the exits. When interviewers couldn't come through with jobs, their booths were trashed.

The ASU continued organizing veterans for the next year, as Soto described:

> And there was the $2,500 or Fight campaign where Julio Ghigliotti and Larry Holmes were [solidly won over] to WWP. Larry was the spokesperson for this activity.[5]

Holmes remembered:

> In April of 1973 we organized and launched a national march of thousands of veterans on Washington, D.C., to demand the $2,500 bonus for each veteran, as well as better benefits and jobs. We had been organizing this march for about a year. It was inspired by the Bonus March that World War I veterans organized in 1933 at the height of the Great Depression.

Veterans also became a highly visible factor in the anti-Vietnam War movement. The ASU had sizable contingents at anti-war protests both at the local level and in Washington, D.C. Often the veterans of ASU wore their military uniforms to let everyone know that they were once military but strongly against the war. Many protesters were inspired to see the Vietnam War veterans in uniform walking arm-in-arm with them at a protest to shut down the war.

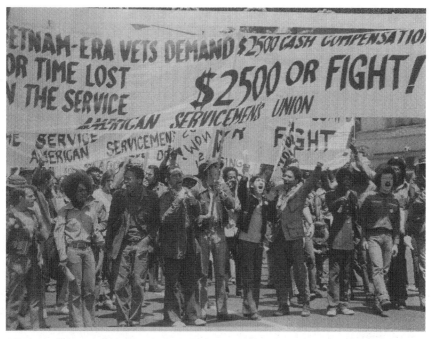

ASU veterans protest in Washington, D.C., April 1973. Tom Soto left of middle in second row, his hand before his mouth. Larry Holmes first row right of center, his left fist in the air. Julio Ghigliotti full face at right. Photo: Richard Wheaton

In the spring of 1973 the government organized what they called the "Home with Honor Parade" along Central Park West in New York. The ASU veterans met about this and decided that it was our duty to once again put on our uniforms and take our anti-war message to this "Home with Honor Parade."

We learned two things that afternoon. One was that the last thing the organizers of this parade wanted to see was uniformed army veterans protesting the war. They were enraged about our plans, but also worried that others would join us or at least sympathize with us.

The other thing we learned is that just because we were veterans wearing uniforms, we would not be immune to a brutal police attack. At one point during the protests along Central Park West, New York City police equipped with riot gear, some on horses, attacked us and beat us. To their surprise these recent veterans did not take it lying down but fought back. One cop was pulled down off his horse.

Quite a few of us went to the hospital that day with busted faces and heads. But we weren't afraid and we didn't regret, not one bit, having come out to protest this ugly pro-war parade.[6]

During the veteran organizing in 1972-73, the ASU added a twelfth demand to its list, focused on the needs of veterans, shown on page 224. (See Appendix D-III for the final list of ASU demands in its program.)

Anti-war demonstration, 1970s. At right, ASU veteran René Imperato.
Photo: ASU collection

Chapter Notes

* Agent Orange was a defoliant employed by the Pentagon. It destroyed tree cover and as a result killed forests — which did grievous harm to the environment and to human beings, including millions of Vietnamese and tens of thousands of U.S. GIs and their families. It continues to disable Vietnamese people. The U.S. has not paid the necessary reparations to decontaminate the entire countryside and aid people disabled by birth defects generations after the war's end. GIs too continue to deal with physical pain and disability this poison inflicted on them and their families.

Chapter 29 Portugal & Africa

April 24, 1974. A popular folk song, serving as a secret signal to the captains in Portugal's Armed Forces Movement (MFA), played on Lisbon's Radio Renascença. Units of the army in and near Lisbon had been scheduled for ordinary maneuvers. This all changed.

Spurred on by the growing war-weariness of their troops, the growing weakness of the police-state regime, the inability of Portugal to win the war against the liberation movements in its African colonies and the growing international isolation of Portugal, the captains acted.

The captains had kept their plans secret from the soldiers they commanded. With troops already in their trucks, they read the new orders: Seize the capital, arrest the government and throw out the fascist gang ruling Portugal. The rank-and-file soldiers, surprised but ecstatic, carried out the new orders, hoping this action might end the wars in Portugal's African colonies.*

Each blow struck by the liberation fighters in Mozambique, Guinea-Bissau/Cape Verde and Angola had weakened the fascist regime in Lisbon. Each strike by Portuguese workers or desertion by Portuguese soldiers boosted the revolutions in the colonies.

The revolt in the armed forces overturned the Portuguese regime in Lisbon. On April 25, 1974, MFA quickly ended the 48-year fascist police state. Still influenced by old habits of respect for power, however, the Portuguese captains politely arrested President Marcelo Caetano and the rest of the top government leaders and later exiled them to Brazil.

They replaced the Caetano gang with a military junta led by Gen. António de Spínola. This officer differed with other fascist generals only because he believed the war was unwinnable. Spínola urged Portugal's rulers to work out a neocolonial relationship with the African colonies, much like French imperialism did in West Africa.†

Despite this deceptively mild beginning, April 25 was no simple replacement of the palace guard. Emboldened by the coup, the masses of workers took over the streets, cheered the soldiers and for the next eighteen months pressed the revolution forward.

Television news in the following days showed groups of workers surrounding and roughing up some individuals. Workers and revolutionaries recognized their former torturers from the notorious PIDE, the Portuguese political police, and dispensed justice.

Defying Spínola's commands to leave prisoners of the old regime in the jails, the crowds, with the support of the troops, emptied the prisons of revolutionaries and anti-fascists, while putting the PIDE thugs behind bars. By May Day — six days later — hundreds of members of the Portuguese Communist Party (PCP) and other revolutionary groups were out of prison or back from exile to organize and agitate in the factories, farms and streets of Portugal.

∞

The armed struggles in Mozambique, Guinea-Bissau/Cape Verde and Angola seeking liberation had undermined the army and made the April 25, 1974, Revolution possible. The African battles had begun on Feb. 4, 1961, when Angolan freedom fighters stormed a prison to free their comrades. As the Popular Movement for the Liberation of Angola (MPLA) sang in its hymn, "The heroes shattered their shackles."

One of the great African Marxists, Amílcar Cabral, was the leader of the liberation struggle in Guinea-Bissau/Cape Verde, Portugal's smallest African colony. Cabral organized a popular army to fight for the freedom of a million people; in a dozen years of people's war, this army had liberated large parts of the small territory and set up a new government.

Amílcar Cabral, Marxist political and organizational leader of the armed struggle of Guinea-Bissau against Portuguese colonialism. Next to him is Constantino Teixeira, Commissioner of State Security of the first independent government of Guinea-Bissau/Cape Verde. Photo: Amílcar Cabral Foundation.

Despite his other priorities organizing a people's war, Cabral knew how important it was to reach out to the soldiers in the colonial army. While fighting the Portuguese, arms in hand, Cabral's organization, the African People's Independence Party of Guinea and Cape Verde also made an appeal to draftees. In a 1963 leaflet, Cabral made it clear the liberation forces would win, and those opposing liberation might well die, but he added:

> Be courageous, refuse to fight our people! Follow the example of your courageous comrades who refused to fight on our land, who revolted against the criminal orders of your leaders, who cooperate with our party or who abandoned the colonial army and found in our midst the best reception and fraternal aid.[1] [Full leaflet in Appendix G-I.]

In a blow that robbed the world's oppressed peoples and workers of a great leader, PIDE agents assassinated Cabral in Conakry, Guinea, in 1973. But even this setback failed to stop the liberation

PORTUGAL & AFRICA

struggle. From tiny Guinea-Bissau/Cape Verde, as well as in much larger Angola and Mozambique, the liberation struggles left their mark on Portugal's army.‡ And the MFA brought the war home. One could claim that the African liberation struggles drove the Portuguese uprising against the fascist regime.

Portugal's ruling class was subordinate to the bankers in Britain and the U.S., who were skimming the cream from the exploitation of workers and resources in both Portugal and Africa.

What distinguished General Spínola from the other top fascist officers was that he urged an end to colonial wars, while being a loyal servant of big capital and acceptable to the Portuguese ruling class. Nevertheless, the April revolution that made him head of state also put Portugal's revolutionaries, many of them from the PCP, back on the streets and in the factories.

Álvaro Cunhal, PCP secretary general, in the mid-1970s. Photo: O Comunista.

The PCP's secretary general from 1961 to 1992 was Álvaro Cunhal, who returned to Lisbon from exile after the coup. Cunhal, who died in 2005, had been imprisoned from 1949 until 1960, when a dramatic escape freed ten party leaders from Peniche maximum-security prison on the Atlantic coast fifty miles north of Lisbon.

Two books Cunhal authored, based on papers he had presented to the party leadership after his escape, succinctly described how the movement in the Portuguese armed forces developed and its relation to the PCP. The movement grew in response to the vicious and arbitrary fascist discipline and in tandem with the actions of the guerrilla fighters trying to free the African colonies.

Cunhal pointed out that Portuguese soldiers in Africa knew they were risking death if they openly resisted the war. The forms of resistance among Portuguese troops during the 1960s were similar to those among U.S. troops during the Vietnam War. Cunhal shows this in his first book discussing events of 1961-1964:

> The resistance of the soldiers against the colonial war is not only one of the most brilliant examples of solidarity of the Portuguese people with the colonial peoples. It is also a new element in the struggle against the fascist dictatorship, an index of the weakened state of the fascist state apparatus, of the radicalization of the politics of the popular masses and the combat readiness of the youth.

> The Angola war gave new reasons for the development and generalization of the struggle of the soldiers. Given the fascist discipline and the political spying that existed in the armed forces, even if only a half dozen mass actions had taken place against the fascist policies, this would have been enough to represent a strong sign of resistance of the people and the youth to the fascist policies and the colonial war. But it wasn't only a half dozen. In the last three years hundreds of struggles of the soldiers have taken place.

> There was also resistance to being sent to the colonies, including work stoppages in the military quarters and barracks, on ships and in military hospitals. ... Desertions reached a significant volume. Sometimes the insubordinations were accompanied by small acts of violence. The soldiers burned their cots or broke windows in their barracks or destroyed the furniture.

> A form of struggle used over and over by the soldiers against arbitrary orders and punishment of the officers, against the bad food and against the colonial war, was the refusal to eat at mess.

> The struggle of the Portuguese people against the colonial war reached the colonies themselves. Risking their lives, many soldiers refused to leave for the front or to participate in atrocities. Pilots refused

to carry out bombings with napalm or bombed off-target. Officers and soldiers organized resistance. Others deserted on the field of battle. Our party has reason to feel proud of these heroic struggles of the soldiers. Without the action of the party they would not have taken place.[2]

In his second book, looking back at the developments immediately leading up to the 1974 Revolution, Cunhal notes that the PCP directed its young members, subject to the draft, to organize and resist, even though the PCP also supported exiled youths.

> Never before in a colonial war did the number of deserters and draft avoiders reach a number comparable with that registered in Portugal. According to some calculations, the number of draft avoiders reached almost a third of the youths of military age. In the great migratory flow a strong contingent was of youths fleeing military service and war.

> Although the PCP placed its members under the obligation to stay in the armed forces (in Portugal and in Africa) in order to conduct revolutionary activity there, the PCP considered the deserter movement as a great movement of resistance to the colonial war and to colonialism.

> In 1973 (despite the surveillance, internal espionage, repression, searches, punishment, trials and imprisonment) the struggles, contradictions and conflicts of opinion in the heart of the armed forces reached a new level with new means of expression.

> Among the commissioned officers a movement developed that rapidly reached a great amplitude and energy. It is under these conditions and atmosphere that the "movement of the captains" (Armed Forces Movement or MFA) took shape.[3]

The Portuguese armed forces nearly tripled in size from 79,000 troops in 1961 to 217,000 by 1974; 149,000 were in Africa.[4] Youth were conscripted for four years, of which they served two in Africa.§

Before the colonial wars, the old professional army in Portugal was filled with pro-fascist officers. When the military tripled in size, many new officers recruited from the middle classes and among professionals were not themselves fascists. Some wanted a more democratic government. Most wanted to end the colonial wars. A core of these junior officers began to gravitate toward planning a military coup to remove the Caetano dictatorship.

Still they looked to higher-ranking sympathetic officers for leadership. One such officer, who saw his role in Africa as preserving the lives and dignity of his troops, was Colonel Vasco Gonçalves. The junior officers invited him to join the MFA in October 1973, long after the captains had already been meeting and just six months before the coup.[5]

General Spínola had seen the sorry state of Portugal trying to defend its old-style colonial empire — the last remaining empire — with an army that was carrying out atrocities against Africans. His book, *Portugal e o Futuro (Portugal and the Future)*, published in early February 1974, advocated a negotiated end to the colonial war. Despite his criticism of the government and the war, Spínola had the confidence of the Portuguese ruling class.

The April coup placed Spínola as president at the head of the military junta of generals and admirals. His role as leader provided a temporary comfort for wealthy Portuguese. The MFA had its own leading body of seven officers, three from the army, including Gonçalves, and two each from the navy and air force.[6]

Right-Wing Coup Attempts Fail

Two major struggles for power took place in the year following April 1974. In both cases, by successfully defending the April revolution, the workers and soldiers opened the door to further revolutionary developments.

The first was on September 28, 1974. Angered by the September 15 liberation of Guinea-Bissau, Spínola and the officers around him called a demonstration supporting the right wing of the junta against the MFA and the rest of the government. They called this a demonstration of the "Silent Majority," borrowing the phrase from the Richard Nixon administration in the United States. Others in the government, including Prime Minister Gonçalves, argued with Spínola to try to neutralize, if not cancel, the rightist demonstration, which was more like an attempted coup.**

In the end, the masses of workers came out and set up road-blocks to stop the demonstration, while enough military units loyal to the MFA stayed in place to defend the government. The Silent Majority demonstration was a flop.††

After his last-minute attempt to get military support from NATO failed, Spínola was forced to resign, and the entire government moved leftward. But the general continued to plot against the MFA and the government. This led to the next confrontation on March 11, 1975. Spínola, working with reactionary forces inside and outside Portugal, planned a military coup.

∞

Helicopter units from the Tancos Airbase sixty miles northeast of the capital rained machine gun bullets on soldiers in the barracks of the First Light Artillery Regiment (RALIS) which was defending Lisbon's government buildings. Spínola depended on his loyal supporters in the National Police, on a Paratrooper Hunter Regiment that had abstained from the April uprising, and on Air Force support from bases around the capital. He apparently hoped Tancos paratroopers would finish off the government that had deposed him the prior fall and crush the MFA.

Captain Diniz de Almeida, who was commanding the RALIS troops as the paratroopers approached the government buildings, ordered his troops to take their machine guns to the higher floors. From the windows and balconies they could control the spaces in front of the buildings. "Hold your fire," he told them. "But if they start shooting, fire back with all you have."[7]

The paratroopers shouted at the defending RALIS troops to surrender. Captain Diniz refused. Both sides wanted to talk. Although nervous that discussions might lead to a "Trojan Horse," Diniz let the paratroopers proceed inside a building. It turned out that the paratroopers were confused about their orders. Their generals never clarified why they should attack, but relied on anti-communist rants.

As both sides drew close enough to talk, they still held their rifles ready to fire.

A television crew happened to be right where the confrontation was taking place. On YouTube you can see Captain Diniz arguing and negotiating. Everyone is still tense. And then all of a sudden the parachutists and the artillery troops are embracing. The paratroopers came over to the revolution.[8] This was at about 3:15 p.m.

At Air Base 3, the sergeants and privates mutinied and refused to take part in the coup. That was another blow to the coup plotters. Once again in history, fraternization among the rank-and-file troops moved the revolution forward.

His coup defeated, Spínola fled to Spain. The MFA purged the pro-Spínola officers from the armed forces. The most progressive period of the revolution followed and was able to begin to redress the grievances of the population.

In Portugal itself, there was reinstatement of rights to labor unions and the nationalization of factories, banks and much of the media, plus wide-reaching agricultural reform that gave legal rights to land seizures by agricultural workers and established collective farms. Begun by actions of workers and other collectives, nearly all these steps were codified under the four parliamentary governments headed by Prime Minister Vasco Gonçalves, who was promoted from colonel to general in 1975.

Overseas, the liberation movements continued on the path to victory. Guinea-Bissau/Cape Verde had become independent on September 15, 1974. Soon Angola and Mozambique won their independence from Portugal. Even East Timor, half of an island in the Indian Ocean, won short-lived independence in November 1975, but was soon occupied by Indonesia, itself under a military dictatorship.

∞

Faced with homegrown reaction and threatened by U.S.-NATO intervention, the Portuguese movement fell short of completing a workers' revolution, as had taken place in Russia in 1917. By the fall of 1975, a more rightist grouping of officers had gained control of the MFA and removed the more revolutionary people from the government. The rightists began eroding the revolutionary gains, a process that has continued through 2016, when the Portuguese working class faces a new crisis of austerity and unemployment.

Nevertheless, it was the 1974 Portuguese Revolution that made the most gains for workers in Western Europe up to that point. The Portuguese experience showed the decisive role of the armed forces as the arbiter of state power and the potential of winning over the rank and file — and, in this case, even the lower officers — to a revolutionary outlook.

Differences, Similarities with U.S. Developments

In the 1960s and 1970s Portugal was the poorest country in Western Europe and in the NATO military alliance. The communist movement there, while underground, was relatively strong and a large section of the working class was pro-communist or at least pro-socialist.

Despite these differences with the political situation in the United States, the Portuguese experience of organizing in the military during a colonial war had many similarities to the ASU experience during the war against Vietnam.

The politically conscious soldiers in Portugal who were anti-fascist also acted in conscious solidarity with the struggles of the colonial peoples against Portuguese colonialism. Many soldier-organizers accepted political direction from the Portuguese Communist Party or from one of the smaller pro-revolutionary organizations. Leading organizers of the American Servicemen's Union also acted in conscious solidarity with the Vietnamese revolutionaries.

The revolutionary energy of the African liberation movements aroused the spirit of struggle among politically conscious Portuguese soldiers, just as the heroic Vietnamese struggle and the Black Liberation Movement inside the U.S. sparked revolutionary feelings among U.S. GIs.

As Cunhal showed, in the 1960s and early 1970s, the PCP had a conscious, sympathetic approach to the soldiers and party activity was geared to support their struggle. The PCP's goal was to involve the soldiers in the revolutionary struggle to overthrow the fascist dictatorship.

Similarly, the goal of Workers World Party organizers and leading ASU cadres was to break the U.S. Armed Forces chain of command so that the U.S. could neither wage imperialist war nor repress workers' struggles or rebellions in oppressed communities.

In 1969, some top U.S. generals requested that the U.S. raise the troop level in Vietnam from 540,000 to one million. Instead, the U.S. administration chose to begin withdrawing troops, relying on airpower and on building a puppet army. This U.S. strategy failed to prevent an eventual Vietnamese victory, but it did decrease tensions inside the U.S. military. Lisbon's rulers chose a different course. By using Portuguese troops to try to win the wars in Africa, they instead provoked the April 1974 Revolution.

Chapter Notes

* Like its neighbor, Spain, Portugal's monarchy, starting in the early 1500s, seized territories in South America, including all of Brazil, plus the three large territories in Africa and some smaller areas: the islands of São Tomé, Principe and East Timor in the Indonesian archipelago and two city enclaves, Goa in India and Macao in China. Little to none of the wealth the Portuguese ruling class robbed from the colonies and the slave trade, however, ever trickled down to Portugal's impoverished peasants and workers. In 1926 a military coup ended Portugal's short-lived republic. By 1932 a regime called the New State was headed by Antonio de Oliveira Salazar, who ran Portugal's fascist-like police state from 1932 until a stroke disabled him in 1968, and then by Marcelo Caetano. As in Spain, the ruling party had close relations with the Catholic Church hierarchy.

† By the 1960s, the big pre-World War II colonial powers, Britain and France, had conceded direct political rule to independence movements in most African colonies. In most of them, the local government, nominally independent, allowed banks and corporations from the former colonial power to continue to exploit the resources of the land and labor of its people.

‡ Portugal was the last colonial power to retain direct rule of all its African colonies, and it faced armed uprisings in all of them.

§ Portugal's total population was less than nine million, meaning that 2.5 percent of the population was in the military; by comparison, at the peak size of the U.S. Armed Forces in 1968, about 3.543 million people or 1.8 percent of the population was in the military. Youth were drafted mainly for two years or enlisted voluntarily for three, and a tour of duty in Vietnam was one year.[9]

** When General Spínola said the demonstration would include a moment of silence to honor the Portuguese soldiers who died in Africa, Gonçalves responded: "Only if it also honors the African fighters who died fighting for liberation." Spínola reconsidered and withdrew the suggestion.[10]

†† Captain Diniz de Almeida wrote about the Silent Majority flop: "The popular movement was decisive in stopping the advance of the reactionary forces. Here with barricades raised, there with support given to the soldiers and to all who were fighting against Spínola and those who he represented, the popular masses showed that they would not permit the return of those who for 48 years had exploited and repressed them."[11]

Chapter 30 'If It's White, I'll Shoot'

My first meeting with Max Watts in the flesh took place as his partner June Van Ingen and I walked through the cottage door in Dilsberg, West Germany, where he was sitting, half as wide as he was tall, buck naked in front of a typewriter. It was late June 1973 and 95°F, but I was still surprised.

I knew Max — I always called him Max — from an exchange of letters starting in late 1967, but hadn't met him until that day. Van Ingen, who shared their Dilsberg cottage, picked me up at the nearby central train station in Heidelberg.

"John Cat - we finally meet," he said without turning to face me. "We're going to the GI center this afternoon. You'll meet the guys. Have you had a coffee yet?"

My first thought was that this was some sort of test. I suppressed surprise, neither stared nor looked away, and said, "I'd like a coffee, Max, thank you. Finish what you're typing and we'll visit the center."

Had I arrived a week earlier Max would have brought me to the special court-martial of PVT Larry Johnson, who was in trouble with his officers because he put the Army on the spot. He objected to U.S. policy of arming Portugal to carry out a colonial war against guerrilla movements in its African colonies, especially in Mozambique. As the key civilian friend of GI organizers in Germany, Max helped coordinate the Larry Johnson Defense Committee.

Max had many adventures throughout his lifetime, but his life's central focus was organizing resistance within the military. The American Servicemen's Union organizers had been working in tandem with Max on different continents to help GIs break the U.S. chain of command. We did it when he was helping deserters in Paris and continued after the French kicked him out and he moved to Germany. We knew we could count on Max. Johnson knew it too.

244

Johnson had grown up in Harlem in New York. According to the defense committee's newsletter that June, after spending his youth addicted to heroin:

> At the age of 21 because of financial pressures and a feeling of responsibility for his wife and child Johnson enlisted in the Army. ... It was after reading the February [1973] issue of Ebony magazine's piece about the liberation struggle in Mozambique that he intensified his research into the relations of colonial powers in Africa, which in turn led to his action disassociating himself from the U.S. Army.[1]

∞

Max's background was a world apart from Johnson's. That didn't mean his life was easy. Born Tomi Schwaetzer in Vienna in 1928 to a family of secular Jews, he, his parents and his sister had to flee Nazi-controlled Austria in 1938. Immigration rules forced the family to split: His mother and sister went to New York while he and his father made it to London. When the British immigration authorities send him a notice that his visa extension had been refused, his father committed suicide in London. Max found out much later this was due to clerical error. He spent a couple years orphaned in England before rejoining his mother and sister in the United States.

Susceptible to the military draft in 1950, Max wanted no part of the U.S. war against Korea. He left the U.S. for Israel, the one place he could go without a passport, but also refused to join the Israel army. As he said, "I don't know any Koreans and I don't know any Arabs, and neither has ever done me any harm." He managed to reach Paris to continue his studies in geophysics.

In Paris in the mid-1960s, when he was still called Tomi Schwaetzer and was beginning to organize aid for U.S. military deserters, he adopted the *nom-de-guerre* Max Watts. Some said it was short for Maximum Wattage, though he never told me that. He had a gift for inventing and promoting names with lively acronyms. One of the GI resisters, Dick Perrin, came up with Resistance Inside the Army or RITA for the Paris group. Max called supporters FRITAs, or Friends of RITAs. In 1972, after the post-Charles De Gaulle French government put the troublesome Max Watts under a sort of house arrest in Corsica in 1972, he slipped his watchers and escaped, first to Denmark and then Germany.

In 1972 Max wound up in West Germany, near Heidelberg, quite close to many of the 220,000 U.S. GIs stationed in that country at that time. His RITA/FRITA work accelerated.

Larry Johnson's case was central to the struggles Max was engaged in. Johnson refused to work, wear his uniform or salute while the U.S. supported Portugal colonialism in Africa. Max and the Lawyers Military Defense Committee supported him. Though I missed the court-martial that June, the ASU staff did get to meet this GI resister after his thirty-day confinement ended in a General Discharge. Johnson preferred to use as his name, Asan Uhuru Akil. This is what *The Bond* carried as a postscript to an article titled "Black GI Defends Africa," which reported on Johnson's June court-martial:

> On August 16, we were very pleasantly surprised to find brother Asan Uhuru Akil at the door of the ASU national office in New York City! While he was doing time in the stockade, the Brass had offered Asan an 'Undesirable' Discharge under Chapter 13, Uniform Code of Military Justice. But the Brass wanted him out so badly, they compromised and Asan was soon out with a General Discharge. The officer who had been most down on Asan, LTC Welch, was relieved of his command and replaced. Legal action is underway to have the whole prosecution overturned. The ASU hails the victory of this righteous brother who would not be intimidated in expressing solidarity with our brothers and sisters fighting for their freedom in Africa.[2]

I never saw Larry Johnson/Asan Uhuru Akil after his visit to the ASU office and don't even know if he knew how his struggle and his teaching had a lasting impact on world history. I hope he did.

Conscious at every moment that the GI struggles were historic, Watts and some comrades in Berlin kept a record of everything associated with these struggles, including Johnson's. He must have imagined hundreds of PhD candidates hunting through them. He named his own notes "Tales of Resistance Days," which he called "TORDs," despite, or perhaps because of, the word's similarity to turds. Currently his TORDs and hundreds of GI newsletters and leaflets are in a library in Amsterdam, Netherlands.*

Max told me at least a half-dozen times how Johnson/Asan's teaching had an impact. It must have been his favorite TORD. In Max's book, *Left Face*, you can read the background and the sequel to that 1973 confrontation with the Army. In brief:

By early 1973 Johnson was a clerk in the small army post, Strasbourg Caserne, in the hills of West Germany near the town of Idar Oberstein. Reading *Ebony* magazine, Johnson learned that some troops in the then fascist-led Portuguese Army's war against the liberation movement in Mozambique were collecting heads of Africans. "He looked in a mirror and thought the heads looked like his," wrote Max. Johnson also learned that this colonial army depended on aid from NATO — principally the U.S., West Germany and Italy.[3]

Johnson studied everything he could find about the liberation struggles in the Portuguese colonies and the role of NATO. He told his commanding officer he would stop cooperating with the Army if the U.S. kept supporting Portugal. After a confrontation with this officer, Johnson was punished and confined to his room. In 1973 punishment had a way of backfiring on the U.S. military command. In that room, he went through a metamorphosis. From PVT Johnson he changed into "Professor" Johnson. In small meetings and discussions, he then began teaching many of his Black and white GI buddies about the Portuguese wars against its African colonies.

The Army then made another mistake. After his trial, Johnson spent thirty days in the Mannheim Stockade and continued his lectures. That punishment also backfired. Troops from the 509th Airborne Infantry, which was 45-percent Black or Brown, heard his explanation of the wars in Africa.

$$\infty$$

Skip forward two years to 1975. A rebellion in the Portuguese Army — the soldiers were fed up with the colonial war — had overthrown Portugal's fascist government in April 1974, and by late 1975 the African colonies wrenched themselves free from Portuguese rule.†

By then a civil war was raging in the former Portuguese colony of Angola in southwest Africa. Outside forces favored by Washington‡ were intervening against the main liberation organization, the Popular Movement for the Liberation of Angola (MPLA). From the north, the CIA-backed forces threatened the MPLA government. From the south, the government of South Africa,§ which then was infamous for its policy of apartheid (extreme segregation), sent thousands of troops to menace Angola's capital, Luanda. South Africa's intent was to smash MPLA rule.

In defense of the Angolan revolution, Cuban troops, invited by the MPLA and given logistical support by the Soviet Union, were aiding Luanda's defense. The South African regime had been counting on the U.S. to send troops to finish off the Cubans and the MPLA.

There were rumors that Washington planned to send the 509th Airborne Battalion to support South Africa against the Cubans. The 509th, with its 3,500 troops, had already been moved from Germany to Carlo Ederli Caserme in Vicenza, northern Italy. Unfortunately for the plans of U.S. strategists, the Pentagon Brass and the South African regime, many in the 509th Airborne had participated in Professor Johnson's classes about Portugal, Africa and NATO.[4]

Max enjoyed repeating what one of the Black GIs in the 509th told him while looking back at that moment: "We don't know much about Angola, but if we are sent there we will shoot it if it's white." And the Black troops wrote something to that effect in the few issues they published of a newsletter out of Florence, Italy, called *Getting the News*.[5]

Nearly all the 509th's officers were white.

The 509th Airborne Battalion stayed in Europe. The South African regime and army hinted that the U.S. betrayed them. Without U.S. intervention, the Cuban-MPLA alliance was able to stop the racist army in its tracks.

The civil war in Angola dragged on for another thirteen years, with hundreds of thousands of casualties. Finally, in 1988 Cuban and Angolan troops handed apartheid South Africa a thorough beating in the battle of Cuito Cuanavale, a small city in southern Angola. This

South African defeat had great repercussions. It forced South Africa to pull out of Namibia, Angola's southern neighbor, which had been the apartheid state's colony. This led quickly to Namibia's independence. The weakened South African apartheid regime then made concessions to the liberation struggle there, and after the African National Congress was unbanned in 1990, it was voted into power in 1994 with Nelson Mandela the country's president.

∞

Max resettled for good in Australia in 1981 and actively supported many struggles of Indigenous peoples in Australia, East Timor, Papua New Guinea and especially PNG's nearby island of Bougainville, where a local ten-year uprising kept the mining monopoly Rio Tinto from pillaging the environment.[6] Max insisted the Bougainville story was the basis for the 2009 movie *Avatar*,[7] because a dissident officer from the Papua New Guinea army, sent to repress the rebellion, instead switched sides and coordinated the military defense of the resistance movement.

My friend Rémy Herrera, a French economist, visited Max in the Australian summer of 2007 in Sydney, and grew enthusiastic over Max's theories about GI resistance. Herrera told me later that Max wore the same outfit in Sydney as he did in Dilsberg – nothing.

Starting in late 1967, Max and I communicated regularly by phone, snail-mail and later email for forty-three years. He signed every letter, "*illegitimati non carborundum*," which he claimed was Latin for "Don't let the bastards grind you down." We had five face-to-face meetings between 1973 and 1981, including one in New York's Upper East Side at the home of his mother, Gisela Barinbaum Schwaetzer, a psychoanalyst trained in Vienna by Sigmund Freud.

To impel me toward some new adventure, Max jarred me out of sleep with a phone call – Sydney is fifteen hours ahead, which means 7 p.m. in Sydney is 4 a.m. in New York. "John Cat," he'd shout, "you sound sleepy. Did I wake you? You have to talk with Jethro."

It was in May 2009. The next afternoon I interviewed Jethro Tulin, the leader of the Indigenous Ipili people from central Papua New

Guinea, in New York for a United Nations meeting. Tulin's people were battling Barrick, a Canadian-based gold-mining company.[8]

The only call I remember initiating was our final conversation on November 20, 2010, after I learned Max was on his deathbed. Max was coherent, but subdued. No more orders.

Following 82 years of a life filled with adventure and intimately entwined with tumultuous events concerning humanity in the 20th century, Watts died in his bed on November 23, 2010, in Sydney, Australia, surrounded at hand-holding distance by friends, comrades and mainly his current and past lovers.**

Asan Uhuru Akil, aka Larry Johnson
Photo: Links Um

I haven't been able to find Larry Johnson/Asan Uhuru Akil, whose resistance may have helped liberate southern Africa. Max's decades of being top FRITA organizer in Europe helped make it possible.†† They both left their mark on history.

Max Watts in Australia, 1994, with the two dogs, Lility and Boulan, on his lap.
Photo: Rosie Kubb

Chapter Notes

* Many of these documents can now be found online at the Wisconsin Historical Society's GI Press Collection. In 2010 Max, working from Sydney, tried to get friends to move to Berlin and manage them after his Berlin colleague, Dieter Brünn, died. Other supporters managed to get them transferred to the International Institute of Social History in Amsterdam, Netherlands. Researcher James Lewes sent digitized versions of the documents from Amsterdam to the University of Wisconsin.

† See Chapter 29.

‡ Washington supported a group of guerrillas operating from the area in and near the Republic of the Congo, also called Zaire, headed by Holden Roberto, as an alternative to the mass-based MPLA, which was receiving support from the Soviet Union. The U.S. wanted to avoid having a Soviet-friendly popular government in this major African country.

§ South Africa was considered one of the most blatant racist governments in the world regarding its oppression of its majority African population and its rule of the nearby territory now the independent country, Namibia.

** When Max's last partner Vivienne Porzolt tried to organize a memorial for him in the summer of 2012, I prepared a video as my contribution to his eulogy. Sydney was too distant for most and the memorial was cancelled. The video became a basis for this book.

†† There was another boomerang from military repression: The Lawyers Military Defense Committee contacted an expert witness, Father Cesare Bertulli, to testify at Johnson's court martial. The 527th Military Intelligence Battalion tapped the call, something illegal under West German law. SP4 Mike McDougal, who did the tapping under orders, was disgusted by his role, and told Max and the LMDC about it. By complaining of this, the LMDC was able to void many sentences, including Johnson's, and got $150,000 compensation from the Army. Johnson got $15,000 compensation. He told Max he was willing to serve the thirty days again, even for only $14,500. (From a Max TORD.)

Chapter 31   Courage

Among the people who grew up in the U.S. and made the greatest contribution to the welfare of humanity were the soldiers, sailors, Marines and airmen and -women who actively resisted the war against Vietnam, those who battled the Pentagon, along with the civilians who stayed at their side.

Young people in the United States are taught it's heroic to go into battle and risk their lives. Risking your life under fire takes physical courage. You have been taught this sacrifice is "for your country."

It is a different level of courage to risk your freedom or your life to defy the existing order, to stand up against the public opinion manufactured by the ruling class and disseminated by its media. All the soldiers who were war resisters in the Vietnam-war era expressed the second type of courage.

Some of the GIs around the ASU did both — that is, they first risked their lives in the war and then became strong and outspoken opponents of that war.

Among the many others in and outside the American Servicemen's Union were individuals who set an example for others with their acts of conscience. The ASU staff appreciated all those who led the way. Later tens of thousands of GIs experienced the war and became committed war resisters.

Many Black GIs, after going through a year in Vietnam, were ready to take their military know-how and join the Black Panthers.* Puerto Rican veterans might join the Young Lords.† If they came from one of the Indigenous nations, they might join the American Indian Movement and in 1973 take part in the armed occupation of Wounded Knee, South Dakota.‡ The Chicano anti-war fighter, Rosalio Munoz, an organizer of the Chicano Moratorium of 1970 in East Los Angeles, wrote the paper "Chale Con El Draft" (No to the Draft), which impacted many Chicano veterans.

They had seen and been nauseated by the violence of the U.S. war machine. If they were to risk their lives again, they wanted it to be on behalf of their people.

As early as 1966, three GIs at Fort Hood, Texas — PFC James Johnson, PVT David Samas and PVT Dennis Mora, who specifically identified themselves as Black, white and Puerto Rican workers, respectively — refused to ship to Vietnam.[1]

At the end of that year, CPT Howard Levy, a medical doctor, refused to train Green Beret Special Forces troops to be medics.[2] He and the Fort Hood 3 did prison time for their courageous refusals.

MSG Donald Duncan, who was in Vietnam in the U.S. Special Forces, opposed the war with a lead article, "The Whole Thing Was a Lie," in February 1966 in *Ramparts* magazine, of which he later became the military editor. Duncan testified against the U.S. at Bertrand Russell's Vietnam Tribunal in 1967.

LT Susan Schnall, a nurse, carried out a dramatic action in a small plane in 1969 when she distributed anti-war leaflets by "air mail" to naval installations and the aircraft carrier USS Ranger.[3]

These actions of conscience set the stage for a massive change in consciousness in the Armed Forces.

Among those whose struggles are reported in this book are GIs who showed the way by their personal example: Marines Bill Harvey and George Daniels who spoke out to other Marines and were jailed; soldiers Ken Stolte and Dan Amick who went to prison just for distributing a leaflet calling for a union; sailor Roger Priest, who took on the Navy at the Pentagon itself, stood up to his commanders, won the case, then slipped quietly into civilian life.[4]

Add to them the dozens of GIs who went absent in Stockholm, London and Paris and the thousands who escaped to

Canada. The hundreds of GIs who rebelled at Danang Prison in the summer of 1968, and the medic Gary Gianninotto who wrote to *The Bond* about the revolt; the other hundreds who rebelled at Long Binh Jail that same summer and those who sent letters to *The Bond* to spread their story; the 160 Black GIs who met all night at Fort Hood in August 1968; Billy Dean Smith, accused of wiping out his "superior" officers in Vietnam in March of 1971;[5] the mutiny of an entire company in the First Cavalry Division at Firebase Pace near the Cambodian border in 1969.[6]

Then there were the 130 sailors on the aircraft carrier Constellation, all but nine of them Black, who on November 9, 1972, refused to board ship.[7] And the 1,200 sailors on the USS Coral Sea who signed a November 1971 petition demanding the ship stay in port.[8]

Not everyone saw eye-to-eye with the ASU's approach. Yet they too contributed to the overall resistance in the military. Jeff Sharlet, a Vietnam veteran, published the newspaper *Vietnam GI*, the only other tabloid paper published on newsprint with a following among thousands of GIs, including in Vietnam. Sharlet founded the paper at the end of 1967 and edited it for a year, stopping only when his untimely death from liver cancer cut his contribution short. One of Sharlet's team, Tom Barton, as late as 2003 began publishing *GI Special*, a GI resistance web newspaper after the U.S. occupied Iraq.

Of the thousands of youth who went to Canada, we remember Dee Knight, who edited *AMEX/Canada* from Toronto.

PVT Andrew Pulley at Fort Jackson, South Carolina, later ran for vice president in 1972 as a candidate of the Socialist Workers Party. At Jackson he helped build GIs United, a group that at one point saw almost an entire unit refuse to go to Vietnam. Among the thousands the ones I knew best were those who became the most active organizers for the ASU —those who joined the ASU because they saw it as the best instrument for taking down the Pentagon.

Role of Women in ASU Organizing

At the top of the list are the contributions of women who worked with the ASU. Early on, women mainly contributed administrative work and to the production and distribution of *The Bond*. Among them were Sue Davis, Jackie Dornbos and Fran Meyers, who also drew political cartoons.

As valuable as their work was to the ASU and *The Bond*, many of the women made even greater contributions to the civilian working-class movement. In May 1968 Davis was protesting in the streets with Youth Against War & Fascism. A photo of her and Deirdre Griswold Stapp decorates the cover of *The Vietnam Songbook,* published in 1969. To protest, they are wearing motorcycle helmets; it's protection from cops' clubs. Davis was a leader in the struggle for women's reproductive rights, and through 2016 has been writing on this topic for *Workers World* newspaper as well as copy editing *Workers World*. Griswold has been editor in chief of *Workers World* for forty years.

Laurie Fierstein's name was on *The Bond* masthead for her technical assistance laying out the paper. She then spent a decade as the main New York branch organizer of Workers World Party, planning meetings and protests and then matching available volunteers with tasks like making signs, pasting up flyers and distributing leaflets.

Unbound by tradition, three women had their names on *The Bond's* masthead during this period as national field organizers: Maryann Weissman, Joyce Betries (Chediac) and Susan Steinman. Weissman, one of the ASU's founding organizers, went to federal prison for six months for supporting GIs when the ASU first got its start at Fort Sill. Later she organized legal defense for the GIs, and proposed and led the 1969 demonstration at the Fort Dix Stockade.

In Chapters 22 and 24, Chediac describes her own work in

an anti-war coffeehouse in Colorado and on the Camp McCoy 3 Defense Committee. She also analyzes the impact of the women's liberation movement on the American Servicemen's Union. After her work with the ASU, Chediac became a leader working for the liberation of the people of the Middle East (West Asia and North Africa) from imperialist and Israeli domination, writing extensively for *Workers World* on that topic. She also overcame dyslexia to work as a managing editor of *Workers World* newspaper for a decade.

Susan Steinman was a field organizer in Hawai'i, where she was studying Chinese and Russian at the University of Hawai'i (see Chapter 13), and later worked out of the New York ASU office. While continuing to volunteer with the ASU, she got a job as a telephone operator at AT&T where she and another Workers World Party member, Gavrielle Gemma, organized their co-workers. Gemma wrote:

> She [Steinman] was a daughter of the working class and a determined revolutionary. Her parents were both deaf, making even more remarkable her outgoing, talkative nature. She became a telephone operator in 1970. At the time the women operators were still captive to the old company "union" set up by AT&T.

> Soon Sue was organizing on all issues of importance to the 100-percent women workforce. At the same time Sue continued to participate in WWP's initiatives against imperialist war, racism and for working women's rights.

> Sue became a lead organizer for the Communication Workers of America. She stood up to the intense male chauvinism of the union and many of the male workers, who were already in the CWA. With tenacity she worked around the union bureaucracy and was able to organize men to support the women who were organizing to join the CWA. Eventually 18,000 women gained union representation.

> Sue was the absolute main driving force in winning the first pregnancy disability laws in the United States. She died in 1985 at the age of thirty-five of cancer, which was truly a loss for working-class women, as well as to her family and the party that

mourned her.[9]

Political Life Post-ASU

In 1970-1973, some of the best "soldiers" of the Vietnam generation were coming into the ASU office in New York and volunteering their time, their little money and risking their security to build the union and stop the war. This includes the ASU founders, those who first met Andy Stapp at Fort Sill, Oklahoma; most stayed as active organizers for years. When the ASU dissolved, after the war ended in 1975, many continued in the struggle for workers and human rights.

Two ASU vets in early May 1973 set out to join the armed defense organized by the American Indian Movement at Wounded Knee on the Pine Ridge Reservation in South Dakota. They had just left New York when the siege ended on May 8 and had to turn back.

Even while working with the ASU, Tom Soto became a leader in the Prisoner Solidarity Committee, a group supporting the rights of prisoners. Due to that work, in September 1971, he was invited by the rebellious prisoners at Attica§ in New York State to be on the observation committee along with people's lawyers and reporters. Soto was 100 percent in solidarity with the rebellion at Attica and was outraged when he saw how the state was preparing to slaughter the inmates.[10] In the 1980s, Soto was a key organizer of demonstrations that mobilized tens of thousands of people opposing U.S. interventions in Central America, especially El Salvador.

Julio Ghigliotti wrote for *Workers World* newspaper and later became a renowned columnist for various newspapers in San Juan, Puerto Rico. AMN Cal Bonner (ret.) also contributed many articles to *Workers World* before retiring to Mississippi.

After his discharge, Bill Roundtree took part in campaigns to win benefits for veterans. Then he became a workers' organizer for the Chicago and later the Detroit branch of Workers World Party, emerging as a national party leader. Once, running for Michigan governor in 1990, he got 28,000 votes.

Larry Holmes said this about how the Vietnam War and the ASU changed his life:

I was about 20 years old in 1972. The day that I got my draft notice in the mail was the worst day of my life up until that point. I was shocked, scared and angry. Today, almost half a century later, I have absolutely no regret over being called for that draft. It turned out to be a life-changing event.

Being drafted radicalized me. It forced me to learn about imperialism and capitalism and exploitation of working people by the ruling class and all the other real reasons young people are forced to die in wars for the rich. It was as a direct result of my being drafted that I became a communist.

From then on I tried as best as I could to dedicate my life to the struggle, not only for social and economic justice but ultimately for a better world where capitalism no longer existed. I have been fighting for a world where socialism based on equality, justice and the ownership of the means of production by the people is a reality.

I learned through the ASU about Workers World Party, a revolutionary communist organization that played a unique role in supporting anti-war GIs, in particular the ASU. I have been a member of Workers World for forty-three years, and since 2012 I have been privileged to serve as the party's First Secretary.[11]

∞

In the U.S. military of 1962-75, there were few GIs who were publicly LGBTQ. Persecution was rampant and LGBTQ GIs faced isolation and bashing along with official punishment. The Stonewall Rebellion that sparked the modern LGBTQ movement only took place in June 1969. Of course there were LGBTQ GIs. Some were brave soldiers, some even braver war resisters and some were both. This chapter honors them, along with the many others named and unnamed who showed their courage by battling the Pentagon.

Chapter Notes

* Wallace Terry, *Bloods. Black Veterans of the Vietnam War: An Oral History*, Ballantine Books, New York 1984, pp. 11-12. "I had left one war and came back and got into another one," one ex-Marine said of joining the Black Panther Party after his bad conduct discharge made it hard for him to find work as a veteran. "I liked their independence. The fact that they had no fear of the police. Talking about self-determination... . This was the first time that black people had stood up to the state since Nat Turner. I mean armed." Terry collected oral histories of twenty African-American soldiers, from draftees to officers, who served in Vietnam between 1965 and 1970. Every one describes experiencing racism in the military: ubiquitous Confederate flags, insults, denial of opportunities, harsher discipline. Alcohol and drug use was widespread in Vietnam. The assassination of Dr. Martin Luther King Jr. in April 1968 left them angry, feeling betrayed by the country they were fighting for. Stories of witnessing or participating in burning of villages, destruction of crops and animals, and murder, rape or torture of civilians were common. Several soldiers described being wounded or seeing comrades killed. Nightmares, flashbacks and other symptoms now recognized as PTSD dogged many long after discharge.

† The Young Lords Party was a revolutionary organization of Puerto Ricans in the United States that began in Chicago and spread in 1969 to New York and other cities. The organization published a newspaper, *Pa'lante (Forward)*. It fought for veterans' rights, and Vietnam veterans joined the Young Lords Party.

‡ The American Indian Movement's armed defense of Wounded Knee in South Dakota in a struggle for Native sovereignty began on February 27, 1973, and ended on May 8 of that year, when some 1,200 people were arrested. Some of the Native people participating with AIM were Vietnam veterans.

§ On September 9, 1971, prisoners at Attica in upstate New York seized nine guards and held the prison for four days, presenting a list of demands to the prison authorities. Governor Nelson Rockefeller sent heavily armed state police into the prison, where they slaughtered 32 prisoners and all nine guards. A book by Heather Anne Thompson, *Blood in the Water: The Attica Prison Uprising of 1971 and Its Legacy*, Penguin Random House, 2016, exposes the crimes of the state and the coverup of these crimes.

Chapter 32 Dempsey's Dilemma

"People say to me, 'You are not the Vietnamese. You have no jungles and swamps.' I reply, let our cities be our swamps and our buildings our jungles." — Iraqi Deputy Prime Minister Tariq Aziz to a researcher from England's Warwick University in the lead-up to the Iraqi War in October 2002.[1]

The Vietnam War smacked the Pentagon on the head. The generals found that keeping hundreds of thousands of troops in a conscript army in combat, even for one-year tours, with the media reporting daily casualties, created a big problem. Civilians rose up in mass opposition. Resistance erupted even within the military. LTC Robert Heinl made that clear in his June 1971 article in *Army Times*, "The Collapse of the Armed Forces." His analysis struck a chord among the Pentagon Brass, especially in the Army. By 1972 they were planning a professional army.

The Pentagon stopped drafting youth on January 27, 1973. That softened the youth rebellion. To defuse GI resistance, the Pentagon also ended many of the minor restrictions the GIs considered "chicken-shit," but which officers and NCOs considered a major part of discipline. They stopped insisting on short haircuts, ended a ban on mustaches, and avoided assigning make-work, like polishing boots and painting and repainting cabinets. Troops returning from Vietnam were returned early to civilian life — these combat veterans were so angry that keeping them in uniform was begging for trouble.

To ensure a supply of volunteers, the Pentagon raised salaries and promised job training. The military shifted its focus to high-tech weapons. The troops needed skills and the training was sold to recruits as job training. Whether the skills were easily transferable to civilian work was questionable, but GIs could re-up. It was a job.

More than before, women were encouraged to join. That step aroused hostility from the male-chauvinist officer corps. And it was accompanied by harassment and even rape of female recruits. But women were present even in combat units.

260

The question remained: Would the volunteer military, smaller and less subject to political resistance, still serve the interests of projecting U.S. power worldwide? That was the Pentagon's dilemma: choosing between sufficient power and political stability.

U.S. imperialist strategy had to take into account what became known as the "Vietnam Syndrome," the popular revulsion to massive land wars. U.S. administrations avoided such wars between 1975 and 1991. The USA confronted the Soviet Union in the nuclear arena or through proxy battles like the CIA war against a secular, progressive government in Afghanistan that began in 1979.

For smaller interventions, as in Central America, Washington provided arms, money and political support to local anti-communist armies, as in El Salvador, Nicaragua and Guatemala in the 1980s.

In 1982 the Pentagon landed 1,800 Marines in Lebanon. They shelled and killed thousands of people in Druze and Shiite villages. As a response, local forces bombed a Marine barracks in Lebanon in October 1983. The explosion killed 241 personnel. President Ronald Reagan ordered a quick withdrawal.

Two days later, the greatest military power on earth invaded tiny Grenada in the Caribbean. The media attention to this quick and overwhelming victory provided a cover for the decision to withdraw from Lebanon.

In 1986 the U.S. bombed Tripoli in Libya and in 1989 bombed and invaded Panama. An intervention in Somalia in 1992 led to the 1993 shoot-down of a U.S. helicopter in Mogadishu and the death of its crew. That battle, made infamous in the feature movie *Black Hawk Down*,[2] ended the U.S. mission.

These were brutal aggressions, but outside of Lebanon and Mogadishu, U.S. casualties were small or hidden and the interventions of short duration — especially compared to thirteen years of war against Vietnam.

The first reversion to massive warfare was against Iraq in January 1991. Washington wrangled the support of the United Nations for the war and mobilized a coalition of forces that included nearly all the countries in and outside the West Asian region with grievances against the Iraqi regime.

The Pentagon followed the doctrine associated with GEN Colin Powell, who was then chair of the Joint Chiefs of Staff. Powell pushed for massive intervention, supported by even more overwhelming air power, to destroy the Iraqi Army that had entered Kuwait. But he insisted this be done with a limited goal that the U.S. population understood — driving the Iraqi Army out of Kuwait. In the process, the U.S. inflicted heavy casualties on the Iraqi troops and the country's infrastructure. It was a war of short duration with little time for opposition to develop either in the U.S. or in the Army.

What made this easier for the U.S. was that in early 1991 the Soviet Union was on the verge of collapse, and the Pentagon no longer had to take into account either Soviet aid to Iraq or the possibility of Soviet intervention, either there or anywhere else.

At that time, the U.S. held back from trying to occupy Iraq and impose a puppet government. This tactic avoided inciting armed guerrilla resistance. Instead, George H. W. Bush's Republican administration pulled U.S. troops out of Iraq and imposed punishing sanctions against the Iraqi people. The sanctions caused more than a million Iraqi deaths, including a half-million Iraqi children, and weakened the Iraqi military and state structure.

With no U.S. casualties, this strategy avoided testing the "Vietnam Syndrome." It also left a U.S. takeover of Iraqi oil fields for a later date.

The next major U.S. intervention, in 1999, this time backed not by the U.N. but only by NATO, aimed at destroying what was left of Yugoslavia. Washington led a NATO air war, with the Democratic administration of Bill Clinton calling it a "humanitarian" intervention. Seventy-eight days of massive bombing of Serbia killed 3,000 civilians and convinced the Yugoslav government to capitulate.[3] This government allowed NATO to occupy the Kosovo province of Serbia, though the Yugoslav Army was still mostly intact.

Washington engineered a coup in September 2000 to overthrow the Yugoslav government, then led by the Socialist Party of Serbia, and replaced it with a government more conciliatory to the West. Subsequent regimes were more and more subservient. War and subversion destroyed multinational Yugoslavia and replaced it with a half-dozen mini-states, virtual colonies of the U.S. and Western Europe. Germany took the lead, establishing a relationship with the new states much like U.S. imperialism's with Central America.

A Professional Army & Wars of Aggression

This set the stage for the next level of U.S. aggressive wars, accelerated by the September 11, 2001, destruction of the World Trade Center buildings in New York and simultaneous attack on the Pentagon near Washington, D.C. The George W. Bush administration exploited the fear and anger these attacks aroused to mobilize a wave of patriotism that neutralized the "Vietnam Syndrome."

U.S. intelligence blamed the attack on individuals mainly from Saudi Arabia in the al-Qaeda organization. The Taliban regime in Afghanistan was hosting al-Qaeda and its leader, Osama bin Laden. The U.S. used the Taliban's hospitality as a pretext to quickly invade and occupy Afghanistan, where it has been mired for fifteen years, as of October 2016. The gang around Bush known as the neoconservatives — Vice President Dick Cheney, Secretary of Defense Donald Rumsfeld and Deputy Secretary of Defense Paul Wolfowitz — then put into effect their plans for the invasion and occupation of Iraq. Iraq had no role in 9/11, but it had a lot of high-quality petroleum.

To sell the war to the U.S. population, the Bush administration continually repeated the lie that Saddam Hussein's Iraqi government of Iraq was allied with al-Qaeda and possessed dangerous "weapons of mass destruction." Meanwhile, the neocon officials prepared to grab massive war plunder — petroleum and the reconstruction projects oil sales would finance — for what they said would be little cost. The military-industrial complex — the banks and oil industries that command U.S. society — looked forward to big profits.

In the first weeks of the war, even as the Iraqi Army was collapsing, the invasion force ran into resistance. *Workers World* newspaper's analyst Fred Goldstein wrote in April 2003, weeks after the invasion began:

> The U.S. military and Secretary of Defense Donald Rumsfeld promised a quick and relatively bloodless war in Iraq. Their plan was based upon a massive "shock and awe" campaign of initial bombing. ...
>
> The bombing took place. It produced only resistance. The most overpowering military machine in the history of humanity faced the heroic opposition of the Iraqi people from day one of the war.[4]

In his 2013 book, *Breach of Trust*,[5] Andrew Bacevich, a 23-year military veteran and professor of history and international relations at Boston University, concurred with Goldstein's words. COL Bacevich (ret.) outlined developments in the Pentagon post-Vietnam and, from the viewpoint of a loyal U.S. Army officer, graphically detailed the disastrous Afghanistan and Iraq experiences.

Goldstein's articles in April 2003, which some thought overestimated the Iraqis' ability to resist, turned out to be prophetic. The neocons' reliance on technology was failing. Bacevich wrote in 2013:

> If technology was changing the nature of warfare in ways that conferred advantages on U.S. forces, someone had forgotten to tell the insurgents. In Iraq, the enemy (or enemies) recovered, regrouped, continued to fight.[6]

In 1968 there were 3.5 million GIs in the U.S. Armed Forces; by 2003 there were only 1.4 million, that is, about 40 percent of the 1968 figure. The Pentagon had become dependent on outsourcing much of the logistics — trucking, food preparation and even some military operations — to private industry and mercenary fighters called "contractors." Bacevich wrote:

> As of 2010, contractors operating in Iraq and Afghanistan had some 260,000 employees on their payrolls — more than the total number of U.S. troops committed to those theaters.[7]

The neocons had promised a quick and cheap victory with little sacrifice to the U.S. population. But only months after the Pentagon's "shock and awe" air destruction of the Iraqi army and infrastructure, Iraqi guerrillas were inflicting casualties on the 150,000-plus U.S. troops in Iraq in 2003. Much of this resistance was organized by members of the Ba'ath Party, including army officers and other leading elements of Saddam Hussein's Iraq that the occupation regime had driven from their jobs and posts.

By the end of 2004, U.S. strategists were discussing how to use "death squad" strategies such as those implemented in Central America in the 1980s to aid the occupation.[8] During 2004 and 2005 a determined Iraqi resistance was killing and wounding U.S. troops. To avoid defeat in an urban guerrilla war, the U.S. occupation regime resorted to sowing and exacerbating ethnic and religious divisions among the Iraqi people.

Troops Begin to Protest

By 2005 individuals in the U.S. Armed Forces began to protest their role in the occupation of Afghanistan and especially Iraq. At first it was just one or two GIs refusing to go to Iraq. Though it never got to the stage of widespread AWOLs and desertions or mass refusals and fraggings, there were the beginnings of military resistance in 2005, just as there had been in Vietnam in 1966.

By the fall of 2006, Navy Seamen Jonathan Hutto and Javier Capella, Petty Officer Dave Rogers and Marine SGT Liam Madden were circulating the "Appeal for Redress," a statement offering a view of the Iraq occupation that differed from that of Bush's neocons. These GI leaders held a news conference on January 15 in Norfolk, Virginia, where twenty-five active duty GIs expressed growing opposition to the U.S. occupation of Iraq by publicly acknowledging that they had signed the appeal. Hutto wrote later that as of June 29, 2007, there were 1,173 signatures from troops who had spent at least one tour in Iraq. (See Appendix H and Hutto's book, Antiwar Soldier.[9])

Anti-war veteran organizations developed more rapidly than resistance within the military. The Iraq Veterans Against the War (IVAW) has played an important role in anti-war actions and declarations. IVAW and Veterans for Peace, for example, support whistleblower Chelsea Manning, who is serving thirty-five years in a military prison for exposing U.S. war crimes in Iraq. Manning, a soldier who worked in Information Technology, leaked electronic data that Wikileaks disseminated. Courage to Resist, another anti-war group, writes of Cian Westmoreland, a drone operator who spoke out in 2015 against "targeted assassinations."*

No Pentagon Victories

While no GI movement comparable to that of the Vietnam period had yet developed, it was still no easy war for the Pentagon. The U.S. is still in Afghanistan as of 2016, with no end in sight. There were as many as 150,000 U.S. troops in Iraq before the major withdrawal in 2011. As of late 2016, there may be as many as 5,000 U.S. troops fighting or training, not counting mercenary contractors.

Contrary to the Bush administration's promises of a cheap war, the Department of Defense has already spent $1.7 trillion for the two interventions in the last 15 years. It's possible that the total "war on terror" may cost as much as $5 trillion,[10] including post-war and Homeland Security costs. And the interventions continue, with no stable U.S. client state in either Afghanistan or Iraq.

In her book, *The Pentagon's Achilles' Heel — U.S. War: Profitable But Unwinnable*, U.S. anti-war leader Sara Flounders wrote the following about the U.S. withdrawal from Iraq in 2011:

> The scale of the U.S. defeat in Iraq can no longer be hidden, nor can the level of animosity towards the U.S. by the overwhelming majority of the Iraqi population. After the U.S. war and eight-year occupation of Iraq, the plans to dominate the region for the next generation are in complete retreat.

> Imperialism's position in Afghanistan is even worse.[11]

From a different viewpoint, Bacevich had a similar assessment of the wars, describing one whole section of his book with this blurb:

> How America's army after Vietnam, seeking reconciliation and relevance, became isolated from society and mired in unwinnable wars.[12]

The media reported "body counts" lower than in Vietnam. Technological and organizational changes kept more severely wounded troops alive. Also, the Pentagon controlled the media by "embedding" reporters in fighting units. Combat still left U.S. veterans suffering, off camera, especially those doing multiple combat tours. Bacevich summarized it this way:

> Troops beset with demons turned increasingly to alcohol and drugs. ... In 2011, the year the Iraq War ended, one out of every five active duty soldiers was on antidepressants, sedatives or other prescription drugs. The incidence of spousal abuse spiked, as did the divorce rate among military couples. Debilitating combat stress reached epidemic proportions. So did brain injuries. Soldier suicides skyrocketed.[13]

The Pentagon's top officer urged the Army to recruit enough so it could limit the combat assignments of its professional soldiers. This was GEN Martin Dempsey, who retired as head of the Joint Chiefs of Staff in 2015, who said in answer to a question about the efficacy of a professional army:

> But there was a period there when we increased the pace of deployments to fifteen months away and a year at home, and **we almost broke the force.** [Author's emphasis] Now we're back to where it's nine months deployed and, generally speaking, two years at home, and it feels to me that that pace is sustainable. So as long as we can keep the force operating at that pace, we can do it in perpetuity. ... But if we make deployments longer and allow less time at home, then I think we will have a huge problem.[14]

Dempsey also discussed the U.S.'s potential "enemies," which he listed as Russia, China, Iran, North Korea and the Islamic State. A war with any of the first four would need a large land army of just the type that the professional army strategy aims to avoid — for fear of reactivating the Vietnam Syndrome.

Dempsey's dilemma is this: While the creation of a smaller, volunteer military has isolated the troops from overall civilian society and allowed the executive to carry out wars without stirring up a major revolt in the military, it has also brought no clear victories.

Bacevich writes that having no conscription leaves the U.S. population out of the equation and allows a small group of political leaders to order wars while ignoring popular opinion. Bacevich advocates reinstating conscription in some form.

Seeds of a New Rebellion

In the first chapter of his book, *Capitalism at a Dead End*, Fred Goldstein wrote in 2012 of those factors driving the U.S. to use its military power for conquest and how the growth of technology influences military strategy:

> The Cold War military strategy has given way to a strategy of reconquering former colonial territories that were lost to imperialism in the 20th century due to liberation struggles and national, antiimperialist revolutions. It is no coincidence that George W. Bush targeted Iraq, Iran, and North Korea as his "axis of evil." In the recent period, Libya and Syria have also been targeted for regime change. ...
>
> The emphasis on high-tech and air warfare is also motivated by a fear of having to mobilize the working class for war at a time of economic decline in U.S. capitalism. A massive war means the draft. The draft and a protracted imperialist war would lead to a rebellion, which could easily go in an anti-capitalist direction.[15]

While a professional military seems much less likely to undergo the kind of change of consciousness discussed throughout this book, not only Goldstein and Flounders, but also Bacevich and Dempsey foresee situations that could change the equation. The main one is a massive land war that requires conscription, for example against Russia, China or even Iran or the DPRK.

The other, which neither Bacevich nor Dempsey mentions, is if the president orders federal troops to break workers' strikes or repress rebellions in communities of color inside the United States. Or turn fire hoses or guns against environmental militants.

Anyone wanting to build a just society should remain alert to such developments. As unlikely as it might seem at this moment in 2016, the rank-and-file soldiers, sailors, Marines and air force troops have a history of not only refusing to fire on their brothers and sisters, but of turning their guns around on the tiny group of wealthy rulers who have put everyone in harm's way.

Chapter Notes

* **Iraq Veterans Against the War (IVAW)** was "founded July 2004 at the annual convention of Veterans for Peace (VFP) in Boston to give a voice to the large number of active duty service people and veterans who are against this war, but are under various pressures to remain silent." Open to those who served after 2001. (ivaw.org) **Veterans For Peace** "was founded in 1985 by ten U.S. veterans in response to the global nuclear arms race and U.S. military interventions in Central America. ... VFP now has veteran and associate members in every U.S. state and several countries. VFP has over 120 chapters." (veteransforpeace.org) **Courage to Resist**, based in Oakland, California, and founded in 2007, "aims to provide political, emotional, legal, and material support to GI resisters and all military objectors critical of the U.S. government's current policies." (couragetoresist.org) A "targeted assassination" by a rocket fired from a drone is a murder of someone deemed an enemy by the U.S. executive power. There is no trial of the individual targeted and often others are killed along with the main target.

Appendix A Black Lives Matter

Racist Police Violence & the Need for Socialist Revolution

By Monica Moorehead, *Workers World Party candidate for president in 2016, (Workers World, Jan. 14, 2016, posted Jan. 5 on workers.org). Here are excerpts from an article showing how the struggle of the Black Lives Matter movement raises the question of the repressive state and how to fight it:*

Under capitalism, the predominant form of class rule, the police as a force cannot be reformed because the super-rich class needs this repressive force to protect its profits out of fear of rebellion by the masses against deteriorating conditions.

All the laws and the courts, which include the judges, prosecutors, grand juries and more, exist to protect the police no matter their criminal behavior. ...

While it is important for the progressive sectors to continue to show the utmost solidarity with the Black Lives Matter movement on a daily basis, especially when a police atrocity occurs, it is also the duty of the movement to help generalize the struggle. It is an important development that many young whites, attracted to the Occupy Movement, which was repressed several years ago by the police, have joined the ranks of the Black Lives Matter struggle.

The movement must agitate for disarming the police, which is part and parcel of the overall demand for community control of the police. It shows a level of understanding that the real aim of the police is not to protect and serve, but to terrorize and oppress the workers and oppressed as a class.

And just as the police cannot be reformed, neither can the capitalist system, which plunders the earth for resources, exploits workers' labor and destroys people's lives to make profits. The interests of the workers and bosses are on opposite ends of the spectrum, and therefore there can be no compromise or mediation, which is why the state is needed.

Appendix B Paris Commune

Excerpted from Chapter 3 of Lenin's *State and Revolution:**

The only "correction" Marx thought it necessary to make to the *Communist Manifesto* he made on the basis of the revolutionary experience of the Paris Commune.

The last preface to the new German edition of the *Communist Manifesto*, signed by both its authors, is dated June 24, 1872. In this preface the authors, Karl Marx and Frederick Engels, say that the program of the *Communist Manifesto* "has in some details become out-of-date," and they go on to say:

> "... One thing especially was proved by the Commune, viz., that 'the working class cannot simply lay hold of the ready-made state machinery and wield it for its own purposes'...."

The authors took the words that are in single quotation marks in this passage from Marx's book, *The Civil War in France.*

Thus, Marx and Engels regarded one principal and fundamental lesson of the Paris Commune as being of such enormous importance that they introduced it as an important correction into the *Communist Manifesto.* ...

Marx's idea is that the working class must break up, smash the "ready-made state machinery", and not confine itself merely to laying hold of it.

On April 12, 1871, i.e., just at the time of the Commune, Marx wrote to Kugelmann [a German gynecologist and member of the First International]:

> "If you look up the last chapter of my Eighteenth Brumaire, you will find that I declare that the next attempt of the French Revolution will be no longer, as before, to transfer the bureaucratic-military machine from one hand to another, but to *smash* it [Marx's italics—the original German is *zerbrechen*], and this is the precondition for every real people's revolution on the Continent. And this is what our heroic Party comrades in Paris are attempting."

The words, "to smash the bureaucratic-military machine", briefly express the principal lesson of Marxism regarding the tasks of the proletariat during a revolution in relation to the state.

Today, in 1917, [not only in continental Europe but] in Britain and America, too, "the precondition for every real people's revolution" is the *smashing*, the *destruction* of the "ready-made state machinery" (made and brought up to the "European," general imperialist, perfection in those countries in the years 1914-17).

Secondly, particular attention should be paid to Marx's extremely profound remark that the destruction of the bureaucratic-military state machine is "the precondition for every real *people's* revolution."

...In Europe, in 1871, the proletariat did not constitute the majority of the people in any country on the Continent. A "people's" revolution, one actually sweeping the majority into its stream, could be such only if it embraced both the proletariat and the peasants. These two classes then constituted the "people." These two classes are united by the fact that the "bureaucratic-military state machine" oppresses, crushes, exploits them. To *smash* this machine, *to break it up*, is truly in the interest of the "people," of their majority, of the workers and most of the peasants, is "the precondition" for a free alliance of the poor peasant and the proletarians, whereas without such an alliance democracy is unstable and socialist transformation is impossible.

As is well known, the Paris Commune was actually working its way toward such an alliance, although it did not reach its goal owing to a number of circumstances, internal and external. ...

2. What is to Replace the Smashed State Machine?

In 1847, in the *Communist Manifesto*, Marx's answer to this question was as yet a purely abstract one; to be exact, it was an answer that indicated the tasks, but not the ways of accomplishing them. The answer given in the *Communist Manifesto* was that this machine was to be replaced by "the proletariat organized as the ruling class," by the "winning of the battle of democracy."

Marx did not indulge in utopias; he expected the *experience* of the mass movement to provide the reply to the question as to the specific forms this organization of the proletariat as the ruling class would assume and as to the exact manner in which this organization would be combined with the most complete, most consistent "winning of the battle of democracy."

Marx subjected the experience of the Commune, meager as it was, to the most careful analysis in *The Civil War in France*. Let us quote the most important passages of this work.

Originating from the Middle Ages, there developed in the 19th century "the centralized state power, with its ubiquitous organs of standing army, police, bureaucracy, clergy, and judicature." With the development of class antagonisms between capital and labor, "state power assumed more and more the character of a public force organized for the suppression of the working class, of a machine of class rule. After every revolution, which marks an advance in the class struggle, the purely coercive character of the state power stands out in bolder and bolder relief." After the revolution of 1848-49, state power became "the national war instruments of capital against labor." The Second Empire [of Louis-Napoleon – JC] consolidated this.

"The direct antithesis to the empire was the Commune." It was the "specific form" of "a republic that was not only to remove the monarchical form of class rule, but [to impose] class rule itself."

What was this "specific" form of the proletarian, socialist republic? What was the state it began to create?

"The first decree of the Commune, therefore, was the suppression of the standing army, and the substitution for it of the armed people."

This demand now figures in the program of every party calling itself socialist. ...

"... From the members of the Commune downwards, the public service had to be done at *workmen's wages*. The privileges and the representation allowances of the high dignitaries of state disappeared along with the high dignitaries themselves.... Having once got rid of the standing army and the police, the instruments of physical force of the old government, the Commune proceeded at once to break the instrument of spiritual suppression, the power of the priests.... The judicial functionaries lost that sham independence... they were thenceforward to be elective, responsible, and revocable."

The Commune, therefore, appears to have replaced the smashed state machine "only" by fuller democracy: abolition of the standing army; all officials to be elected and subject to recall. But as a matter of fact this "only" signifies a gigantic replacement of certain institutions by other institutions of a fundamentally different type. ... It is still necessary to suppress the bourgeoisie and crush their resistance. This was particularly necessary for the Commune; and one of the reasons for its defeat was that it did not do this with sufficient determination. The organ of suppression, however, is here the majority of the population, and not a minority, as was always the case under slavery, serfdom, and wage slavery. And since the majority of people itself suppresses its oppressors, a 'special force" for suppression is no longer necessary! ..."

*V.I. Lenin, *State and Revolution*, 1917, excerpted from Chapter 3.

Appendix C Black Liberation at Fort Hood
Black GIs Stand Firm at 'Riot-Duty' Refusal Trial
By Ellen Catalinotto, excerpts (*Workers World*, Nov. 10, 1968).

Fort Hood, Oct. 25 [1968]. – The court-martial of six Black GIs who demonstrated along with 100 others against racism and riot control duty ended here tonight after four days. Two men were acquitted, two got sentences of three months hard labor and the others received bad conduct discharges. The sentences, considerably less than the maximum, were an indication of the Army's fear that harsher punishment might backfire and lead to open rebellion.

The convictions were the expected outcome of military "justice" so the real climax of the trial came when the convicted men took the stand and put the Army on trial for racism.

The six men on trial today – PFC Guy Smith, SGT Robert Rucker, SP4 Tollie Royal, PVT Ernest Frederick, PFC Ernest Bess and SP4 Albert Henry – were the first of 19 soldiers who face more serious general courts-martial, which can hand down maximum sentences of five years hard labor and a dishonorable discharge. Twenty-two others were tried by special court-martial, in which six months hard labor and a fine is the maximum penalty. Civilian lawyers for all the men were arranged for by the American Servicemen's Union so the accused would not have to depend on Army officers to "defend" them, as is customary.

Tension built up outside Building 2230 – Fort Hood Courtroom – this afternoon as the defendants, civilian supporters from the Committee for GI Rights, *The Bond* and the Oleo Strut [anti-war coffee house], and GI sympathizers awaited the verdict. The court (equivalent of a civilian jury) of 17 officers and noncommissioned officers – the latter are called "enlisted men" to pretend that the accused are before a jury of their peers – deliberated from 10:25 a.m. until 1:15 p.m. before declaring Smith, Frederick, Royal and Henry guilty of "willfully disobeying the lawful command of a superior officer." Rucker and Bess were acquitted of the same charge.

Throughout the four-day proceedings, Black and white GIs came to the courtroom to show their solidarity with the men on trial. They were subjected to constant harassment by the unsettled Brass for doing so. ...

After the verdict was returned, defense attorney Michael Kennedy of

274

the [National] Emergency Civil Liberties Committee called those convicted to the stand to testify on their own behalf.

SP4 Tollie Royal told the court he had studied biology in college for a year before beginning a two-year hitch in the Army. He was the outstanding soldier of his cycle in basic training and was assigned to the infantry. Royal is married and the father of three young sons.

Royal stood up and said with emotion, "I know I am innocent. ... Tell me how you found me guilty." The court was apparently stunned by this. Their eyes were averted and no one answered. After repeating his question, Royal was interrupted by the law officer (similar to a civilian judge), Col. Barry. Barry said the question was improper since the court was bound not to reveal how it reached its conclusion during secret deliberations, etc., etc.

SP4 Albert Henry took the stand next. Henry, 19, was wounded twice in Vietnam, once while pulling a wounded comrade out of fire despite an order to stay behind. He told the court, "I know I was innocent but you found me guilty and I will accept your punishment. ... This won't stop anything. What is going on at Fort Hood is not right."

PVT Frederick let the court have it. "I'm no angel and don't claim to be one," he said. (His record, which included such "crimes" as taking an unauthorized Christmas leave, had been read to the court.) He defended the demonstration by Black GIs and ended by saying, "I am not guilty."

PFC Guy Smith was the last to speak. He had spent two months in the stockade in Vietnam for refusing the order of a racist NCO who assigned him to guard duty when Smith was due for R&R after four months in the field. He told the court, "I demonstrated against Army policy here and in Vietnam. ... There is racism and prejudice here. General Bowles said he would do something about it, but nothing has been done. ... There are clubs in Killeen [the base town] where Black GIs can't go. ... The Black man has been held back because of his color. Your convictions add to the injustice." And he warned, "Too many Black people are taking too much now."

In summing up the testimony for mitigation and extenuation, attorney Kennedy said, "The Army's racist policies are on trial. Indicate that you will work to end racism in the Army."

Morale was high as the men left the courtroom, shaking hands and gathering around the jeep that was to take Henry to the stockade. The relatively lenient sentences were a victory – not of justice, but of the strength and determination of the Black soldiers not to be used against their brothers.

TURN THE GUNS AROUND

Appendix D-I

Order to the Garrison of Petrograd (March 1, 1917)

To the garrison of the Petrograd District. To all the soldiers of the Guard, army, artillery and fleet for immediate and precise execution, and to the workers of Petrograd for information.

The Soviet of Workers' and Soldiers' Deputies has decided:

a. In all companies, battalions, regiments, depots, batteries, squadrons and separate branches of military service of every kind and on warships immediately choose committees from the elected representatives of the soldiers and sailors of the above-mentioned military units.

b. In all military units which have still not elected their representatives in the Soviet of Workers' Deputies, elect one representative to a company, who should appear with written credentials in the building of the State Duma at ten o'clock on the morning of March 2.

c. In all its political demonstrations a military unit is subordinated to the Soviet of Workers' and Soldiers' Deputies and its committees.

d. The orders of the military commission of the State Duma are to be fulfilled only in those cases which do not contradict the orders and decisions of the Soviet of Workers' and Soldiers' Deputies.

e. Arms of all kinds, as rifles, machine-guns, armored automobiles and others must be at the disposition and under the control of the company and battalion committees and are not in any case to be given out to officers, even upon their command.

f. In the ranks and in fulfilling service duties soldiers must observe the strictest military discipline; but outside of service, in their political, civil and private life, soldiers cannot be discriminated against as regards those rights, which all citizens enjoy. Standing at attention and compulsory saluting outside of service are especially abolished.

g. In the same way the addressing of officers with titles: Your Excellency, Your Honor, etc., is abolished and is replaced by the forms of address: Mr. General, Mr. Colonel, etc. Rude treatment of soldiers of all ranks, and especially addressing them as "thou,"* is forbidden; and soldiers are bound to bring to the attention of the company committees any violation of this rule and any misunderstandings between officers and soldiers.

This order is to be read in all companies, battalions, regiments, marine units, batteries and other front and rear military units.

* Familiar form used for intimates or in an insulting way to subordinates.

Source: https://www.marxists.org/history/ussr/government/1917/03/01.htm

Appendix D-II

Ultimatum From Sailors of North Sea Fleet, Germany
November 1918

1. The release of all those arrested and all political prisoners.

2. Complete freedom of speech and press.

3. Abolition of censorship of sailors' letters.

4. Appropriate treatment of the sailors by their officers.

5. Sailors return to ships and barracks without punishment.

6. Prohibition under all conditions that the fleet should set sail.

7. Take all preventive steps to avoid bloodletting.

8. Withdrawal from Kiel of all troops not in the Kiel garrison.

9. Sailors' Council has the authority to protect private (personal) property.

10. When off-duty there is no recognition of superior officers (no saluting, saying "sir").

11. Unlimited personal freedom for all enlisted men off duty.

12. Officers who accept the authority of the sailors' Council are welcomed; the others are dismissed without claim to compensation.

13. Members of the Council are exempt from any service.

14. All future orders must be countersigned by the Council.

All these demands must be recognized as general military orders.

From Kuttner, p. 17. Repeated here for comparison with ASU demands.

Appendix D-III

Program of the American Servicemen's Union

WE DEMAND*

1. The right to disobey illegal orders — like orders to fight in the illegal imperialist war in Southeast Asia.

2. Election of officers by vote of the rank and file.

3. An end to saluting and sir-ing of officers.

4. The right of Black, Latin and other national minority servicemen and women to determine their own lives free from the oppression of racist whites. No troops to be sent into Black, Latin or other national minority communities.

5. *An end to the systematic attempt by officers and NCO's to create prejudice against women, both in and out of the military. An end to the prostitution and rape of Vietnamese and all other women, which is conducted and incited by the military. We demand an end to the degradation of women, and their treatment as sexual objects rather than equal human beings.*

6. *No troops to be used against anti-war demonstrators.*

7. *No troops to be used against workers on strike.*

8. Rank and file control over court-martial boards.

9. The right of free political association.

10. Wages for rank-and-file enlisted men and women adequate to maintain them and all dependents at a decent standard of living. Adequate housing for dependents, supplied by the military. Free day care centers for dependent children, controlled by their parents. Free and decent medical care for rank-and-file dependents, equal to that of officers' dependents.

11. The right of collective bargaining.

12. *Full employment for veterans of both sexes; adequate employment benefits to last until such employment is provided. Special measures to provide decent jobs for Black, Puerto Rican and other national minority veterans. Free medical, dental and hospital care, and free education benefits or job training with financial support. Abolition of all "less-than-honorable" discharges.*

*Demands in italics were added to the original eight demands, whose wording was also altered to reflect new developments in the struggle from 1967 to 1973, when the twelve demands above were published in *The Bond*.

Appendix E Pentagon at the Crossroads

Excerpts From Hawai'i Resistance's 'Crossroads Sanctuary' Chronology*

August 6, 1969 Following a noon press conference, Buffy Parry entered sanctuary at Crossroads Church, ending what he termed his complicity with the U.S. military and its crimes against humanity. ...

August 9. 1969 John Catalinotto, national ASU representative, arrived in Honolulu and joined evening planning session for the march.

August 10, 1969 Celebration of Life, Love and Revolution held at Crossroads Church, led by Rev. Bob Warner. Following the service, some 350 to 400 people, including many GIs, participated in the Walk for Peace from Kapiolani to Ala Moana Park, a distance of three miles. Led by Buff Parry, the march stretched several long blocks through heavily populated Waikiki. Across the street, thirteen Young Americans for Freedom zealots countermarched for their beliefs. A rally followed at Ali Moana Park, featuring folk music and the statements of concerned GIs. Buffy and John Catalinotto gave keynote speeches. ... Army Spec. 4, Dan Overstreet, AWOL from R & R leave from Vietnam, rose to state his determination not to return to the war zone and his intent to join the sanctuary. Marine private Vince Ventimiglia, military police undercover agent assigned by the military to undermine the march and apprehend the AWOLs, instead announced his decision to join them in sanctuary. Navy airman Eric Harms, foregoing the crime of continued silence, declared his intent to join the sanctuary. Navy Seaman John Veal, Army Pfc. Bob Schultz, and Navy Seaman Howard Pallaske also announced their active "retirement" from the armed services and their entry into sanctuary. Seaman Apprentice Bob Matheson joined these seven back at Crossroads Church later that night and brought the total to eight men in sanctuary.

August 11, 1969 Marine Cpl. Lou Jones, Jr., Marine Pfc. Curt Trendell, and Ron Allen, stationed with the Army in Vietnam, entered the sanctuary. Community celebrated joyfully by dancing in the courtyard. August 12, 1969 Pvt. Jim Morris declared his active retirement from the Marine Corps and entered sanctuary. ... Black Marines at Kaneohe Marine Corps Air Station rebelled against prejudicial job assignments and racist harassment by white Brass and MPs. Crossroads GIs issued statement in support of just black grievances. Support community people demonstrated outside Kaneohe and later received calls of approval from black military leaders.

TURN THE GUNS AROUND

August 14, 1969 Rally at U.H. campus, 12:00 noon; Dan Overstreet and Lou Jones risked apprehension to speak with U.H. students and faculty and garner support. Matthew Biggerstaff and Alan Porter, both from the army, and Randy Reese of the Navy joined the sanctuary, bringing the number of men in sanctuary to 15. Church officials and members expressed concern about the "carnival nature" of the sanctuary. ...

August 15, 1969 Oscar Kelley (Navy), Bryan Bohannon (Army) and Art Parker (Navy) joined the sanctuary. Student-Faculty and Univ. Democrats support the sanctuary.

August 17, 1969 The eighteen GIs in sanctuary received a standing ovation from the 350 people who attended Crossroads Church Sunday morning. Mike Waters and Ad Hoc Committee formed, including 6 Church members, 3 GIs, and 2 members of the Resistance community. Ultimatum from Executive Board of Church establishing limits on the support community and declaring a 3-day moratorium created a crisis situation, with the Church and the Resistance support community at odds. Church policy of remaining "autonomous" but becoming "involved", and being "with" the men.

September 6, 1969 - The social event of the movement of 1969 took place as the Sanctuary Community celebrated the marriage of Resistance leader John Witeck, former East-West Center grantee and Lucy Hashizume. ... All the GIs acted as best man along with Wayne Hayashi, who just returned from a Far East trip. Lucy brought the house down when she asked, "Will you accept me and my rice as I accept you and your potatoes."
In the gray light of the Hawaiian dawn on September 12, 1969, military police, in the tradition of Hitler's SS, descended upon the Church of the Crossroads and the Unitarian Church of Honolulu to wipe out the Sanctuaries where men of conscience had come to publicly protest the War in Vietnam and the injustice of the military system. The sleeping men were caught up in the swiftness of that injustice as 40 armed MP's swept through the Freeway Coffeehouse building into what the GIs had moved the night before to comply with city zoning regulations.

* Hawai'i Resistance anti-war movement published a chronology of the *Crossroads Sanctuary*. Fall of 1969. Text is left in original style.

Appendix F Women's Liberation

Anti-Women Propaganda: How the Brass and Their Flunkies Use It Against Us

By SP4 Tom Chase (ret.) and SP4 Steve Geden (ret.), in *The Bond*, December 24, 1971.

Remember in basic training, one of the worst insults that a sergeant could make towards a man involved some kind of reference to women? 'You sound like a bunch of old women!' "You're nothing but a bunch of p——-s!" We heard this as often as we showed any sign of hesitation, or what they considered "weakness." One officer in basic liked to make us sing "Jody's Got Your Girl and Gone," songs designed to make us feel hostile and distrustful of our wives or girlfriends. At the rifle range we were told by the range NCOs to "squeeze the trigger like you squeeze your girl's t—s," separating sex from love and relating it to violence.

WACs (women in the Women's Army Corps) are singled out for special abuse by lifers, especially in basic training. According to the warped officers, a WAC is a woman "who couldn't make it" with men on the outside. ... Lesbian baiting them, and calling them "pigs."

We must reject this trash....The reason for enlisting: no skills, no jobs, no money, a bad family situation, the outrageous lies of a true pig — the recruiting NCO. These are the reasons why both men and women enlist...

The Brass say they are trying to make us into highly-trained and disciplined fighting men. The truth is that every step of the way, lifers and officers try to jam filthy anti women bullshit down our throats. Take a look through "PS," the monthly maintenance magazine put out by the Army. In this official publication, you can see...Vietnamese women portrayed as a 'local purchase item.' ... This is racism and anti-woman propaganda wrapped into one sick lesson. And it's the officers and NCOs who teach these lessons.

We have each spent a year in Vietnam, and we know for a fact that in some units, rape, torture and murder of Vietnamese women and children is SOP [standard operating procedure].

Anti-woman prejudice is not simply a matter of the attitude of certain officers and NCOs. It is a conscious policy of the high-ranking generals who run the military. Just as the military pursues a deliberate racist policy to keep whites divided from Blacks and other national minority peoples, so also does it pursue a deliberate sexist policy, that is, a policy of male superiority, to keep men and women divided. This policy is designed to keep male GIs from uniting with their equally oppressed sisters called "dependents," and their sisters within the military. When combined with racism, the result of this anti-woman policy is genocide — like thousands of Vietnamese women being raped, tortured and murdered.

We must not play into the hands of the Brass. We must realize that any dehumanization of women... is doing what the Brass want.

We demand an end to all anti-woman propaganda, especially in basic training. We demand that officers and NCOs stop inciting, encouraging and ordering us, rank-and-file GIs, to commit crimes against women.

We must also understand that we, as men, will have to start now to change our attitude and actions. By our changes, we can start to build a trust and unity among brothers and sisters in the military and military dependents. Only the unity we build ensures the downfall of the Brass and their flunky NCOs.

∞

The response from readers was thoughtful and positive. Carlos wrote in the January 27, 1972 issue:

I am working as hard as ever for the union. I have been talking to all I meet on the ASU...I must confess to being a bit of a sexist, although I wasn't consciously aware of it until I read [in the] Bond on the training of young men in boot camp. Yes, they do make one feel very anti-female...I had to readjust my thinking as to women's role in the movement, as have we all, as to their value as human beings in our eyes.

Legalized prostitution—Brass's new weapon against GIs and Vietnamese Women

By PVT John Lewis (ret.) in *The Bond*, January 27, 1972.

[As] in all their wars, the Brass's interest is to make sure we GIs remain their willing tools. To do this, the Brass will use any and every means at their disposal to keep GIs ready to fight and kill whenever and wherever they issue the order.

In Vietnam, the means the Brass have used—which the American Servicemen's Union denounces as their crimes—are numerous. They have used heroin, when it suited their purposes. They have used body counts and prizes for the GIs who killed the most Vietnamese, in order to totally dehumanize the Vietnamese people in the eyes of GIs. They have always used racism, to stir up race hatred among white GIs in order to prevent the white and nonwhite GIs from uniting to get the Brass off their backs. And they have always used the oppression of women.

In South Vietnam, a country of about 17 million people, over 400,000 women are now prostitutes. These women have had no choice. In order to survive over the course of the last decade that the U.S. has occupied, exploited, and destroyed their country, they have been forced to become prostitutes.

The U.S. military, through the use of devastating bombs and defoliants, has ruined, in many cases forever, the lands of Vietnam and has caused large number of Vietnamese, totaling in the millions, to leave their homeland and move to population centers. In most cases, the people were forced to move, just as hundreds of thousands were recently forced from I Corps in northern South Vietnam to the Mekong Delta. The economy of South Vietnam is basically agricultural; so once the land is ruined or the people forced out, they must find another means of living.

South Vietnam is virtually a colony of the U.S. There is an occupying force of over 200,000 men, counting the ships off the coast.... all the economic aspects of the society are controlled by the U.S. military directly or by the large U.S. monopolies that have factories or other business interests there. So the Vietnamese people must either work for the U.S. military directly, or work for some U.S. corporation, or, as in the case of over 400,000 South Vietnamese women, they must be prostitutes in order to live.

The Vietnamese women can be blamed in no way for being prostitutes. If they could find another way to feed, clothe, and shelter themselves and their families, they would take it. The answer to this problem for the entire Vietnamese people is that the U.S. military must leave their country at once. Only when the people of Vietnam are free to solve their own problems will prostitution stop. There is no prostitution in North Vietnam, and there won't be any in the South either after the U.S. imperialists leave and the people take over their government.

The American Servicemen's Union goes on record unequivocally denouncing the Brass's use of legalized prostitution of Vietnamese women as another in the Brass's long list of crimes against the Vietnamese people. Only through the total liberation of their country will all the Vietnamese people be able to have a decent life.

These two articles are referred to in Chapter 24 as part of the ASU's effort to combat male chauvinism and misogyny imposed by the Brass on the GIs.

Appendix G-1 Portugal and Africa

Amílcar Cabral's January 23, 1963 Message to

SOLDIERS, SERGEANTS AND OFFICERS OF THE PORTUGUESE COLONIAL ARMY*

The hour of truth has arrived, the hour in which you will see the proof of all that our Party announced to you in advance with the humanitarian intention to help you defend your lives against the criminal lies and orders of your colonialist masters.

In this hard time, one that finds our people filled with hopes and confidence, and you overcome with desperation and doubt, we want to repeat what we have already told you:

Our people, who will fight until victory for our country's independence, is no enemy of the Portuguese people. You are the sons of the Portuguese people, but the colonialists are using you as weapons to kill our people, to attempt to stop us from being free people and masters of our own land.

We want peace, freedom and cooperation between human beings and among all the peoples. But for that reason and because of that, we must end Portuguese colonialism on our land, we must eliminate all the obstacles to our national independence, we fight and we will eliminate all those who, with arms in hand, undertake a futile attempt to prevent the liberation of our people.

PORTUGUESE SOLDIERS, SERGEANTS AND OFFICERS

You know, everyone knows – and first of all the Portuguese government itself knows – that the colonialist cause is an unjust and lost cause. It also knows that no force in the world will be able to stop the liberation of our people from the colonial yoke.

We are conscious of this truth: we shall battle courageously against you and we will fight until victory. Experience has already shown you that all the children of our lands – young and old, women and men, including the young children – are ready to give their lives for freedom, for progress and for the happiness of our people.

And you – Portuguese soldiers, officers and sergeants, youth of Portugal, the hope of your people – why and for what are you dying on our land?

Among the dozens of your compatriots who have already died on our territory – and soon there will be hundreds and they may become thousands – look at the case of the soldiers No. 834/59 Veríssimo GODINHO RAMOS and No. 224/60, Fernando Cristiano PEREIRA; of First Corporal Francisco MOREIRA and of Corporal Abílio MONTEIRO de BRITO. Many of you will remember these four youths, the hopes of their families who, by the way, live a life of suffering and sorrow in Portugal.

Like all of you, they were corralled, deceived and forced to come to our land to carry out a war of colonial domination against us. Despite our advice, they committed with impunity, during a long period, the worst crimes against our people. They tortured, killed, massacred and burned. They used at will, against our defenseless population, your modern and heavy arms, certain there would be no response.

But today, under the direction of our great party and guided by its best children, our people also have powerful modern arms – and they get more every day – to defend themselves against the crimes of the colonialists and to develop our struggle and to win freedom.

Why did your compatriots listed above die, along with many others? Why the mourning and unhappiness in so many households, especially in so many poor households? Why?

Because your colonialist masters deceived you and continue to deceive you. Because your government and your military superiors act against the interests of your people and force you to take up arms to battle our desire for freedom, to destroy our people who, like all peoples, want to be the ruler of their own land and master of their destiny. Because – and I have to tell the whole truth – you accepted and continue to accept the shameful and ignoble role of unconscious instrument in the service of colonial oppression and repression, instead of acting as courageous and aware human beings at the service of the true interests of your people.

For what did your compatriots die, for what are you continuing to run the permanent risk of dying on our land? For what?

To serve the exploitive and criminal interests of the C.U.F., of the Commercial Overseas Company, of the National Overseas Bank – of the Portuguese colonialists and of their imperialist masters. To serve, in the end, the interests of some few rich families in Portugal, which have nothing at all to do with the interests of your families and your people.

APPENDICES

PORTUGUESE SOLDIERS, SERGEANTS AND OFFICERS

You know that your people, who must fight for freedom and democracy on their own land, need your help. Your families, who for the most part belong to the poor classes of Portugal, fervently desire your return, to guarantee their future – and the future of your fathers, mothers, sisters, fiancées, sons and daughters. It is indispensible that you act.

As youths, you have a sacred mission to carry out in your homeland, which is to struggle in order to construct a future worthy of your people, who still live in misery, in ignorance and suffering.

As conscious human beings, you have the right to unmask the colonial lie, to disobey the impositions of an unjust and lost cause, to help humanity to build a world of freedom, of peace and of social welfare.

As Portuguese and as patriots, you have the duty to do all you can to preserve the possibility of a friendly cooperation between the peoples of Africa and of Portugal, between our people and yours, based on the equality of rights, of duties and of benefits.

SOLDIERS, SERGEANTS AND OFFICERS OF THE PORTUGUESE COLONIAL ARMY

The hour of truth has arrived, the hour of great decisions.

There is still time to make a correct, conscious and courageous decision, to act in your own interest and in the interest of your people.

Because of this – and because we have firmly decided to carry out our duties as conscious human beings, as African patriots – we address once again this message to you of fraternity, of understanding, of encouragement and with wishes of a long life in your homeland, at the service of your people.

REFUSE TO SERVE AS INSTRUMENTS OF COLONIALISM, DISOBEY THE ORDER TO TAKE UP ARMS AGAINST THE FREEDOM AND INDEPENDENCE OF A PEACEFUL PEOPLE!

BE COURAGEOUS, REFUSE TO FIGHT OUR PEOPLE!

DON'T WILLINGLY SERVE AS WATCHDOGS OF THE UNJUST INTERESTS OF C.U.F. AND THE OTHER COLONIALIST MONOPOLIES; THESE ARE NOT YOUR INTERESTS NOR THOSE OF YOUR PEOPLE!

DON'T WILLINGLY ACCEPT THE LOT OF YOUR COMPATRIOTS WHO HAVE FALLEN INGLORIOUSLY AT THE SERVICE OF AN INJUST AND IR- REMEDIABLY LOST CAUSE!

REVOLT AGAINST YOUR FASCIST AND COLONIALIST RULERS WHO ORDER YOU TO YOUR DEATH!

SHOW THAT YOU ARE CONSCIOUS HUMAN BEINGS COMMITTED TO SERVING THE TRUE INTERESTS OF YOUR PEOPLE!

FOLLOW THE EXAMPLE OF YOUR COURAGEOUS COMRADES WHO RE- FUSED TO FIGHT ON OUR LAND, WHO REVOLTED AGAINST THE CRIM- INAL ORDERS OF YOUR LEADERS, WHO COOPERATE WITH OUR PARTY OR WHO ABANDONED THE COLONIAL ARMY AND FOUND IN OUR MIDST THE BEST RECEPTION AND FRATERNAL AID!

DEMAND YOUR IMMEDIATE RETURN TO REJOIN YOUR FAMILIES IN PORTUGAL!

LONG LIVE PEACE, FRIENDSHIP AND COOPERATION AMONG ALL PEO- PLES!

LONG LIVE THE STRUGGLE FOR NATIONAL AND SOCIAL LIBERATION OF ALL OPPRESSED PEOPLES!

LONG LIVE THE AFRICAN PARTY OF INDEPENDENCE!

DOWN WITH PORTUGUESE COLONIALISM AND ALL ITS LACKEYS!

* Mário de Andrade, coordinator, *Collected Works of Amílcar Cabral (vol. II)/Unity and Struggle/Revolutionary practice*, Seara Nova, Lisbon, 1977, pp. 23-25. Reissued Cabo Verde: Amílcar Cabral Foundation (*Selected Works of Amílcar Cabral*).

Carlos Lopes Pereira, former editor of the magazine, *O Militante*, and who had been a member of the Secretariat of the Cabral's party, the African Party for the Inde- pendence of Guinea and Cape Verde (PAIGC) in Bissau, Guinea, sent Cabral's texts for translation and publication. Pereira wrote: "Amilcar Cabral (aka Abel Djassi, his underground name) wrote these texts in Portuguese that the PAIGC distributed in the form of leaflets. Most of it was reproduced in the newspaper *Libertação*, the PAIGC organ established on December 1, 1960."

Cabral's appeal was translated by the author and left in the style of the original.

288

Appendix G-II Vietnam Liberation Front

Carrying out the policy of the South Vietnam National Front for Liberation and the Provisional Revolutionary Government of the Republic of the South Vietnam towards anti-war GI's, captured or wounded American servicemen on the battlefields, the Command of the South Vietnam People's Liberation Armed Forces on April 26, 1971 ordered its officers and men:

1. Not to attack those anti-war U.S. servicemen-individuals or groups- who demand repatriation, oppose orders of the U.S. Commanders, and abstain from hostile actions against the People's Liberation Armed Forces, from supporting or coming to the rescue of the Saigon army, encroaching on freedoms, property and lives of the South Vietnamese people, interfering in their internal affairs, hindering their struggles against the Thieu-Ky-Khiem clique.

2. To give proper treatment to those U.S. servicemen- individuals or groups – who in action refrain from opposing the People's Liberation Armed Forces, and those who carry with them anti-war literature.

3. To stand ready to extend aid and protection to those anti-war U.S. servicemen who have to run away for their oppositions, to harsh discipline and to discriminatory policy in the army.

4. To welcome and give good treatment to those U.S. servicemen who cross over to the South Vietnam people and the People's Liberation Armed Forces; to stand ready to help them go home or seek asylum in another country if requested by them.

5. To welcome and to grant appropriate rewards to those U.S. servicemen – individuals or groups- who support the National Front for Liberation and the Provisional Revolutionary Government of the Republic of South Vietnam.

The Command of the South Vietnam People's Liberation Armed Forces calls on the officers and men in all services of the U.S. army in South Vietnam to make their best efforts to demand their repatriation, to refuse to go submissively to a useless death in the unjust war in Vietnam and Indochina, to try by every means to enter into contact with and to inform the South Vietnam people and the People's Liberation Armed forces of their anti-war actions in order to receive assistance.

THE COMMAND OF THE SOUTH VIETNAM PEOPLE'S LIBERATION ARMED FORCES*

* The Bond, May 26, 1971. "Vietnamese Make Peace Offer to GIs," p. 1.

TURN THE GUNS AROUND

Appendix H Dempsey's Dilemma

Active-duty GIs speak out on Iraq war*

By John Catalinotto

Norfolk, Va. [Jan. 15, 2007]

Twenty-five active duty GIs reflected the growing opposition to the U.S. occupation of Iraq at a news conference Jan. 15 in Norfolk, Va., by publicly acknowledging that they had signed the "Appeal for Redress," a statement offering a view of the Iraq occupation that differs from that of President George W. Bush. The appeal has been circulating since last October.

Organizers had chosen the date to connect their appeal with the legacy of Rev. Martin Luther King Jr.'s struggle for justice and peace. Some 35 active-duty troops and reservists, including Iraq veterans and other veterans, and the day's speakers filled the stage at the Unitarian Universalist Church. Banners around the walls of the church greeted the 100 people filling it, including one banner with the message: "Support the troops; listen to them."

And those who came, along with Norfolk's TV stations and some national and international media, listened. They heard, if they listened carefully, that a new movement of active-duty troops was starting to speak with its own voice. They heard that those in the civilian anti-war movement were pledging to support this new GI movement and to welcome it.

Some of the appeal's drafters and early organizers spoke out at the meeting and clarified their position with a four-hour series of nonstop interviews with television and press media and documentary filmmakers. These active-duty troops included Navy Seamen Jonathan Hutto and Javier Capella, Petty Officer Dave Rogers and Marine Sergeant Liam Madden.

Hutto and Capella are stationed on the aircraft carrier Theodore Roosevelt with a complement of more than 3,000 officers and enlisted sailors stationed in Norfolk. Hutto, who grew up in Atlanta under the strong influence of that city's movement for civil rights, helped focus the conference on Martin Luther King and his opposition to the Vietnam War.

Madden, who is stationed at the Marine base in Quantico, Va., and has only a week of active duty left in his contract, spoke about the need to pay attention to King's words more than one day a year. He read the Appeal for Redress, which the movement drafted in such a way that active-duty troops have the legal right to sign, protected by the Military Whistleblower Protection Act (DOD directive 7050.6).

The simple statement makes it clear that "staying in Iraq will not work and is not worth the price. It is time for U.S. troops to come home." Madden added, "Not one more of my brothers should die for a lie. This is not politics. It is our generation's call to conscience."

Hutto said that among the 1,029 signatures that the group has verified, 35 are from troops in Iraq.

Among the main supporters were at least a dozen members of the Iraq Veterans Against the War (IVAW). This group had up to now focused on organizing returning veterans of the Iraq occupation and getting them involved in the anti-war movement. The IVAW now also uses the appeal to reach out to active-duty personnel.

Jabbar Magruder of IVAW, still active in the National Guard in California, said he would be joining Madden and others on Jan. 16 to meet with Dennis Kucinich and other representatives in Congress and present the signatures to them. Nancy Lessin of Military Families Speak Out and Michael McPherson of Veterans for Peace also had representatives supporting the new active-duty movement.

Phil Wilayto of the Virginian Anti-War Network (VAWN) spoke, along with Fabian Bouthillette of the Military Project in New York, which has been reaching out to National Guard troops at armories in the city.

"We must listen to the men and women" who are in the military and who are taking the courageous move of speaking out against the war, said David Cortwright, author of the book "Soldiers in Revolt." A year earlier, Hutto had read this book about the GI movement during the Vietnam War, which inspired him to begin the Appeal for Redress.

Before the conference ended, Hutto pointed out that before King made his famous April 1967 anti-war speech from Riverside Church in New York, King himself had come to a realization: if he were going to advise non-violence as a tactic in the movement for civil rights, he would have to start by insisting that the U.S. government—"the greatest purveyor of violence"—desist from its warlike foreign policy.

Hutto then introduced three active-duty GIs who read portions of King's April 1967 talk.

* _Workers World,_ Jan. 25, 2007, online at workers.org on Jan 20, 2007.

ENDNOTES

Prologue 1
[1] http://www.latinorebels.com/2015/03/15/the-soldiers-of-st-patrick/
[2] Gill H. Boehringer, "Black American Anti-Imperialist Fighters in the Philippine American War," Sept. 15, 2009, blackagendareport.com.
[3] Richardson, *The GI's Handbook on Military Injustice*, p. 39.
[4] Monica Moorehead, "At Standing Rock: 'We're not going anywhere,'" *Workers World*, Dec. 15, 2016, p. 1.
[5] Ibid.

Prologue 2
[1] *Pentagon Papers*.
[2] Lt. Col. Robert Debs Heinl, "The Collapse of the Armed Forces," in *Armed Forces Journal*, June 7, 1971. An October 2009 article in the Naval Institute blog called the 27-year Marine veteran Heinl "one of the finest writers of military literature ever to emerge from the profession of arms in the United States" and "a contributor to the *Encyclopaedia Britannica, The National Geographic*, other professional journals, and author of a history of the *Marine Corps, Soldiers of the Sea* (U.S. Naval Institute, Annapolis, Maryland) and *Victory at High Tide*."
[3] Heinl, "Collapse."

Introduction
[1] Pinto, *Soldiers and Strikers, pp. 40-43.*
[2] Chin, *Haiti, a Slave Revolution,* for a full discussion of this revolution.
[3] Lembcke, *The Spitting Image,* see for a discussion of this Big Lie.
[4] digitalcommons.lasalle.edu/cgi/viewcontent.cgi?article=1017&context=vietnamgeneration

Chapter 1
[1] Andy Stapp, "Letter From 3 GIs," *Workers World*, Feb. 6, 1967,
[2] Richard Wheaton, letter November 2014, resent by email to author, Jan. 19, 2016.
[3] Terry Klug, Andy Stapp, John Catalinotto and Ellen Catalinotto, December 2007 video interview ASU veterans organized for Derek Seidman's doctoral dissertation.
[4] Stapp, *Up Against the Brass,* pp. 52-53.
[5] Richard Wheaton, letter.
[6] Tucker, *Encyclopedia of the Vietnam War.*
[7] United States Dept. of Defense, *Annual Report, 1968,* p. 66.
[8] Russell F. Weigley, *New York Times Book Review,* April 11, 1993. In review of *Working-Class War: American Combat Soldiers and Vietnam,* by Christian Appy, Weigley writes: "Appy reminds us of the disturbing truth that some 80 percent of the 2.5 million enlisted men who served in Vietnam—out of 27 million men who reached draft age during the war—came from working-class and impoverished backgrounds."
[9] Eddie Oquendo letter, November 2014.

Chapter 2

[1] Stapp, *Up Against*, p. 72.
[2] Stapp, *Up Against*, p. 73.
[3] Richard Wheaton letter, November 2014.
[4] United States Census Bureau.
[5] Stapp, *Up Against*, p. 96.
[6] Dave Zirin, "Don't Remember Muhammad Ali as a Sanctified Sports Hero. He Was a Powerful, Dangerous Political Force," *Los Angeles Times*, June 4, 2016, Op Ed.

Chapter 3

[1] Stapp, *Up Against*, p. 102.
[2] Deirdre [Griswold] Stapp, "Anti-War Soldiers Solid at PVT Stapp's Hearing," *The Bond*, Feb. 18, 1968.
[3] Ibid.
[4] Ibid.
[5] Richard Wheaton, "About the Author," *Court Martial Turned Around*, by Bill Smith.
[6] Zinn, *People's History*, "The Impossible Victory – Vietnam," p. 483.

Chapter 5

[1] Marx, *The Civil War in France*, from Frederick Engels' 1891 Introduction.
[2] http://history-world.org/franco_prussian_war.htm
[3] Ibid. "On October 27 Marshal Bazaine surrendered at Metz with 173,000 men."
[4] Marx, *The Civil War in France, pp. 50-52*.
[5] Marx, *The Civil War in France*, Introduction, p. 7.
[6] *Le journal officiel de Paris pendant la Commune*, leaflet of March 10, 1871.
[7] Jellinek, *Paris Commune*, p. 113.
[8] Maclellan, *Rebel Lives - Louise Michel*, pp. 34-35.
[9] March, *History of the Paris Commune*, p. 103.
[10] March, *History of the Paris Commune*, p. 104.
[11] Jellinek, *Paris Commune*, p. 115.
[12] Lenin, *Paris Commune*, p. 19.
[13] *Le journal officiel de Paris pendant la Commune, 24 mai*, translation by author.
[14] Maclellan, *Rebel Lives – Louise Michel*, page 101 (Louise Michel: 'I have finished... If you are not cowards, kill me.'")
[15] Ibid. p. 95.

Chapter 9

[1] Klug et al, December 2007 video.

[2] Perrin, *GI Resister*, pp. 65-66.

[3] Klug et al, December 2007 video.

[4] Michael T. Kaufman, "Stokely Carmichael, Rights Leader Who Coined 'Black Power,' Dies at 57," *New York Times*, Nov. 16, 1998.

[5] Klug et al, December 2007 video.

[6] Klug et al, December 2007 video.

[7] Bill Smith, "Terry Given 3 Years, Says, 'We're Going To Win'", *The Bond*, Vol. 3, No. 5, May 20, 1969.

[8] "Terry Writes," *The Bond*, May 20, 1969, letter from Klug, p. 4.

Chapter 10

[1] http://www.americanwarlibrary.com/vietnam/vwc10.htm

[2] https://www.archives.gov/research/jfk/select-committee-report/part-2d.html, Findings on MLK Assassination.

[3] http://chicago68.com/c68chron.html, 1968, April 15.

[4] Stapp, *Up Against the Brass*, p. 152.

[5] Ibid, p. 155.

[6] Ellen Catalinotto, "Black GIs Stand Firm at 'Riot-Duty' Refusal Trial," *Workers World*, Nov. 10, 1968, p. 6.

[7] www.history.com, This Day in History, July 23, 1967, "The 12th Street Riot."

Chapter 13

[1] *Hawai'i Resistance Chronology*, section on "The Sanctuary GI's Speak."

[2] , "Black Marines Rebel at Kaneohe; White Servicemen Take Sanctuary," *The Bond*, Aug. 25, 1969.

[3] Cortright, *Soldiers in Revolt*, p. 35.

[4] Olsen, *Liberate Hawai'i*, Chapter 5, "The Annexationist Plot and Hawaiian Resistance."

[5] Members of the Hawai'i Resistance in 1968, Jon Olsen and John Witeck, in early 2016 provided much of the written sources for this chapter.

[6] *Hawai'i Resistance Chronology, p.* 1, Feb. 9, 1969.

[7] *Resistance chronology*, p. 1, July 1969.

[8] Tillich, Doctoral dissertation, p. 82.

[9] *Resistance chronology*, p. 2, Aug. 17.

[10] Laxer, unpublished memoir, chapter 7.

[11] Laxer, chapter 7.

[12] *Resistance chronology*, p. 6, Sept. 6.

[13] *Resistance chronology*, p. 7, "Bust Starts," Sept. 12.

[14] Louis "Buff" Parry, email to author, Nov. 19, 2016.

[15] *Resistance chronology*, p. 2, Aug. 17.

Chapter 14

[1] Engels, preface to *In Memory of the German Arch-Patriots of 1806-1807, by* Sigismund Borkheim, https://www.marxists.org/archive/lenin/works/1918/jun/29b.htm.
[2] Marcy, *The Bolsheviks and War*, p. 7.
[3] Marcy, Appendix, p. 138.

Chapter 15

[1] Raskol'nikov, *Kronstadt and Petrograd in 1917*, p. 1.
[2] 1914-1918-Online. *International Encyclopedia of the First World War* (WW1). http://encyclopedia.1914-1918-online.net/home/, "Counting Russia's Laborers."
[3] Ibid., "War Losses."
[4] Ibid., "Wartime Mobilization and Maintaining the Workforce."
[5] Sukhanov, *The Russian Revolution 1917*, p. 19.
[6] Sukhanov, p. 29.
[7] Sukhanov, p. 61.
[8] Sukhanov, p. 66.
[9] https://www.marxists.org/history/ussr/government/1917/03/01.htm.
[10] 1914-1918-Online, *International Encyclopedia of the First World War (WW1)*.
[11] Raskol'nikov, *Kronstadt and Petrograd in 1917*, p. 34.
[12] Raskol'nikov, p. 64.
[13] https://www.britannica.com/event/June-Offensive.
[14] Sukhanov, *The Russian Revolution 1917*, p. 596.

Chapter 16

[1] Kuttner, *Von Kiel bis Berlin,* pp. 12-13.
[2] Toller, *Eine Jugend in Deutschland*, pp. 11-54.
[3] Lutz, *The German Revolution,* pp. 8-9.
[4] Lutz, p. 11.
[5] Toller, p. 78.
[6] John Black, "A Servicemen's Revolt – Fifty Years Ago This Month, the German Sailors Rebelled and Told Their Officers to Go to Hell," *Workers World*, Aug. 31, 1967. Forty of the mutinous sailors were sentenced to death; most of these sentences were not carried out. (Von Forstner argued that it was an error to withdraw the sentences.)
[7] Toller, pp. 78-79.
[8] Forstner, *Die Marine-Meuterei*, p. 7.
[9] Kuttner, *Von Kiel bis Berlin*, p. 14.
[10] Kuttner, p. 15.
[11] Forstner, p. 12.
[12] Kuttner, p. 15.
[13] Kuttner, p. 16.
[14] Kuttner, p. 17.
[15] Lutz, p. 34.
[16] Kuttner, pp. 22-24.
[17] Lutz, pp. 46-47.
[18] Kuttner, pp. 26-29.

Chapter 18

[1] David Cortright, *Soldiers in Revolt,* p. 40.

[2] "Jailed Men in Nam Rebel Against Brass," *The Bond*, Sept. 18, 1968, p. 1.

[3] "Inmates Smuggle Letter from LBJ Stockade; Tell What Brass Hide," *The Bond*, Oct. 16, 1968.

[4] Sentencingproject.org, Number incarcerated in federal and state prisons increased by seven times or 600 percent between 1968 and 2000; the total population of the U.S. only increased by 40 percent.

[5] *Workers World*, April 3, 1969.

[6] Andy Stapp, "Escaped Presidio 'Mutineers' Tell Their Story," *The Bond*, March 17, 1969.

Chapter 19

[1] Andrew O'Hehir, "How 'Battleship Potemkin' Reshaped Hollywood ... Eisenstein's Soviet-era classic as pioneering action cinema," *Salon.com*, Jan. 11, 2011.

[2] *Encyclopedia Britannica*, "Russian Revolution of 1905."

[3] *The Bond*, Jan. 21, 1969, "Dix Prisoners Rebel Over Lousy Food," by Eugene Sylvester.

[4] Bill Smith, "Stockade Prisoners Organize," *The Bond*, Feb. 17, 1969.

[5] *The Bond*, March 17, 1969, "Voices of Defiance – from Inside Fort Dix Stockade," by an anonymous prisoner.

[6] Ibid.

[7] Joe Walker (New York editor of *Muhammad Speaks*), "The Black Liberation Army Is The Only Army I'm Interested In," *Workers World*, April 3, 1969, reprinted from *Muhammad Speaks* of February 21, 1969.

[8] PVT John Lewis, "Rebellion In SPB at Fort Dix,"*The Bond*, Oct. 20, 1969.

Chapter 20

[1] *The AWOL Press, vol. 1, No. 6,*
http://www.sirnosir.com/archives_and_resources/galleries/cover_pages/awol_press/01.html

[2] "38 Prisoners Charged in Fort Dix Rebellion," *The Bond*, July 22, 1969, p. 4.

[3] Naomi Goldstein, "Heroes of Dix Invasion – Women's Brigade," *Workers World*, Oct. 23, 1969.

[4] *The Bond*, Oct. 20, 1969, p. 1.

[5] *The Bond*, Dec. 16, 1969, p. 1.

Chapter 21

[1] Pinto, *Soldiers and Strikers, pp. 40-43*.

[2] SP4 Gene Weixel (Ret.), "As Nixon Sends Troops to New York," *The Bond*, April 22, 1970, p. 2.

[3] Cortright, *Soldiers in Revolt*, pp. 10-11.

[4] Cortright, *Soldiers in Revolt*, p. 9.

[5] Defense Manpower Data Center, Office of the Secretary of Defense, U.S. Department of Defense. Since 2012 this number has been fewer than 1.4 million or about 40 percent of the 1968 number.

Chapter 22

[1] *Camp News: News of the GI Movement,* January-February 1972.

[2] Andrew Gelman, "How Many Vietnam Veterans Are Still Alive?" *New York Times,* March 25, 2013.

[3] http://www.americanwarlibrary.com/vietnam/vwfrg.htm

[4] *Camp News: News of the GI Movement,* January-February 1972.

[5] "The Murder of George Doakes," *The Bond*, July 21, 1972, p. 3.

[6] *Camp News: News of the GI Movement,* January-February 1972.

[7] *The Bond*, July 21, 1972, p. 3.

[8] *Camp News: News of the GI Movement,* January-February 1972.

[9] Ibid.

Chapter 24

[1] Joyce Beatries, Sandi Kreps and Peggy Geden, *Army Dependents Speak: Women and the Military.*

[2] $60 in 1968 is roughly equivalent to $420 in 2016, which is inadequate.

[3] *The Bond*, March 31, 1972, p. 2.

[4] *Army Dependents Speak.*

[5] http://www.wintersoldier.com

[6] SP4 Tom Chase (ret.) and SP4 Steve Geden (ret.), "Anti-women propaganda: How the Brass and their flunkies use it against us," *The Bond*, Dec. 24, 1971.

[7] "Women in the Forefront of the Struggle," *The Bond*, Jan. 27, 1972, letter, p.5.

[8] *The Bond*, March 31, 1972, p. 2.

Chapter 25

[1] Mike Gill, wrote Oct. 18, 2013, report based on a talk in New York City.

[2] Ibid.

[3] SGT (E4) B. Dorsey, "Airmen and Supporters Shake Brass – Griffiss Air Force Base." *The Bond*, May 26, 1971.

Chapter 27

[1] Tom Soto, email July 14, 2016 to author.
[2] Ibid.
[3] Ibid.
[4] PFC Tom Soto (ret.), "Ft. Meade, Md.: Black Brothers and Sisters Tell About Rebellion,"*The Bond*, June 30, 1971.
[5] AMN Calvin T. Bonner, "Neo-Colonialism in the Armed Forces," *The Bond*, June 30, 1971.
[6] PVT John Lewis (ret.), "Chanute AFB – Black ASU Organizer Busted; Brothers Take Action Against Racism," *The Bond*, June 30, 1971.
[7] Bill Roundtree, Aug. 16, 2016, phone interview with author.
[8] Ibid.
[9] Larry Holmes interview with author, Aug. 3, 2015.

Chapter 28

[1] Larry Holmes interview with author, Aug. 3, 2015.
[2] Tom Soto email July 14, 2016.
[3] "Flee Vets Righteous Anger at Chicago Job Hoax," *The Bond*, May 19, 1972, p. 4-5.
[4] Ibid., p. 5.
[5] Tom Soto email July 14, 2016.
[6] Larry Holmes interview with author, Aug. 3, 2015.

Chapter 29

[1] *Collected Works of Amílcar Cabral,* p. 23-25, *see* Appendix G for full leaflet.
[2] Cunhal, *Rumo à Vitória,* pp. 191-193, author's translation.
[3] Cunhal, *A Revolução Portuguesa,* pp. 51-53, author's translation.
[4] John P. Cann, *Counterinsurgency in Africa: The Portuguese Way of War 1961-74, (Helion Studies in Military History, No. 12),* Solihun, England: 2012, p. 26
[5] Gonçalvez, *Um General na Revolução,* pp. 51-52
[6] Diniz, *Ascensão, Apogeu e Queda do M.F.A., Vol 1,* p. 89.
[7] Ibid., pp. 310-327 (Diniz tells story in detail, summarized here).
[8] http://media.rtp.pt/memoriasdarevolucao/acontecimento/ral-1-lisboa/
[9] historyinpieces.com/research/us-military-personnel-1954-2014.
[10] Diniz, *Ascensão, Vol 1,* p. 167.
[11] Ibid. p. 198.

Chapter 30

[1] Wisconsin Historical Society, RITA notes 309, newsletter from Larry Johnson Defense Committee, Heidelberg, Germany, June 1973.

[2] "Black GI Defends Africa," *The Bond*, Aug-Sep, 1973, pp. 2,8.

[3] Watts, *Left Face*, p. 34.

[4] *Left Face*, p. 35.

[5] *Left Face*, p. 36.

[6] Rhiannon Hoyle, "Rio Tinto Walks Away From Closed Bougainville Copper Mine," *Wall Street Journal*, June 29, 2016: "Rio Tinto PLC (RIO.AU) said it is walking away from a closed copper mine on the South Pacific island of Bougainville that was at the center of a decadelong civil war."

[7] James Cameron, director, *Avatar*, 20th Century Fox, 2009.

[8] John Catalinotto, *Workers World*, June 6, 2009, "Papua New Guinea's Indigenous people v. Barrick Gold."

Chapter 31

[1] "Servicemen Need Help," *The Bond*, June 23, 1967.

[2] Joseph P. Fried, "Following Up, A 60's Lightning Rod, Now on History TV," *New York Times*, July 21, 2002.

[3] *Independent* (newspaper), Long Beach, California. Feb. 4, 1969.

[4] Wisconsin Historical Society, *Biographical facts on Roger L. Priest: chronology of repression.*

[5] AMN Cal Bonner, "Prosecution Suffers Serious Setback," *The Bond*, Sept. 30, 1972.

[6] Richard Boyle, *Flower of the Dragon – The Breakdown of the U.S. Army in Vietnam* (Ramparts Press, 1972)

[7] "130 Sailors Refuse to Board Ship,"*The Bond*, Nov. 24, 1972.

[8] Wisconsin Historical Society, *Stop Our Ship (SOS)*, leaflet 1971

[9] Gavrielle Gemma, email Feb. 13, 2016 to author.

[10] Tom Soto, interview, *Workers World*, Sept. 17, 1971, Special 8-page section on Attica, centerfold.

[11] Larry Holmes, Interview, Aug. 3, 2015, with author.

Chapter 32

[1] *San Francisco Chronicle*, March 31, 2003, and cited in an article in *Workers World* from April 10, 2003, "The death of a delusionary doctrine — Iraqi resistance and the Rumsfeld strategy," by Fred Goldstein.

[2] Ridley Scott, director, *Black Hawk Down*, Germany 2002.

[3] Catalinotto, *Hidden Agenda,* pp. xxiv, xxv.

[4] Fred Goldstein, "To rescue failed Rumsfeld doctrine, U.S. massacres Iraqi civilians," *Workers World*, April 17, 2003.

[5] Bacevich, Andrew J., *Breach of Trust*, p. 45.

[6] *Breach of Trust*, p. 103.

[7] *Breach of Trust*, p. 127.

[8] John Barry, "The Pentagon May Put Special-Forces-Led Assassination or Kidnapping Teams in Iraq," Newsweek, Jan. 14, 2005.

[9] Jonathan Hutto, *Antiwar Soldier, p. 149.*

[10] Neta C. Crawford, "Costs of War," Brown University's Watson Center, Sept. 2016.

[11] Sara Flounders, *U.S. War: Profitable But Unwinnable*, p. 1. (Flounders is a co-coordinator of the International Action Center, whose founder is former U.S. Attorney General Ramsey Clark, an international human-rights activist.)

[12] Bacevich, *Breach of Trust*, p. 45.

[13] *Breach of Trust*, p. 105.

[14] Gideon Rose, editor, interviews Dempsey, *Foreign Affairs*, June 2016.

[15] Fred Goldstein, *Capitalism at a Dead End*, pp. 15-16.

Bibliography

1914-1918-Online. *International Encyclopedia of the First World War (WW1)* http://encyclopedia.1914-1918-online.net/home/

Adoratskiĭ, V.V. and Dona Torr. *Karl Marx and Frederick Engels Selected Correspondence 1846-1895*. New York: International Publishers, 1942.

An Illustrated History of the Great October Socialist Revolution: 1917. Moscow, USSR, 1988. Translated: Unk. Pub. Dom: Soviet History Archive 2005. www.marxists.org

Aponte, Walter and Shirley Jolls. *Kangaroo Court-Martial: George Daniels and William Harvey, Two Black Marines Who Got 6 and 10 Years for Opposing the Vietnam War*. New York: Committee for GI Rights, 1969.

Bacevich, Andrew J. *Breach of Trust: How Americans Failed Their Soldiers and Their Country*. New York: Metropolitan Books, 2013. henryholt.com.

Beatries, Joyce; Peggy Geden and Sandi Kreps. *Army Dependents Speak: Women and the Military – The Wives of Low-Ranking Enlisted Men Tell of Their Oppression*. Madison, WI, 1972.

Boyle, Richard. *GI Revolts: The Breakdown of the U.S. Army in Vietnam*. San Francisco: 1973. Originally in *Flower of the Dragon – The Breakdown of the U.S. Army in Vietnam*. Ramparts Press, 1972.

Cabral, Amílcar. *Collected Works (vol. II)/Unity and Struggle/Revolutionary practice*. Seara Nova, Lisbon, 1977, coordinated by Mário de Andrade. Translations of excerpts by the author.

Catalinotto, John and Sara Flounders, editors. *Hidden Agenda: U.S./NATO Takeover of Yugoslavia*. New York: International Action Center, 2002.

Chin, Pat, Greg Dunkel and Sara Flounders. *Haiti, a slave revolution: 200 years after 1804*. New York: International Action Center, 2004.

Cortright, David. *Soldiers in Revolt – GI Resistance During the Vietnam War*. Chicago: Haymarket Books, 2005 edition.

Cortright, David and Max Watts. *Left Face: Soldier Unions and Resistance Movements in Modern Armies*. Westport, Connecticut: Greenwood Press, 1991.

Crawford, Neta C. "Costs of War." Brown University's Watson Center, September 2016.

Cunhal, Alvaro, *Rumo à Vitória (Path to Victory)* first presented to the PCP Central Committee in April 1964, Lisbon, Portugal: Edições "Avante!" 1964. Translation of excerpts by the author.

301

Diniz de Almeida, Eduardo. *Ascensão, Apogeu e Queda do M.F.A. (Rise, Apogee and Fall of the Armed Forces Movement, Vol 1 and Vol 2.)* Lisbon: Edições sociais [no date given] (A two-volume detailed history of Portugal's Armed Forces Movement MFA by one of the captains of April; Translations of excerpts by the author.)

Flounders, Sara. *The Pentagon's Achilles Heel: U.S. War: Profitable But Unwinnable.* New York: World View Forum, 2012.

Forstner, George Günther, Freiherr von, 1882-1940. *Die Marine-Meuterei.* Berlin: K. Curtius, 1919. Translations of excerpts by the author. http://hdl.handle.net/2027/mdp.39015013491900

Goldstein, Fred. *Capitalism at a Dead End, Job Destruction, Overproduction and CRISIS in the High-Tech Era, a Marxist View.* New York: World View Forum, 2012.

Gonçalvez, Vasco. *Um General na Revolução. Entrevista com María Manuela Cruzeiro (A General in the Revolution. Interview with MMC).* Lisbon: Editorial Notícias, 2002. Translations of excerpts by the author.

Hawai'i Resistance. *Crossroads Sanctuary.* A chronology. 1969.

Hutto, Jonathan. *Antiwar Soldier: How to Dissent Within the Ranks of the Military.* New York: Nation Books, 2008.

Jellinek, Frank. *The Paris Commune of 1871.* New York: Grosset & Dunlap Universal Library Edition, 1965

Kuttner, Erich (1887-1942), *Von Kiel bis Berlin: der Siegeszug der deutschen Revolution.* Berlin: Verlag für Sozialwissenschaft, 1918. Translations of excerpts by the author. http://hdl.handle.net/2027/wu.89098683527

Laxer, Greg, unpublished memoir as of December 2016.

Le journal officiel de Paris pendant la Commune (20 Mars-24 Mai 1871): histoire, extraits, facsimile du 10 mars. Paris: L. Beauvais, 1871. Translations of excerpts by the author.

Lembcke, Jerry. *The Spitting Image: Myth, Memory and the Legacy of Vietnam.* New York: NYU Press, 2000.

Lenin, V.I. (Vladimir Ulyanov). *Collected Works, Volume 25.* p. 381-492 "The State and Revolution." First published 1918. Excerpts from Chapter 3: Lenin Internet Archive (marxists.org) 1993, 1999

Lenin, V.I. *The Paris Commune.* New York: International Publishers, 1934.

Lutz, Ralph Haswell, (1886-1968) *The German Revolution, 1918-1919.* Stanford University Publications, 1922.

Maclellan, Nic, *Rebel Lives - Louise Michel.* Melbourne; New York; [St. Paul, Minn.]: Ocean Press ; Consortium Book Sales and Distribution [distributor], 2004.

March, Thomas. *The History of the Paris Commune of 1871.* London: 1895

Marcy, Sam. *The Bolsheviks and War: Lessons for Today's Anti-War Movement*. New York: World View Forum, 1985

Marx, Karl. *The Civil War in France*. Bejing: Foreign Languages Press, 1966.

Olsen, Jon. *Liberate Hawai'i: Renouncing and Defying the Continuing Fraudulent U.S. Claim to the sovereignty of Hawai'i*. Waldoboro, ME: Goose River Press, 2014.

Pentagon Papers. www.americanwarlibrary.com

Perrin, Dick, with Tim McCarthy. *GI Resister: The Story of How One American Soldier and His Family Fought the War in Vietnam*. Printed in Victoria, Canada: 2001. (Published on-demand in cooperation with Trafford Publishing.)

Pinto, Vincent. *Soldiers and Strikers*. San Francisco: United Front Press, second edition, 1973.

Raskol'nikov, F.F. (Fedor Fedorovich), translated and annotated by Brian Pearce. *Kronstadt and Petrograd in 1917*. London: New Park Publications, 1982. First published 1925.

Richardson, F.O. *The GI's Handbook on Military Injustice: Why Rank and File GIs Need an Organization of Their Own*. New York: American Servicemen's Union, 1971.

Smith, Bill. *Court Martial Turned Around. Pvt. M. Smith Charges Military Harassment*. New York: American Servicemen's Union, 1970.

Stapp, Andy and Shirely Jolls. *Black Marines Against the Brass: Interview with William Harvey and George Daniels*. New York: American Servicemen's Union, 1969. [check]

Stapp, Andy. *Up Against the Brass*. New York: Simon and Schuster, 1970.

Sukhannov, Nikolai Nikolaevich. Edited, abridged and translated by Joel Carmichael. *The Russian Revolution 1917: A Personal Record*. Princeton, New Jersey: Princeton University Press, 1982.

Terry, Wallace. *Bloods. Black Veterans of the Vietnam War: An Oral History*. New York: Ballantine Books, 1984.

Tillich, Linda Meyerson. *The Crossroads Sanctuary*. August 1977. Manuscript of doctoral dissertation. Psychologist Tillich led group sessions for Sanctuary members.

Toller, Ernst (1893-1939). *Eine Jugend in Deutschland*. Berlin, Hamburg: rororo, 2012. Translations of excerpts by the author.

Tucker, Spencer C., editor. *Encyclopedia of the Vietnam War: A Political, Social, and Military History*. Oxford, UK: ABC-CLIO, 1998.

Watts, Max, David Harris, Dieter Brünn. *US-Army-Europe: Von der Desertion zum Widerstand in der Kaserne oder wie die U-Bahn zur RITA fuhr*. West Berlin: Harald Kater Verlag, 1989. Translations of excerpts by the author.

Zinn, Howard. *A People's History of the United States, Third Edition*. London: Pearson Education Limited, 2003.

Acknowledgments

A video message on GI resistance prepared for a memorial to honor Max Watts in 2012 was the seed that grew into *Turn the Guns Around*. Naomi Cohen, Fred Goldstein and Ellen Catalinotto's encouragement and aid provided water and sunlight. Deirdre Griswold and Sue Davis, my co-editors on *Workers World* newspaper over the past decades, edited and copy edited my drafts, adding political insight along with craft. Lallan Schoenstein, a true political artist, designed the cover and tutored the typography. Sara Catalinotto proofread the final proof.

Like the organization of the American Servicemen's Union, this book resulted from teamwork. Former GIs and civilians who founded the ASU, noted throughout the text, contributed interviews, letters, emails, photos and feedback that aided and vetted the narrative. I thank them and also:

ASU founder Andy Stapp, who died in 2014, for his permission and encouragement to quote liberally from *Up Against the Brass* and his other writing and recorded interviews. Larry Holmes, Tom Soto and Bill Roundtree, who described veteran organizing. Joyce Chediac for writing on the Camp McCoy 3 and on women's liberation as it affected the military.

Hawai'i Resistance veterans John Witeck and Jon Olsen, for original sources verifying the Crossroads Sanctuary chapter. Carlos Pereira, Miguel Urbano, Jorge Cadima and Manuel Raposo for texts of original documents on the history of Portugal and Africa, and David Raposo for reviewing my translations from Portuguese. Ocean Press publishers for permission to cite their book of Louise Michel's life and writings.

Richard Wheaton, Ellen Catalinotto, Brenda Sandburg, Rosie Kubb and David Felton for permission to use their photos, and the anonymous ASU and *Workers World* volunteer photographers and political cartoonists and all who offered advice, instruction or feedback on my writing and map-making.

The late Sam Marcy for conceiving of the ASU and all the comrades of Workers World Party for their aid and solidarity.

I take responsibility for the result, which I hope will contribute to teaching how a change of political consciousness among rank-and-file troops can turn a weapon of oppression into a tool for human liberation.

INDEX

G

H

I

J

K

P

R

Q

About the Author

Speaking at a memorial for Andy Stapp on Nov. 30, 2014 in New York City.
Photo: Brenda Sandburg

Active in the anti-war movement in the United States since 1962, a civilian organizer with the American Servicemen's Union from 1967-70 and a managing editor of *Workers World* weekly newspaper since 1982, John Catalinotto has also co-edited the books *Hidden Agenda: U.S./NATO Takeover of Yugoslavia* and *Metal of Dishonor - Depleted Uranium: How the Pentagon Radiates Soldiers & Civilians with DU Weapons.*

Capitalism at a Dead End

Job destruction, overproduction and crisis in the high-tech era

El capitalismo en un callejón sin salida

Destrucción de empleo, sobreproducción y crisis en la era de la alta tecnología

For more information on these books and other writings by the author, Fred Goldstein, go to www.**LowWageCapitalism**.com

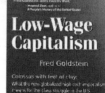

Low-Wage Capitalism

Fred Goldstein

Colossus with feet of clay: What the new globalized high-tech imperialism means for the class struggle in the U.S.

Hidden Agenda
U.S. /NATO TAKEOVER OF YUGOSLAVIA
Edited by Sara Flounders and John Catalinotto
The hypocrisy and lies behind the alleged humanitarian war waged by the U.S. and NATO are exposed in this anthology of carefully documented critiques of the Balkan conflict. Evidence is presented to conclude that divide-and-conquer tactics were used to stimulate war in Yugoslavia; critical essays examine the Hague Tribunal, the occupation of Kosovo, media deception, war crimes, and blatant NATO aggression. Contributors include Ramsey Clark, Slobodan Milosevic, and Michael Parenti.

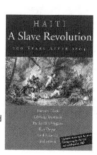

HAITI
A Slave Revolution
200 Years After 1804
Essays include those written by Ramsey Clark, Edwidge Danticat, Frederick Douglass, Ben Dupuy and Paul Laraque. Drawn from a wide range of authors, and historical texts. Book also contains a time line and photo essay, This revised edition also includes context surrounding the response to the tragic 2010 earthquake disaster.

MARXISM, REPARATIONS
& the Black Freedom Struggle

An anthology of writings from Workers World newspaper.
Edited by Monica Moorehead.

Racism, National Oppression & Self-Determination
Larry Holmes

Black Labor from Chattel Slavery to Wage Slavery
Sam Marcy

Black Youth: Repression & Resistance LeiLani Dowell

The Struggle for Socialism Is Key Monica Moorehead

**Domestic Workers United Demand Passage
of a Bill of Rights** Imani Henry

Cover graphic: Sahu Barron

Black & Brown Unity: A Pillar of Struggle for Human Rights & Global Justice!
Saladin Muhammad

Harriet Tubman, Woman Warrior Mumia Abu-Jamal

Haiti Needs Reparations, Not Sanctions Pat Chin

Alabama's Black Belt: Legacy of Slavery, Sharecropping & Segregation
Consuela Lee

Are Conditions Ripe Again Today? Anniversary of the 1965 Watts Rebellion
John Parker

WAR WITHOUT VICTORY

by Sara Flounders

*"By revealing the underbelly of the empire, Flounders sheds
insight on how to stand up to the imperialist war machine
and, in so doing, save ourselves and humanity."*

– Miguel d'Escoto Brockmann,
President, U.N. General Assembly, 2008-2009;
Foreign Minister of Nicaragua's Sandinista government.

For more go to **www.PentagonAchillesHeel.com**

Books are published by World View Forum,
147 West 24th Street, 2nd Floor, New York, N.Y. 10001

They are available online at major booksellers and in bookstores
around the country.

➜ SP4 RICHARD WHEATON

'Every once in a while a book comes along that lifts us high by reminding us that people struggling together can accomplish momentous things. I consider myself fortunate to have been part of the GI anti-war movement, and a founding member of the ASU; we are all fortunate to have this book.'
  U.S. Army, Sept. 7, 1965 to Sept. 6, 1968

➜ SARA FLOUNDERS

'The radical shift in consciousness fifty years ago within the U.S. military has invaluable lessons as a new period of resistance unfolds. In *Turn the Guns Around,* rank-and-file GIs, who suddenly emerged as leaders of a movement, describe their determination to risk all, refuse orders and sabotage the military machine. By rooting them in past resistance, this "How to" manual' arms the people's movements of today to combat new wars.'
  Co-Director of International Action Center, Author of War Without Victory

➜ SP4 GREG LAXER

'Catalinotto's book digs up historical precedents for troop revolts contributing to the ending of imperialist wars. That was certainly our aim through the actions of the American Serviceman's Union. The best people I met in the army were my fellow stockade inmates!'
  U.S. Army, prisoner of conscience, Forts Devins, Dix and Riley, 1968-70

➜ FRED GOLDSTEIN

'In the present period of reaction it is difficult to imagine the undoing of the powerful capitalist state. Catalinotto reaches back in history to vividly demonstrate how social and economic crises can and will lead to the disintegration of the capitalist military. He shows that the forces of social revolution lie embedded in the very structure of imperialism and it's insatiable drive for conquest.'
  Author of Low-Wage Capitalism *and* Capitalism At A Dead End

Made in the USA
San Bernardino, CA
09 February 2017